Multiculturalism and Interculturalism

From Nasar to Aiisha and Katherine.

From Tariq to Jasmin and Ghizela.

From Ricard to Isabel and Samjana.

MULTICULTURALISM AND INTERCULTURALISM

Debating the Dividing Lines

Edited by
Nasar Meer, Tariq Modood and Ricard Zapata-Barrero

EDINBURGH
University Press

This edited collection includes papers first presented at a two-day European Science Foundation (ESF) exploratory workshop organised by Ricard Zapata-Barrero and Tariq Modood, held in Barcelona, 29–30 May 2014. We would like to thank the ESF for their generous funding and support.

Edinburgh University Press is one of the leading university presses in the UK. We publish academic books and journals in our selected subject areas across the humanities and social sciences, combining cutting-edge scholarship with high editorial and production values to produce academic works of lasting importance. For more information visit our website: www.edinburghuniversitypress.com

Edinburgh University Press Ltd
The Tun – Holyrood Road
12 (2f) Jackson's Entry
Edinburgh EH8 8PJ

Typeset in 11/14 Sabon by
Servis Filmsetting Ltd, Stockport, Cheshire,
and printed and bound in Great Britain by
CPI Group (UK) Ltd, Croydon CR0 4YY

A CIP record for this book is available from the British Library

ISBN 978 1 4744 0708 3 (hardback)
ISBN 978 1 4744 0709 0 (paperback)
ISBN 978 1 4744 0710 6 (webready PDF)
ISBN 978 1 4744 0711 3 (epub)

Contents

Foreword

Charles Taylor

This book opens out and explores further a constellation of questions which are essential to the integration and health of contemporary liberal democracies. In one sense, these debates are intra-mural: all of the participants, however they situate themselves on the gamut of multi- to interculturalism, are agreed on some basic goals. They want to bring about the integration of our increasingly diverse societies, on an equal basis, rather than pursuing the assimilation of all new arrivals to some (supposed) ancestral identity.

I say 'new arrivals', and one usually thinks 'immigrants'. But it is worth noting that the increasing diversity of our contemporary democracies also arises from long-established and disadvantaged groups and populations pressing for their rights. The feminist movement, the gay movement and aboriginal populations, in all their inner diversity, have also raised demands in the name of unrecognised or suppressed differences to which justice must be done.

That being said, what are the differences between multi- and interculturalism? Here we see a wide variety of definitions of the issue. This is to be expected and is not a bad thing. The issues around (to use a slogan) 'seeking integration without assimilation' arise in rather different ways in different societies: different among the societies of the Western hemisphere and other overseas societies peopled by Europeans, which have been receiving immigrants regularly for generations, on the one hand, and many of the societies of Western Europe, on the other, many of which have been until recently more or less homogeneous ethnically, and have

recently started to admit immigrants in large numbers. Among
European societies we can see the important role of the existing
political culture in framing the question of how to integrate newcomers (the contrast between the UK and France is an obvious
case); the chapter by Ana Solano-Campos then shows how differently the societies of Latin America approach these questions. And
I can't help mentioning in this context my own dual country, where
a different term is established in Canada as a whole, on the one
hand, and in Quebec on the other.

But can we define the difference between inter- and multiculturalism in a way which can cast light on all these different situations,
and offer clear advice on which term to adopt in each context?
Maybe we'll be able to do this one day, but that moment has not
yet arrived. Whether it ever arrives or not, the different chapters
in this book offer important insights into the dynamics of diverse
situations, and the difficult choices people have to face in them.

Will Kymlicka offers the suggestion that the differences between
the two terms are greatly exaggerated; that they generate a host
of more detailed policy measures which are common to them
both – measures to integrate immigrants, to combat discrimination
and stereotypes, and so on. He suspects that the differences are
often invoked for the purpose of rhetorically discrediting one or
the other. He obviously has a point, both in seeing the substantial
overlap between the two, and in denouncing the largely ignorant
rhetoric of anti-multiculturalism. In one short period in recent
years, first Merkel, then Cameron, then Sarkozy informed us that
multiculturalism had 'failed' in their respective societies, where
it would have been much more accurate to say that it had never
been tried. And the discourse of certain Quebecers denouncing
Canadian multiculturalism is also rather loosely related to reality.

Nevertheless, I think that there do remain differences between
what the two terms suggest – whether it be the focus on intercultural exchange, which is perhaps the main semantic ground for
using this term, or the need to reassure a historic majority against
its (often exaggerated) fears of dissolution. And here I want to
recur to a third point Kymlicka makes: the crucial objective for all
of us, whatever the label, has to be the redefinition of the nation,
expanding it beyond its ethno-historical, 'traditional' image to a
more inclusive one. And beyond a brace of good policies, fostering integration, combating stereotypes, encouraging exchange, this

requires a story, an account of where we came from, where we are, and where we're going.

I mean a story that everyone, or at least the majority, can sign on to. Otherwise the best policies will lack legitimacy. In the nature of things, Canada and Quebec can't adopt an identical story: in one case it's a story of rupture – we used to have a dominant ethno-national identity, and now we've broken with that and have no established 'culture'; in the other case there is such a historic identity, which we want to continue, but which can only survive by redefinition in each generation, and in this redefinition everyone, regardless of origin, has an equal voice. This difference in narrative would exist even if we agreed on labels.

In any case, whatever the differences, how they work out in practice will depend on the particular history and culture of each society, and one of the strengths of this book is the rich and varied descriptions it offers of the ways the distinction can cast light on a host of different contexts.

List of Contributors

Gérard Bouchard is Professor at the Université du Québec à Chicoutimi, Canada. He has published 37 books and 280 papers in scientific journals. With the political philosopher Charles Taylor, he co-chaired in 2007–8 a governmental commission of inquiry on intercultural relations in Québec (*Building the Future. A Time for Reconciliation*). In 2008–9, he was visiting professor of sociology at Harvard and holder of a Canada–US research chair. He has been awarded a number of prestigious distinctions, including the French Légion d'honneur and several *honoris causa* doctorates. He has also published three novels.

Ted Cantle is Professor at the Institute of Community Cohesion (iCoCo), UK. He led the development of community cohesion in the UK following his seminal report (known as the Cantle Report). His book *Community Cohesion: A New Framework for Race and Diversity* (Palgrave Macmillan 2005) builds on this approach. For the last few years, he has been developing the notion of interculturalism, and his new book on this subject, *Interculturalism – The New Era of Cohesion and Diversity* (Palgrave Macmillan 2012). Ted has previously worked in the local government, health, private and voluntary sectors. He was Chief Executive of Nottingham City Council from 1990–2001 and was awarded the CBE in 2004.

Alain-G. Gagnon is Canada Research Chair in Quebec and Canadian Studies and Professor of Political Science, Université du Québec à Montréal. He is a founding member of the Research Group on Multinational Societies (1995–) and is director of an emerging research centre on diversity (CRIDAQ: Centre de recherche interdisciplinaire sur la diversité au Québec) that brings together thirty researchers. He is the editor of *Débats*, an established book collection with Québec Amérique, which already counts more than ten titles. Gagnon has held visiting appointments at the Universidad Autonoma de Barcelona, the Institut d'études politiques de Bordeaux and the Institute for Research on Public Policy.

Raffaele Iacovino is Associate Professor in the Department of Political Science at Carleton University where his research interests include Canadian and Quebec politics, federalism, citizenship and immigration, and citizenship education. Recently, he held the position of Invited Professor of Quebec Studies in the Quebec Studies Program at McGill University. His publications include: *Federalism, Citizenship and Quebec: Debating Multinationalism* (with Alain-G. Gagnon) (2007).

Will Kymlicka is the Canada Research Chair in Political Philosophy at Queen's University, where he has taught since 1998. He has published eight books and over 200 articles, which have been translated into thirty-two languages, and has received several awards, most recently the 2009 Premier's Discovery Award in the Social Sciences. His books include *Contemporary Political Philosophy* ([1990] 2002), *Multicultural Citizenship* (1995), which was awarded the Macpherson Prize by the Canadian Political Science Association, and the Bunche Award by the American Political Science Association; *Multicultural Odysseys: Navigating the New International Politics of Diversity* (2007), which was awarded the North American Society for Social Philosophy's 2007 Book Award, and most recently *Zoopolis: A Political Theory of Animal Rights* (2011), co-authored with Sue Donaldson.

Geoffrey Brahm Levey is an Australian Research Council Future Fellow and Associate Professor in Political Science, Faculty of Arts and Social Sciences, University of New South Wales (UNSW), and was the Foundation Director of the UNSW Program in Jewish Studies. He has held a wide range of visiting fellowships and is currently a Robert Schumann Fellow in the Global Governance Programme of the Robert Schumann Centre for Advanced Studies, European University Institute in Florence.

Patrick Loobuyck studied religious studies at the Catholic University of Leuven and ethics at Ghent University. He is Associate Professor in Religion and Worldviews at the Centre Pieter Gillis of the University of Antwerp and Guest Professor in Political Philosophy at Ghent University. His research focuses on political liberalism, church state regimes, religion in the public sphere, religious education, multiculturalism, and liberal nationalism. He has published widely in several national and international journals.

Nasar Meer is a Reader at Strathclyde University, and a Royal Society of Edinburgh Research Fellow. His publications include *Citizenship, Identity and the Politics of Multiculturalism* (2nd edition 2015), *European Multiculturalisms* (co-ed.) (Edinburgh University Press 2011), *Racialization and Religion* (ed. 2014) and *Race and Ethnicity* (2014). He has been a Minda de Gunzburg Fellow at Harvard University, a Fellow with the Institute for Advanced Studies in the Humanities (IASH) at the University of Edinburgh, and a member of the British Council's Outreach Program. In 2014 he was elected to the RSE Young Academy. http://www.nasarmeer.com

Tariq Modood is Professor of Sociology, Politics and Public Policy at the University of Bristol, UK and Founding Director of the University Research Centre for the Study of Ethnicity and Citizenship. He has held over forty grants and consultancies (UK, European and US), has written over thirty (co-) authored and (co-) edited books and reports and over 150 articles or chapters in political philosophy, sociology and public policy. He is also the co-founding editor of the international journal *Ethnicities*. He was awarded an MBE for services to social sciences and ethnic relations in 2001 and elected a member of the Academy of Social Sciences in 2004. He served on the Commission on the Future of Multi-Ethnic Britain, the IPPR Commission on National Security and the National Equality Panel, which reported to the UK Deputy Prime Minister in 2010. http://www.tariqmodood.com

Lord Bhikhu Parekh is a fellow of the Royal Society of Arts and of the Academy of the Learned Societies for Social Sciences and a Professor of Political Philosophy at the University of Westminster. Lord Parekh was Chair of the Runnymede Commission on the Future of Multi-Ethnic Britain (1998–2000). He is Vice-

Chairman of the Gandhi Foundation, a trustee of the Anne Frank Educational Trust, and a member of the National Commission on Equal Opportunity. Lord Parekh is the recipient of the Sir Isaiah Berlin Prize for lifetime contribution to political philosophy by the Political Studies Association (2002); the Distinguished Global Thinker Award by the India International Centre Delhi (2006); the Inderdependence Prize from the Campaign for Democracy (New York 2006), and the Padma Bhushan honours in the 2007 Indian Republic Day Honours list.

Ana Solano-Campos is Assistant Professor in the Department of Curriculum and Instruction at the University of Massachusetts Boston. She received her PhD in Educational Studies from Emory University (2014). She also holds degrees in Applied Linguistics, Teaching English as a Foreign Language (TEFL), and Teaching English to Speakers of Other Languages (TESOL). She works at the intersection of critical, qualitative, interdisciplinary, and comparative approaches to the study and design of culturally and linguistically responsive education, and is Co-Chair of the Latin America Special Interest Group (LASIG) of the Comparative and International Education Society (CIES).

Charles Taylor (CC GOQ FRSC) is a Canadian philosopher from Montreal, Quebec known for his contributions to political philosophy, the philosophy of social science and intellectual history. This work has earned him the prestigious Kyoto Prize and the Templeton Prize, in addition to widespread esteem among philosophers. In 2007, Taylor served with Gérard Bouchard on the Bouchard–Taylor Commission on Reasonable Accommodation with regard to cultural differences in the province of Quebec.

Ricard Zapata-Barrero is Professor at the Department of Political and Social Sciences, Universitat Pompeu Fabra (Barcelona, Spain). Director of Gritim UPF (Interdisciplinary Research Group on Immigration) and of the Master Degree on Immigration Studies. His main lines of research deal with contemporary issues of liberal democracy in contexts of diversity, especially the relationship between democracy, citizenship and immigration. He is also a member of several government advisory boards, and occasional contributor to media and policy debates. For his research publications, see http://dcpis.upf.edu/~ricard-zapata/

A Plural Century:
Situating Interculturalism and Multiculturalism

Nasar Meer, Tariq Modood and Ricard Zapata-Barrero

Introduction

This book explores the topics of interculturalism and multiculturalism, including their relationships to each other and to public philosophies more broadly. In many respects it is a timely and perhaps
overdue intervention that locates the debate about interculturalism and multiculturalism in amongst a series of sociological and
political developments. It is widely accepted that the significant
movement and settlement of people outside their country of birth
'is now structurally embedded in the economies and societies of
most countries' (Pécoud and de Guchteneire 2007: 5). The prevailing context is that the majority of the world's population resides in
175 poorer countries relative to the wealth that is disproportion-
ately concentrated in around twenty. With levels of migration fluc-
tuating but anxieties constant, it is common to hear governments
and other agencies favour 'managed migration' and strategies for
'integration', which, though meaning different things in different
places, registers migration and post-migration settlement as an
intractable feature of contemporary society.

As we show below, this has immediate implications for the
approaches that interculturalists and multiculturalists adopt, but
this sociological development is matched by a political tendency,
in so far as any story of the 'plural century' cannot be restricted
to migration only, and must also take account of what we might
think of as state *remaking*. One illustration is found in modes of
substate national and federal governance that resist the drive for a
unitary and centralised state citizenship, and so challenge how one

'dominant group organises the common life in a way that reflects its own authority and culture' (Walzer 1997: 25; cf. Hepburn and Zapata-Barrero 2014). Large territorially concentrated communities who see themselves as autonomous nations within nation-states are the most obvious example of this. Despite what is sometimes claimed, therefore, these remind us that all of today's nation-states reflect some longstanding internal diversity (notwithstanding what status non-majority cultural forms may have enjoyed). A second form of state-remaking has less to do with territory and autonomy and more to do with overarching collective membership. This is about legal rights but also about symbols and political equality and remaking citizenship to include 'difference'. What it shares with the first expression of state remaking flows from an underlying concern that minorities will 'feel crucially left out [when] the majority understand the polity as an expression of their nation, or agreed purpose, whatever it may be' (Taylor 2001: 123). In this respect it is striking that there seems to be greater minority integration in countries with more multiculturalist policies than in those with none. So controlling for other factors, when the same ethnic minority group (with the same pre-arrival characteristics) enters two different countries at the same time, it has been shown that the group which is in the multicultural context fares much better (Bloemraad 2006).[1]

---

[1] In her study, Bloemraad (2006) compared the integration of two Vietnamese groups in Toronto and Boston, and then repeated this for Portuguese minorities. According to Kymlicka (2012: 46), in these cases Canada's proactive multicultural policies 'sent a clear message that Vietnamese [and Portuguese] political participation is welcome, and have also provided material and logistical support for self-organization and political representation of the community'. Elsewhere, Berry et al. (2006) use the International Comparative Study of Ethnocultural Youth (which focuses on thirteen countries and takes in 5,000 young people) to argue that polices and discourses of multiculturalism (e.g. plural national identities, equal opportunity monitoring, effective anti-discrimination legislation and enforcement) encourage a more successful and deeply established integration in those settings. In the British case, this is supported by Heath and Roberts (2008: 2), who, in their analyses of the UK government's citizenship survey, report: 'We find no evidence that Muslims or people of Pakistani heritage were in general less attached to Britain than were other religions or ethnic groups. Ethnic minorities show clear evidence of "dual" rather than "exclusive" identities.' They point instead to hyphenated identities, in showing that 43 per cent of Muslims belong 'very strongly' to Britain and 42 per cent say that they belong to Britain 'fairly strongly', and taken together these figures are higher for Muslim respondents than they are for Christian ones and those of 'no religion' (for an overview of some recent studies see Meer 2014: 88–9 and Modood 2013: 145).

Taken together, what we describe further complicates long-established tensions 'between the universalistic principles ushered in by the American and French Revolutions and the particularities of nationality, ethnicity, gender, "race", and language' (Benhabib 2002: vii). The point being that all liberal democratic citizenship has been cut from a cloth coloured by prevailing national cultures and identities, and new modes of citizenship have developed that seek to correct this. In their own ways both interculturalists and multiculturalists offer such a move, and both register 'a third generation norm of legitimacy, namely respect for reasonable cultural diversity, which needs to be considered on a par with the [first and second generation] norms of freedom and equality, and so to modify policies of "free and equal treatment" accordingly' (Tully 2002: 102). While different political contexts express distinct stories, something that is emphatically brought out in the proceeding focus on post-migration multicultural settlements and the status of nationalist settlements, both interculturalism and multiculturalism seek to be a vehicle for what Tully (2000) calls 'citizenisation' – the processes of incorporation into and (as a consequence) revision of prevailing citizenship settlements.

It is against this background that our concepts of interculturalism and multiculturalism have developed their normative and political content. While this content unfolds throughout the rest of this chapter and indeed the book more broadly, it would be useful at this juncture to provide a pocket overview of how we understand the provenance of each. For the purposes of our discussion, interculturalism's core meaning refers to support for cross-cultural dialogue. Bouchard and Taylor (2012: 118) state that the first record of the term 'interculturalism' in Quebec is in 1985, prior to which they could find only two references, a Council of Europe document and a Belgian government document, both dated 1981. It is worth noting that 'intercultural education' was being used by German educationalists from the late 1970s (Kraus and Schönwälder 2006) and also seems to have European origins of the same vintage as 'multicultural education', while the first documented uses of the term 'intercultural' in Latin America may have been in Venezuela's 1979 bilingual intercultural education policy (see Chapter 8). Whilst in Canada interculturalism developed as a reaction to the multiculturalism of federal Canada (see Chapter 5), in Europe it emerged as a city policy strategy in the Intercultural

Cities programme of the Council of Europe in 2008.[2] On 15 January 2015 the Committee of Ministers of the Council of Europe adopted a recommendation on the Intercultural Cities approach, proposing it to cities and governments.[3] Multiculturalism, meanwhile, although used differently across varying contexts, has more broadly been focused on the accommodation and integration of migrant and post-migrant groups typically termed 'ethnic minorities'. To confuse matters, however, multiculturalism has also taken in multinational questions – for example, multiculturalist Canada focused from the outset on constitutional and land issues too. To further narrow the conceptual span of multiculturalism, Laegaard (2014) has recently argued that Euro-multiculturalism is a useful differentiation from the other modes (cf. Triandafyllidou, Modood and Meer 2013), but we might nonetheless summarise that multiculturalism can simultaneously describe

> the political accommodation by the state and/or a dominant group of all minority cultures defined first and foremost by reference to race or ethnicity, and, additionally but more controversially, by reference to other group-defining characteristics such as nationality, aboriginality, or religion. The latter is more controversial not only because it extends the range of the groups that have to be accommodated, but also because it tends to make larger political claims and so tends to resist having these claims reduced to those of immigrants. (Modood and Meer 2013: 113)

In ways that have both overlapped and diverged, therefore, both interculturalism and multiculturalism are seeking to engender certain kinds of unity in polities that have seen what Arnold Toynbee (1958: 87) termed 'the annihilation of distance'. This problematic emerges across a multifaceted set of arguments presented throughout the chapters of this book, and takes up intel-

---

[2] A pilot programme of the Council of Europe jointly with the European Commission that examines practical tools for the management of interculturalism in eleven European towns and cities.

[3] See Recommendation CM/Rec(2015)1 of the Committee of Ministers to member states on intercultural integration; available at <https://wcd.coe.int/ViewDoc.jsp?Ref=CM%2FRec%282015%291&Language=lanEnglish&Ver=original&Site=CM&BackColorInternet=C3C3C3&BackColorIntranet=EDB021&BackColorLogged=F5D383#> (last accessed 2 June 2015).

lectual and policy debates that span Europe, and South and North America.

Debating the dividing lines

This book is presented in the context of a widespread (but contested) view that there has been a retreat from relatively modest approaches of multicultural citizenship across a variety of citizenship regimes (Meer, Mouritsen, Faas and de Witte 2015). The reasons are various, but include how, for some, multiculturalism has facilitated social fragmentation and entrenched social divisions; for others it has distracted attention away from socio-economic disparities or encouraged a moral hesitancy amongst 'native' populations. Some even blame it for international terrorism (Phillips 2006; Prins and Salisbury 2008). While the theory and practice of interculturalism has its own provenance too, especially outside English-speaking contexts such as in Latin American debates about *interculturalidad* (see Chapter 8, and Tubino 2013) and Quebec scholarship about distinguishing it from federal multiculturalism (see Chapter 4), it has become especially prominent as a distinct alternative to prevailing approaches of multiculturalism in Europe. As Irena Guidikova (2014: 4), coordinator of the Intercultural Cities programme, puts it, multiculturalism 'is increasingly being challenged as eroding the foundations of community cohesion and the universality of human rights and equal dignity, and accused of being unable to forge a common identity'.[4] For Zapata-Barrero (Chapter 3), too, interculturalism 'enters into this negative diagnosis of MC [multiculturalism], offering a lifeline'. While advocates of both are in favour of recognising and accommodating diversity, interculturalists arguably share the view that interculturalism, minimally, addresses multiculturalist shortcomings, and in stronger versions no longer sees multiculturalism as a persuasive intellectual approach or policy goal. For example, one of the leading advocates and policy practitioner of 'community cohesion', Ted Cantle (2012: 2), has described interculturalism as 'an opportunity to replace multiculturalism as a conceptual and policy framework'. Others such as Maxwell et al. (2012: 429) maintain

---

[4] <http://www.coe.int/t/dg4/cultureheritage/culture/Cities/Publication/BookCoE06-Guidikova.pdf> (last accessed 2 June 2015).

that 'interculturalism represents a gain over Multiculturalism while pursuing the same set of mostly uncontroversial political ends' (see also Chapter 6).

Outside academic quarters, the Council of Europe's 2008 White Paper on Intercultural Dialogue, *Living Together as Equals in Dignity*, includes reports that practitioners and NGOs across Europe have come to the conclusion that multiculturalism is no longer fit for purpose and needs to be replaced by a form of interculturalism. Similar views were expressed in the UNESCO World Report *Investing in Cultural Diversity and Intercultural Dialogue* (2008). The former report facilitated the creation of the Intercultural Cities programme, which seeks 'a strategic reorientation of urban governance and policies to encourage adequate representation, positive intercultural mixing and interaction, and institutional capacity to deal with cultural conflict' (Guidikova 2014: 1). As is stated in its founding documents, it places emphasis on the fact that interculturalism is basically seen as a local and especially city-level means of responding to diversity (Zapata-Barrero 2015a). In this framing, '[o]ne of the defining factors that will determine, over coming years, which cities flourish and which decline will be the extent to which they allow their diversity to be their asset . . . Whilst national and supra-national bodies will continue to wield an influence it will increasingly be the choices that cities themselves make which will seal their future' (COE 2008: 22). The British Council (quoted in Phipps 2014: 109) too has insisted on the need for interculturalism, specifically in order to 'develop a deeper understanding of diverse perspectives and practices; to increase participation and the freedom and ability to make choices; to foster equality; and to enhance creative processes'.

Despite the fact that the evidence is that there has not been a wholesale or even a significant retreat from multiculturalism,[5]

---

[5] For example, let us take two countries seen as multiculturalist (the UK and the Netherlands) and two countries that are not seen as multiculturalist (Denmark and Germany). Using Banting and Kymlicka's (2013) Multiculturalism Policy Index, which monitors multicultural public policies across twenty-one Western democracies across three intervals (1980, 2000 and 2010), we see that in 2000, the Netherlands and Britain each scored 5.5 out of a possible 8, and Denmark and Germany scored 0.5 and 2 respectively. By 2010, the score for the Netherlands had been reduced to 2, Britain remained the same, Denmark was at 0, and Germany had increased to 2.5. This offers a mixed picture of the fate of multiculturalism that is given qualitative

statements such as these above have invited the question: how are interculturalism and multiculturalism similar or different, substantively or otherwise, from each other? In this collection we bring together two parallel – but largely unrelated – attempts to answer this question. The first centres not in Europe but in North America, and includes the Report of the Consultation Commission on the Accommodation of Practices Related to Cultural Differences, commissioned by the Quebec government, widely known as the Bouchard-Taylor report (2008). This maintains that Quebec as a nation has developed a distinctive intercultural approach to diversity that is quite distinct from federal Canadian multiculturalism. As one of the authors of the report puts it, 'The crucial point here is that there really is a majority culture within the nation of Quebec whose fragility is a permanent fact of life. This results in a specific vision of nationhood, identity and national belonging' (Bouchard 2011: 463; see also Chapter 4). Thus while multiculturalism remains the official policy of the Canadian federal government, named as such in section 27 of the Canadian Charter, 'all Quebec governments since 1981, as well as the Quebec population in general, have rejected it' (Tremblay 2009: 2).

In important respects the Quebec case begins to explain how the normative debates around interculturalism and multiculturalism have been quite political and less about normative practice. One of the contributions of this book therefore is to bring more contextualised policy concerns into view. In Europe the concept of interculturalism is now found in places as diverse as German, Greek and Italian education programmes (Luchtenberg 2003; Portera 2012), Spanish urban governance (a Spanish network of Intercultural Cities was created in 2011[6]), Belgian commissions on cultural diversity, and Russian teaching on world cultures (Froumin 2003), and is principally oriented towards addressing questions of migration-related diversity. A prominent symbolic example could be how 2008 was designated the European Year of Intercultural Dialogue (EYID), with the European Commission's

support in Vertovec and Wessendorf's reading that while the term 'multiculturalism' has 'disappeared from the political rhetoric' (2010: 18), this is something that is not paralleled by the 'eradication, nor much to the detriment, of actual measures, institutions, and frameworks of minority cultural recognition' (2010: 21).

[6] See <http://www.ciudadesinterculturales.com> (last accessed 2 June 2015).

stated objective being to encourage 'all those living in Europe to explore the benefits of our rich cultural heritage and opportunities to learn from different cultural traditions'. The aforementioned Intercultural Cities programme places emphasis on interculturalism as an integration policy (Guidikova 2015) and a way to manage city-level public spaces (Wood 2015). It was nurtured in management and urban studies on diversity, focusing on policy and implementation (Zapata-Barrero 2015b), and assumed that diversity is itself a culture that should be promoted through an intercultural strategy (Zapata-Barrero 2015a).

In both cases, although expressed differently, advocates of interculturalism wish to emphasise its positive qualities in terms of addressing a gap that multiculturalism allegedly misses. Multiculturalists have in turn responded to this characterisation by restating what multiculturalism is (see Chapter 2) and challenging the argument that interculturalism offers a substantive advance. Outside of Canada, which we have already noted, in the USA, the UK and later the Netherlands multiculturalism was initially centred on issues of schooling, both in terms of the curriculum and as an institution, to include features such as minority languages, non-Christian religions and holidays, halal food, dress and so on. In this respect there was an ambition to remake the common institution and curriculum to include minorities too. This became married to a parallel equality focus that had a civil rights provenance, and which together developed more broadly into the contemporary meaning of multiculturalism as a critique of 'the myth of homogeneous and monocultural nation-states' (Castles 2000: 5), and an advocacy of the right of minority 'cultural maintenance and community formation, linking these to social equality and protection from discrimination' (ibid.). The political multiculturalism of Modood (2006: 61), for example, insists that 'when new groups enter a society, there has to be some education and refinement of . . . sensitivities in the light of changing circumstances and the specific vulnerabilities of new entrants'.

Multiculturalists, however, argue that much of this is consistent with interculturalist objectives. Kymlicka (Chapter 7) presents an especially challenging response: 'The interculturalism-as-remedy-for-failed-multiculturalism trope is not offered as an objective social science account of our situation, but rather, I believe, is intended to serve as a new narrative, or, if you like, a new myth.' A series of debates have therefore emerged, but too often these have remained spatially restricted to either Europe or North America, and so are rarely bridged and connected to each other, or are restricted to broad categories which locate interculturalism and multiculturalism in, for example, a 'duality' and 'diversity' paradigm respectively (see Chapter 4). This means that while the intercultural-multicultural debate is now widely established, there remains untapped potential for intellectual dialogue and policy engagement for audiences across (and also within) both approaches. This edited collection addresses this gap by engaging with real-world cases that move us beyond pure theory to ask: what are the dividing lines between interculturalism and multiculturalism?

Let us begin with where there is agreement:

- First, both interculturalism and multiculturalism not only register the undeniable fact of cultural pluralism but see this as an asset even while each is committed to reconciling this diversity with unity.
- Second, each has a shared adversary in assimilationist and unreconstructed ideas of membership and policy perspectives concerning citizenship.
- Third, there is a common aversion to formalist (or deontological) notions of liberalism that do not take into consideration the role and function of culture and identity.
- Fourth, each seeks to remake the terms of fair and equal treatment through the inclusion of cultural difference.

Where there appears to be more tension is explicitly taken up in the various chapters that follow and can perhaps also be identified in terms of four themes:

- First, the status of dialogue, contact and interpersonal relations within respective approaches.
- Second, the position of historical majority cultural forms – or majority precedence.
- Third, the normative significance of recognising groups in addition to individual citizens.
- Fourth, the status of minority religious communities and organisations.

On the second issue, Bouchard (2011: 438) usefully summarises how 'interculturalism concerns itself with the interests of the majority culture, whose desire to perpetuate and maintain itself is perfectly legitimate, as much as it does with the interests of minorities and immigrants'. In this respect interculturalism addresses multiculturalism's alleged asymmetry in focusing only on the 'minority'. What is interesting is that this broadly stays within conventional parameters, for example it means that it is not only liberal nationalists who think that historical 'elective affinities' (Canovan 1998) mean nation-states are the best guarantors of a type of liberal citizenship. While multiculturalists too want to retain the link between culture and citizenship, they would seek to remake both (see Chapters 9 and 11).

In relation to the third issue, the status of groups, as Meer and Modood (Chapter 2) show, some interculturalists are more hostile to the recognition of minority group claims (indeed, to group categories more broadly). This is clearly expressed in this volume by the chapter from Ted Cantle (Chapter 6). Ricard Zapata-Barrero (Chapter 3) also argues that a prevailing differentia of interculturalism (from multiculturalism) is that the former prioritises individual over group rights. Yet it is easily shown that other interculturalists, such as Bouchard (Chapter 4) and Gagnon and Iacovino (Chapter 5), want to build around groups and nations.

In relation to the fourth issue of disagreement, the orientation towards the ethno-religious, interculturalists broadly do not include religious groups within their framework, preferring to leave new religions to prevailing approaches of toleration within existing secularist arrangements. However, on this some interculturalists and some multiculturalists complement each other. Kymlicka's liberal secularism, for example, is quite consistent with this view (Meer and Modood 2016). In his view most matters to do with the needs of religious minorities seem to fall within the ambit of the traditional freedoms of worship, association and conscience (see Modood 2007/13). The only additional questions that his political multiculturalism considers in relation to religious minorities are exemptions (such as allowing Sikh men to wear turbans when others have to wear motorcycle helmets) rather than, as in the case of other cultural groups, demands for democratic participation, for public resources or institutional presence.

Turning in detail to the first issue of contention, the status of dialogue and contact for interculturalists, the argument is best put by Zapata-Barrero (Chapter 3), to whom

> the core of intercultural citizenship is essentially one basic idea: that the interaction among people from different diversity attributions matters, and that this has been overlooked by the multicultural citizenship paradigm, which has mainly concentrated on ensuring the cultural rights of diverse groups.

To explore this further, the next section of this chapter locates intercultural and multicultural concerns within the wider intellectual landscape. The important point to bear in mind at the outset, however, and as the subsequent chapters betray, is that neither interculturalists nor multiculturalists occupy a position of unanimity amongst themselves, and interculturalists and multiculturalists can and do agree. A good place to begin to understand why concerns the common denominator of the role and nature of pluralism, something that has both shared and diverging implications for interculturalism and multiculturalism, and it is to this we next turn.

Inter- and multicultural pluralism

The fact of pluralism, to paraphrase Rawls, emerges as self-evident in a world comprising over six hundred languages, five hundred ethno-cultural groups and innumerable religions spread across nearly two hundred recognised sovereign states. By definition, therefore, pluralism is an inescapable feature of human societies, and 'can neither be wished out of existence nor suppressed without an unacceptable degree of coercion, and often not even then' (Parekh 2000: 196). Different kinds of polities have long struggled with reconciling cultural pluralism with an idea of collective membership. In one respect this is odd because the intermingling of cultural (including religious and ethnic) diversity is as old as we can record. On the other hand it may well be anticipated that unsettling established social and identity configurations creates challenges, something that is no less apparent in modern polities. The way pluralism is conceived obviously has implications for understanding the relationships between interculturalism and multiculturalism and other ways of reconciling unity and diversity. Minimally, we might build on the distinction Isaiah Berlin (1991: 10) put forward between pluralism and relativism. While the latter flattens out our capacity to make value judgements, according to Berlin, the former retains this capacity but anchors it in an ability to imagine and empathise with that which is different to us. He elaborates:

> Members of one culture can, by the force of imaginative insight, understand . . . the value, the ideals, the forms of life of another culture or society, even those remote in time or space. They may find these values unacceptable, but if they open their minds sufficiently they can grasp how one might be a full human being, with whom one could communicate, and at the same time live in the light of values widely different from one's own, but which nevertheless one can see to be values, ends of life, by the realisation of which men could be fulfilled.

This value pluralism can endow agents with a capacity to see the world from different vantage points, which is quite different to how pluralism is sometimes understood, as, say, a set of governmental approaches. The latter are not purely theoretical, though they take in theory, but instead centre on an understanding of democracy as a competition between rival elites (Dahl 1961), or a conception of organised groups which form a link between the governed and representative government (Bentley 1948). In Berlin's statement, in contrast, pluralism bestows a certain insight into real and imagined cultural differences, ways of life and forms of social organisation.

Contact and dialogue

This insight is not neutral – that is to say, it is not without judgement on our part – but it is nonetheless able to register a utility in different approaches. Our interest here primarily concerns how both interculturalism and multiculturalism appeal to a common register of pluralism on which contact and dialogue can proceed. In one respect this is an obvious ambition. As Carbaugh (2013: 10) asks, 'Who, indeed, would be against "dialogue"?' The challenge is surely to make an abstract ambition not only operable but also politically meaningful. Dialogue, to paraphrase Augustine on charity, is no substitute for justice. And the complaint arises that in recent years we have seen a significant intellectual investment in dialogue in a manner that is sometimes uncoupled from wider political contexts (see Phipps 2014). Differences in status and power relations more broadly mean that dialogue(s) do not proceed on an equal footing. This can easily imply what Young (1990: 165) called 'coming to the game after it is already begun, after the rules and standards have been set, and having to prove oneself accordingly'. This of course spills over into the manner in which different kinds of contact can proceed. As Pettigrew et al. argue:

> Not all intergroup contact reduces prejudice. Some situations engender enhanced prejudice. Such negative intergroup contact has received less research attention ... Negative contact typically occurs in situations where the participants feel threatened and did not choose to have contact. These situations frequently occur in work environments where intergroup competition exists as well as in situations involving intergroup conflict. (2011: 277)

As Zapata-Barrero (Chapter 3) argues, contact and dialogue are understood in functional terms as 'interaction', defined roughly as acting together, sharing a public sphere and working for some common purpose, and he extensively deals with the place of 'interaction' in founding several strands within interculturalism. A compelling attempt to bring pluralism and dialogue together is once more found in Parekh's argument. Here the intrinsic value of pluralism lies in how cultures other than one's own have something to teach us, such that members of minority cultures should be encouraged to cultivate their moral and aesthetic insights for humanity as a whole. He offers the following explanation:

> Since human capacities and values conflict, every culture realizes a limited range of them and neglects, marginalizes and suppresses others. However rich it may be, no culture embodies all that is valuable in human life and develops the full range of human possibilities. Different cultures thus correct and complement each other, expand each other's horizon of thought and alert each other to new forms of human fulfillment. The value of other cultures is independent of whether or not they are options for us ... inassimilable otherness challenges us intellectually and morally, stretches our imagination, and compels us to recognize the limits of our categories of thought. (Parekh 2000: 167)

Going further than Berlin's 'imaginative insight', Parekh uses the idea of intercultural dialogue as a basis to widen the horizons of our thought or of a way of life. Moreover, Parekh thinks dialogue rather than an appeal to universal truths is the way to handle multicultural conflicts like those over free speech and protecting minorities from demeaning speech, or the virtues of exclusively legalised monogamy over the inclusion of polygamy. This can be contrasted with rationalist conceptions of dialogue. In the latter camp Habermas (1987), most prominently, deems dialogue a powerful regulative ideal that appeals to reason and reciprocity rather than equality per se. What this under-emphasises in practice are existing and entrenched hierarchies (and, more broadly, it suffers from problems of abstractness). In contrast, dialogue for both interculturalists and multiculturalists is 'bi-focal' (Parekh 2000: 271) in so far as it centres on both 'the minority's and wider society's way of life'. Whilst multiculturalists like Parekh make intercultural dialogue at philosophical and political levels central to their theories, interculturalists have offered an alternative: dialogue in terms of local encounters. Here, then, is a perfect example of where multiculturalists and interculturalists usefully complement each other, even if the latter sometimes believe that the emphasis on dialogue is an interculturalist innovation (see Chapters 9 and 11). One possible explanation is that sustaining a minority language has been central where interculturalism has developed; this is certainly the case in minority nations such as Quebec and Catalonia, and this is also true of Latin America, where Intercultural Bilingual Education has been a key element of *interculturalidad*.

Groups and nations

At this juncture some interculturalists and multiculturalists diverge on the status of historical majorities, for, as Modood (2014: 306; Chapter 11) observes, the intercultural 'emphasis on majoritarian anxieties is a radically different starting point from [multiculturalism]'. Perhaps this is best brought out not by comparing multiculturalism and interculturalism, but by two forms of the latter. Here we find a marked divergence between Quebec and European interculturalism. The former makes a moral and policy case for the recognition of relatively distinct substate nationalisms (see Chapters 4 and 5). Gagnon and Iacovino (Chapter 5), for example, contrast interculturalism positively with multiculturalism in a way that relies upon a strong formulation of groups, yet for Cantle

(Chapter 6) this 'mirrors much of the reified, static and defensive form of identity management found in European forms of multi-culturalism'. That Quebec has developed a distinctive intercultural political approach to diversity in opposition to federal Canadian multiculturalism, however, is now a widely established argument. As Bouchard neatly summarises:

> Since the middle of the nineteenth century, francophones in Quebec have fought to gain acceptance of the idea that Canada is composed of two nations (anglophone and francophone). This vision of the country was undermined by the introduction of multiculturalism, which made fran-cophones in Quebec simply one ethnic group among others throughout Canada. In this sense, multiculturalism weakened Quebec and for this reason it is the source of keen opposition from the francophone popula-tion. (Bouchard 2011: 462).

This framing and the wider distinction between Quebec intercul-turalism and Canadian multiculturalism is certainly a contested one (see Chapter 7), and might be illustrative of the difference between what Levey (Chapter 9) sees as 'hard' and 'soft' distinc-tions. Quebec interculturalists insist that there should be a public space and identity that is not merely about individual constitutional or legal rights, and this public space is an identity for those who share it and so qualifies and counterbalances other identities valued by citizens. So far, so republican. The important point is that this is deemed to have an inescapable historical character, such that Quebec, and not merely federal Canada, is an object immigrants need to have identification with and integrate into in order to main-tain Quebec as a nation and not just a federal province.[7] While for some Quebec is a nation within federal Canada, this intercultural-ism argument is not predicated on minority nationalism or multi-nationalism, but on a paradigm of minority/majority relations that are applicable to any nation and certainly would be asserted in an independent mononational Quebec. As such, and quite unlike their European counterparts (see Chapters 3 and 6), Quebec intercul-turalists are not minded to begin with the diversity of the location that migrants and ethnic minorities are from, or the super-diversity

---

[7] The same point may apply in other multinational states, but there are different degrees and variations of 'multinationalism'.

that this is alleged to cultivate. Guidikova (2014: 14), for example, insists that interculturalism in its European moulds 'thrives on a dynamic and constantly changing environment in which individuals and collectives express multiple, hybrid and evolving identities and needs'. This is very different to sustaining and elevating historically sedimented ad hoc majority precedence.

The difference between the two types of interculturalism instead bears resemblance to how Levey (Chapter 9) draws out the differences between 'parity multiculturalists' and 'liberal nationalist multiculturalism' which, as he understands it, turns on the treatment of majority cultures. On this view, since a Rawlsian neutral state organised by liberal principles alone is impossible, the best means of achieving liberal goals – including personal liberties, autonomy, freedom for cultural diversity, liberal constitutionalism and the welfare state – is through the stable basis of a nation or a nation-state or a multi-nation (Miller 1995). As Loobuyk (Chapter 10) puts it: 'distributive justice and deliberative democracy require that citizens share more than simply political principles, but less than a shared conception of the good life. A shared but "thin" national identity should and can be sufficient.' The difference between this 'liberal national multiculturalism' and what Levey terms 'parity multiculturalism' in fact seems a smaller cleavage than that between Quebec and European conceptions of interculturalism.

This should not imply, however, that there are *not* significant differences between the liberal nationalist, interculturalist and multiculturalist camps. Like a Venn diagram, they can simultaneously occupy common and distinct areas. If we take up Levey's challenge of contrasting liberal nationalists with political multiculturalists, beyond the issue of majority precedence that he uses to distinguish the two, a number of observations can be made. It is clear that political multiculturalism can be more receptive to the place of religion in public life, or more precisely that religion is not precluded a priori on the grounds that it makes claims of a different order to those relating to ethnicity or culture. Furthermore, and in a manner that returns us to the discussion of the majority, the terms of common membership – especially, though not exclusively, in relation to national identity – are deemed more fluid and changeable. Thirdly, and perhaps at a more foundational level, political multiculturalists such as Modood (2013) do not ground their politics in an ethics of autonomy, or certainly an ethics of *individual* autonomy. This joins together with a fourth concern relating to the capacity of communities and groups, and their roles in forging conceptions of the good life. Perhaps sharing something with McLaughlin (1992: 123) here too, the third and fourth distinctions mean that multiculturalists, much more so than liberal nationalists, consider there to be *multiple* launch pads for autonomy, in which 'a legitimate starting point is from the basis of experience of a particular "world view" or cultural identity; a substantiality of belief, practice or value'.

Neither liberal nationalists nor interculturalists give religious groups the importance they give to ethnicity, preferring to leave new religions to prevailing norms of toleration within existing secularist arrangements – this is especially true in Quebec, where some interculturalists respond by reaffirming a conception of *laicite*, or at least reinterpreting *laicite* as 'open secularism' (see Chapter 4) – while others allow exemptions, for example in relation to the Sikh turban. Here some interculturalists and some multiculturalists also complement each other. Kymlicka's liberal secularism, for example, is quite consistent with this view (see also Chapter 2). Yet here European interculturalists (see Chapter 6) seek to change the frame from one of accommodating ethnoreligious groups to one of globalisation, young people, hybridity, cosmopolitanism, individualism and so forth, and so are part of this larger consensus of not fully including religion within policies of diversity.

Chapter overviews

The first substantive chapter, by Meer and Modood, sets the challenge that constitutes this book, namely the relation between multiculturalism and interculturalism, specifically in identifying in what ways the latter is different from and/or an advance on multiculturalism. Meer and Modood critically examine some of the ways in which conceptions of interculturalism are being positively contrasted with multiculturalism, especially as political ideas. They argue that while some advocates of a political interculturalism wish to emphasise its positive qualities in terms of encouraging communication, recognising dynamic identities, promoting unity and critiquing illiberal cultural practices, each of these qualities is also an important (on occasion foundational) feature of multiculturalism.

Importantly, they explore the provenance of multiculturalism as an intellectual tradition, with a view to assessing the extent to which its origins continue to shape its contemporary public 'identity', to show how some of the criticism of multiculturalism is rooted in an objection to earlier formulations that displayed precisely those elements deemed unsatisfactory when compared with interculturalism. They maintain, however, that interculturalism – as a political discourse – does not, intellectually at least, eclipse multiculturalism, and so should be considered as complementary to multiculturalism.

To some extent Zapata-Barrero reframes this challenge in arguing that the multicultural debates of the late twentieth century tended to follow a cultural rights-based approach to diversity. He maintains that these were mistakenly centred on questions such as the rights of cultural recognition in the public sphere, and how to reassess equality and cultural rights of non-national citizens with different languages, religions and cultural practices. This approach characterised multicultural citizenship studies until the emergence of a 'new paradigm of interculturalism', which, in his reading, offers a lifeline to all those who see diversity as an asset in the public square. In providing a theoretically driven account of the 'intercultural turn', Zapata-Barrero proposes an overarching political theory that can function as a normative framework.

In the first of our chapters tackling the interculturalism/multiculturalism nexus from a Quebec perspective, Gérard Bouchard returns us to the view that pluralism provides the general background of interculturalism, which translates into respect for human rights, support for immigration, assistance to minority languages and cultures, wider practices of accommodation, and so forth. He moves on from this to insist that at the micro level, a second defining trait of interculturalism is its emphasis on exchange and interaction between citizens of all origins, with a view to activating diversity as a resource, fighting stereotypes, avoiding 'groupism' and preventing social exclusion. His model of interculturalism, moreover, stresses integration as a two-way process but, in addition, is designed for societies where perceptions of ethnocultural realities are structured on the basis of a majority/minorities relationship. In this view the protection of minority rights *must* be reconciled with majority rights, which also calls for some forms of ad hoc, contextual precedence in favour of the majority culture.

In the second of our readings of interculturalism in a Quebec context, Gagnon and Iacovino frame the merits of interculturalism as an explicit model for integration. They contrast this with how they see Canadian multiculturalism as being a product of nation-building efforts, rather than a genuine commitment to the main tenets of multiculturalism. They maintain it is a framework for the promotion of cultural pluralism. They contend that a model of cultural pluralism along the lines of Quebec interculturalism makes a more serious effort to balance the requirements of unity with the preservation, recognition and flourishing of minority cultures. At the same time they note the enduring problem confronting the Quebec model, one that would have to be taken into account in any future attempts at empirical verification, namely the idea of competing interpretations of citizenship by those identified for integration in the first place. The Quebec model is, they maintain, placed to address this because it is embedded in a larger project for national affirmation. The fact that it can legitimately be included as a model for integration at the very least demonstrates the strides that Quebec has made in the area of citizenship.

A contrasting reading of interculturalism comes from Ted Cantle's contribution, which begins with the view that multicultural policies, in Europe at least, are not fit for purpose and have slowed, if not inhibited, both integration and the acceptance of difference. Interculturalism for Cantle is based upon an entirely different conceptual and policy framework and offers a new and progressive approach to how we learn to live with diversity. In this view the Bouchard and also Gagnon and Iacovino readings of interculturalism have been the most difficult to sustain because they mirror what he argues is a reified, static and defensive form of identity management in European forms of multiculturalism. Interestingly, Cantle sees the Canadian government form of multiculturalism as being closer to the European idea of interculturalism. Cantle (2012: 79) nonetheless maintains that 'Interculturalism should . . . build upon the essential elements of multiculturalism – the framework of rights to equal treatment and non-discrimination are critical – as well as developing the interaction and belonging programmes initiated by community cohesion.' In this regard, while multiculturalism's focus on inequalities was justified, he argues it has failed to adapt to 'super-diversity' and the multifaceted aspects of difference and 'otherness', including those based on disability, age, sexual orientation and gender – what we might otherwise call 'intersectionality'. Further, for Cantle multiculturalism remains firmly rooted in intra-national differences, between minority and majority populations, and can be contrasted with interculturalism, which recognises that 'difference' now crosses national boundaries and also reflects the heterogeneity of national, ethnic and faith groups.

These robust challenges are met with an equally vigorous rejoinder from Will Kymlicka. In his contribution Kymlicka argues that interculturalists may think they are defending diversity, but their 'crude anti-multiculturalist rhetoric may play into the hands of xenophobes who reject both multiculturalism and interculturalism' (Chapter 7). He focuses on the intercultural strategy to build a new political narrative in which interculturalism emerges from the alleged failed extremes of multiculturalism. 'Can this new narrative work to energize pro-diversity forces and to undercut support for populism?' he asks. The answer is uncertain, for in his reading interculturalist narratives have too often left untouched exclusionary accounts of nationhood, and unintentionally legitimised populist narratives about the untrustworthy nature of mainstream elites on issues of diversity. In this respect, he concludes, 'The search for new narratives of diversity will have to continue.'

Stepping outside the North American/Western European nexus, Ana Solano-Campos's chapter brings in Latin American academic debates about multiculturalism, interculturalism and *interculturalidad*, identifying patterns, similarities and differences among them. Her chapter provides an introduction to a form of interculturalism, Latin American *interculturalidad*, which emerged as a response not to post-immigrant social formations but to colonial and postcolonial dynamics and relationships, including but not limited to indigenous groups. She argues that across the continent, academic discussions largely 'prescribe and dichotomise models of diversity' (Chapter 8). In contrast, she advocates a contextual approach that opens up potential avenues for dialogue and cross-pollination, focusing especially on how Latin American scholars define *interculturalidad*, and especially its capacity for 'equitable relations among members of different cultural universes' (Godenzzi Alegre 1996: 15, in Chapter 8). There is, however, no one simple or agreed-upon definition of *interculturalidad* among scholars, particularly because *interculturalidad* in the Latin American context is conceived as a work in progress. The important acknowledgement is that interculturalism also exists in contexts other than North America (especially Canada) and Europe, and that it emerges in contexts where multiculturalism has not been the predominant diversity paradigm. In these cases it is not necessarily a reaction to dissatisfaction presumably caused by multiculturalism, which means that *interculturalidad* in Latin America is not as recent as some scholars might assume.

Our final three chapters return us to the theme of possible reconciliations between interculturalism and multiculturalism. In the first, by Geoff Levey, we observe that the tensions *between* interculturalism and multiculturalism can also run *across* interculturalism and multiculturalism. So while the issue of 'ad hoc majority precedence' is central between multiculturalism and interculturalism, at least on the Quebec model, in Levey's reading it runs across liberal nationalist multiculturalism and parity multiculturalism too. The second, by Patrick Loobuyck, understands interculturalism neither as an anti-multiculturalist position nor as a remedy for the alleged failures of multiculturalism, but instead as an additional strategy that might rest alongside modes of liberal nationalism and constitutional patriotism. The challenge that each sets itself, in this reading, is to create a sense of belonging as a necessary condition for solidarity and deliberative democracy in multicultural societies. Loobuyck understands this as presently expressed across three intercultural policy applications concerned with social mixing, language and civic integration programmes, and integrative religious education. In this account, while multiculturalism and interculturalism do not contradict each other on the theoretical level, there may be some tensions on the policy level.

In the final chapter Tariq Modood, a European multiculturalist, directly engages with Quebecan interculturalism. He acknowledges that Quebecan interculturalists have raised the question of the normative significance of the majority in the way that multiculturalists have not, and that multiculturalists can learn from those interculturalists. However, he holds that multiculturalists can take on board this concern with the majority without changing or adapting multiculturalism. He accepts the starting points of the 'ad hoc majority precedence' argument but not the conclusions. To underline the point, he concludes by reaffirming a commitment to accommodate ethno-religious minorities that is very different from what is advocated by Quebecers. So, despite emphasising the over-laps and dialogical connections between Quebecan intercultural-ism and multiculturalism as he understands it, he is of the view that they clearly differ on majority and minority entitlements.

This, indeed, could also be said to be the message of the book: there are different versions of multiculturalism and intercultural-ism; within each set there are differences even while there is sig-nificant common ground across the two sets. This is a sentiment shared in the afterword by Bhikhu Parekh, whose own position is one which marries interculturalism and multiculturalism. He is nonetheless willing to acknowledge that there are some other things that we can learn from more recent interculturalist critics, while rejecting the view that multiculturalism is flawed and needs to be replaced, or that interculturalism is a successor position. In this respect there are not fundamental differences between the two 'isms', so that while interculturalisms add to multiculturalisms, they do not always understand the latter, and certainly cannot be said to supersede political multiculturalism as it has been built up in theory and practice over the decades on both sides of the North Atlantic.

Acknowledgements

This edited collection includes papers first presented at a two-day European Science Foundation (ESF) exploratory workshop organised by Ricard Zapata-Barrero and Tariq Modood, held in Barcelona 29–30 May 2014. We would like to thank the ESF for their generous funding and support. The collection also incorpo-rates some materials first developed in an earlier form in the *Journal of Intercultural Studies*, 33 (2), and we gratefully acknowledge that here. Ana Solano-Campos provided very helpful comments on an earlier draft, and Jenny Daly at Edinburgh University Press has provided excellent support throughout the review process; we would also like to thank her and EUP more broadly. The image appearing on this cover belongs to the weekly broadcast television programme 'Tot un món', from Televisió de Catalunya (TV3), http://www.ccma.cat/tv3/tot-un-mon/ We are very grateful to Televisió de Catalunya for allowing its use here. Finally, we have been very fortunate to be able to include a foreword and afterword respectively from Professor Charles Taylor and Professor Lord Bhikhu Parekh. We are delighted to include their participation.

References

Banting, K., and W. Kymlicka (2013), 'Is There Really a Retreat from Multiculturalism Policies? New Evidence from the Multiculturalism Policy Index', *Comparative European Politics*, 11, 577–98.

Benhabib, S. (2002), *The Claims of Culture: Equality and Diversity in a Global Era*, Princeton: Princeton University Press.

Bentley, A. (1948), *The Process of Government*, Evanston, IL: Principia.

Berlin, I. (1991), *The Crooked Timber of Humanity: Chapters in the History of Ideas*, London: Fontana Press.

Berry, J. W., J. S. Phinney, D. L. Sam and P. Vedder (2006), 'Immigrant Youth: Acculturation, Identity and Adaptation', *Applied Psychology: An International Review*, 55 (3), 303–32.

Bloemraad, I. (2006), *Becoming a Citizen: Incorporating Immigrants and Refugees in the United States and Canada*, Berkeley: University of California Press.

Bloomfield, J., and F. Bianchini (2004), *Planning for the Intercultural City*, Stroud: Comedia.

Bouchard, G. (2011), 'What Is Interculturalism?', *McGill Law Journal*, 56 (2), 435–68.

Bouchard, G., and C. Taylor (2008), *Building the Future: A Time for Reconciliation*, Report of the Consultation Commission on Accommodation Practices Related to Cultural Difference, Quebec City: Government of Quebec.

Canovan, M. (1998), *Nationhood and Political Theory*, Cheltenham: Edward Elgar Publishing.

Cantle, T. (2012), *Interculturalism: The New Era of Cohesion and Diversity*, Basingstoke: Palgrave Macmillan.

Cantle, T. (2013), 'Interculturalism: What Makes it Distinctive?', in M. Barrett (ed.), *Interculturalism and Multiculturalism: Similarities and Differences*, Strasbourg: Council of Europe, pp. 69–92.

Carbaugh, D. (2013), 'On Dialogue Studies', *Journal of Intercultural Studies*, 1 (1), 9–28.

Castles, S. (2000), *Ethnicity and Globalisation: From Migrant Worker to Transnational Citizen*, London: Sage.

Clarijs, M. A. J. L., I. Guidikova and T. Malmberg (2011), *Diversity and Community Development: An Intercultural Approach*, Amsterdam: SWP.

Council of Europe (COE), Committee of Ministers (2008), *Living Together as Equals in Dignity: White Paper on Intercultural Dialogue*, Strasbourg: Council of Europe, <http://www.coe.int/t/dg4/intercultural/source/white%20paper_final_revised_en.pdf> (last accessed 1 June 2015).

Dahl, R. A. (1961), *Who Governs? Democracy and Power in an American City*, New Haven: Yale University Press.

Froumin, I. (2003), 'Citizenship Education and Ethnic Issues in Russia', in J. A. Banks (ed.), *Diversity and Citizenship Education: Global Perspectives*, San Francisco: Jossey-Bass, pp. 273–98.

Gagnon, A.-G., and R. Iacovino (2007), *Federalism, Citizenship and Quebec: Debating Multinationalism*, Toronto: University of Toronto Press.

Guidikova, I. (2014), *Cultural Diversity and Cities – The Intercultural Integration Approach*, EUI: RSCAS Policy Paper 2014/02.

Guidikova, I. (2015), 'Intercultural Integration: A New Paradigm for Managing Diversity as an Advantage', in R. Zapata-Barrero (ed.), *Interculturalism in*

Cities: Concept, Policy and Implementation, Cheltenham: Edward Elgar Publishing, pp. 136–51.

Habermas, J. (1987), *Theory of Communicative Action Volume Two: Liveworld and System: A Critique of Functionalist Reason*, trans. T. A. McCarthy, Boston, MA: Beacon Press.

Heath, A., and J. Roberts (2008), *British Identity, Its Sources and Possible Implications for Civic Attitudes and Behaviour*, research report for Lord Goldsmith's Citizenship Review, London: HMSO.

Hepburn, E., and R. Zapata-Barrero (eds) (2014), *The Politics of Immigration in Multi-Level States: Governance and Political Parties*, Basingstoke: Palgrave Macmillan.

James, M. R. (2003), 'Communicative Action, Strategic Action, and Inter-Group Dialogue', *European Journal of Political Theory*, 2 (2), 157–82.

Kraus, P. A., and K. Schönwälder (2006), 'Multiculturalism in Germany: Rhetoric, Scattered Experiments, and Future Chances', in K. Banting and W. Kymlicka (eds), *Multiculturalism and the Welfare State: Recognition and Redistribution in Contemporary Democracies*, Oxford: Oxford University Press, pp. 202–21.

Kymlicka, W. (2012), 'Multiculturalism: Success, Failure, and the Future', in Migration Policy Institute (ed.), *Rethinking National Identity in the Age of Migration*, Bielefeld: Verlag, pp. 33–78.

Laegaard, S. (2014), 'Multiculturalism and Contextualism: How is Context Relevant for Political Theory?', *European Journal of Political Theory*, DOI: 10.1177/1474885114562975.

Luchtenberg, S. (2003), *Migration, Education and Change*, London: Routledge.

McLaughlin, T. H. (1992), 'The Ethics of Separate Schools', in M. Leicester and M. Taylor (eds), *Ethics, Ethnicity and Education*, London: Kegan Paul, pp. 114–36.

Maxwell, B., D. I. Waddington, K. McDonough, A.-A. Cormier and M. Schwimmer (2012), 'Interculturalism, Multiculturalism, and the State Funding and Regulation of Conservative Religious Schools', *Educational Theory*, 62 (4), 427–47.

Meer, N. (2014), *Race and Ethnicity: Key Concepts*, London: Sage.

Meer, N., and T. Modood (2016), 'Religious Pluralism in United States and Britain: Its Implications for Muslims and Nationhood', *Social Compass*, 62, 526–40.

Meer, N., P. Mouritsen, D. Faas and N. de Witte (2015), 'Examining Post-Multicultural and Civic Turns in the Netherlands, Britain, Germany and Denmark', *American Behavioural Scientist*, 59 (6), 702–26.

Miller, D. (1995), *On Nationality*, Oxford: Oxford University Press.

Modood, T. (2006), 'Obstacles to Multicultural Integration', *International Migration*, 44 (5), 51–62.

Modood, T. (2013), *Multiculturalism: A Civic Idea*, Cambridge: Polity Press.

Modood, T. (2014), 'Multiculturalism, Interculturalism and the Majority', *Journal of Moral Education*, 43, 302–15.

Modood, T., and N. Meer (2013), 'Multiculturalism', in J. Krieger (ed.), *The Oxford Companion to Comparative Politics*, Oxford: Oxford University Press, pp. 11–116.

Parekh, B. (2000), *Rethinking Multiculturalism: Cultural Diversity and Political Theory*, Basingstoke: Macmillan.

Pécoud, A., and P. de Guchteneire (2007), 'Introduction: The Migration without Border Scenario', in A. Pécoud and P. de Guchteneire (eds), *Migration*

Without Borders: Essays on the Free Movement of People, Paris: UNESCO, pp. 1–32.

Pettigrew, T. E., L. R. Tropp, U. Wagner and O. Christ (2011), 'Recent Advances in Intergroup Contact Theory', *International Journal of Intercultural Relations*, 35, 271–80.

Phillips, M. (2006), *Londonistan: How Britain Created a Terror State Within*, London: Gibson Square Books.

Phipps, A. (2014), '"They Are Bombing Now": "Intercultural Dialogue" in Times of Conflict', *Language and Intercultural Communication*, 14 (1), 108–24.

Potera, A. (2012), 'Intercultural Education and All-Day Schools in Italy', in N. Palaiologou and G. Dietz (eds), *Mapping the Broad Field of Multicultural and Intercultural Education Worldwide: Towards the Development of a New Citizen*, Newcastle: Cambridge Scholars Publishing.

Prins, G., and R. Salisbury (2008), 'Risk, Threat and Security: The Case of the United Kingdom', *RUSI Journal*, 153 (1), 22–7.

Taylor, C. (2001), 'Multiculturalism and Political Identity', *Ethnicities*, 1, 122–8.

Toynbee, A. (1958), *Christianity among the Religions of the World*, London: Oxford University Press.

Tremblay, L. B. (2009), *The Bouchard-Taylor Report on Cultural and Religious Accommodation: Multiculturalism by Any Other Name?*, EUI Law Working Papers, 2009/18, <http://cadmus.eui.eu/handle/1814/12971> (last accessed 1 June 2015).

Triandafyllidou, A., T. Modood and N. Meer (eds) (2011), *European Multiculturalism(s): Cultural, Religious and Ethnic Challenges*, Edinburgh: Edinburgh University Press.

Tubino, F. (2013), 'Intercultural Practices in Latin American Nation States', *Journal of Intercultural Studies*, 34 (5), 604–19.

Tully, J. (2000), 'The Challenge of Reimagining Citizenship and Belonging in Multicultural and Multinational Societies', in C. McKinnon and I. Hampsher-Monk (eds), *The Demands of Citizenship*, London: Continuum, pp. 212–34.

Tully, J. (2002), 'The Illiberal Liberal', in P. Kelly (ed.), *Multiculturalism Reconsidered*, Cambridge: Polity, pp. 102–13.

UNESCO (2008), *Investing in Cultural Diversity and Intercultural Dialogue: World Report on Cultural Diversity*, Paris: UNESCO.

Vertovec, S. (1999), 'Conceiving and Researching Transnationalism', *Ethnic and Racial Studies*, 22 (2), 1–24.

Vertovec, S., and S. Wessendorf (eds) (2010), *The Multiculturalism Backlash: European Discourses, Policies and Practices*, London: Routledge.

Walzer, M. (1997), *On Tolerance*, New Haven: Yale University Press.

Weller, P. (2012), 'The End of Multiculturalism? A Riposte', in Dialogue Society (eds), *Debating Multiculturalism I*, London: Dialogue Society, pp. 21–38.

Wilson, R. (2013), 'The Urgency of Intercultural Dialogue in a Europe of Insecurity', in M. Barrett (ed.), *Interculturalism and Multiculturalism: Similarities and Differences*, Strasbourg: Council of Europe, pp. 53–68.

Wood, P. (2004), *The Intercultural City Reader*, Stroud: Comedia.

Wood, P. (2015), 'Meet Me on the Corner? Shaping the Conditions for Cross-Cultural Interaction in Urban Public Space', in R. Zapata-Barrero (ed.), *Interculturalism in Cities: Concept, Policy and Implementation*, Cheltenham: Edward Elgar Publishing, pp. 53–75.

Young, I. M. (1990), *Justice and the Politics of Difference*, Princeton: Princeton University Press.

Zapata-Barrero, R. (ed.) (2009), *Immigration and Self-Government of Minority Nations*, Brussels: Peter Lang.

Zapata-Barrero, R. (2015a), 'Introduction: Framing the Intercultural Turn', in R. Zapata-Barrero (ed.), *Interculturalism in Cities: Concept, Policy and Implementation*, Cheltenham: Edward Elgar Publishing, pp. viii–xvi.

Zapata-Barrero, R. (2015b), 'Exploring the Foundations of the Intercultural Policy Paradigm: A Comprehensive Approach', *Identities: Global Studies in Culture and Power*, 22 (1), DOI: 10.1080/1070289X.2015.1006523.

2

Interculturalism, Multiculturalism and Citizenship

Nasar Meer and Tariq Modood

Introduction

In this chapter we engage with some recent authors who believe that an alternative to multiculturalism must be sought in order to understand and live with diversity.[1] These authors are not anti-diversity – on the contrary, in fact – but they share the view that multiculturalism is no longer a persuasive intellectual or policy approach. For example, the Council of Europe's White Paper on Intercultural Dialogue (2008) included the finding that the majority of practitioners and NGOs across Europe had come to the conclusion that multiculturalism was no longer fit for purpose, and needed to be replaced by a form of interculturalism. Similar views were expressed in the UNESCO World Report *Investing in Cultural Diversity and Intercultural Dialogue* (2008). More recently still, Ted Cantle (2012: 2) has described interculturalism 'as an opportunity to replace multiculturalism as a conceptual and policy framework', while Maxwell et al. (2012: 429) maintain that 'Interculturalism represents a gain over Multiculturalism while pursuing the same set of most uncontroversial political ends'. These statements therefore invite the question: in what ways – if at all – is interculturalism different, substantively or otherwise, from multiculturalism?

[1] This chapter uses materials from Meer and Modood 2011 and Meer and Modood 2012. We are grateful to Routledge and to the European Council for allowing their reproduction here and would also like to thank Geoff Levey, Per Mouritsen and Varun Uberoi for their very helpful comments on earlier drafts.

Is it merely the case, as Lentin (2005: 394) has suggested, that interculturalism is an 'updated version' of multiculturalism? If so, what is being 'updated'? If not, how do they differ (if, indeed, they do)? With a specific focus on the political, in this chapter we tentatively sketch out and critically evaluate four ways in which conceptions of interculturalism are being positively contrasted with multiculturalism (while these four positive evaluations of interculturalism overlap, we also consider them to be sufficiently distinct to be discussed separately). These are, firstly, as something greater than co-existence, in that interculturalism is allegedly more geared toward interaction and dialogue than multiculturalism. Secondly, that interculturalism is conceived as something less 'groupist' or more yielding of synthesis than multiculturalism. Thirdly, that interculturalism is something more committed to a stronger sense of the whole, in terms of such things as societal cohesion and national citizenship. Finally, that where multiculturalism may be illiberal and relativistic, interculturalism is more likely to lead to criticism of illiberal cultural practices (as part of the process of intercultural dialogue).

It is important to register at the outset that the chapter is concerned with what we understand as 'political interculturalism', by which we mean the ways in which interculturalism is appropriated in the critique of multiculturalism (Booth 2003; Powell and Sze 2004; Wood, Landry and Bloomfield 2006), in a manner that is not necessarily endorsed by wider advocates of interculturalism. Moreover, the purpose of this chapter is not to offer a comprehensive account of the topic, but to provide an entry point in developing a discussion, especially in relation to multiculturalism and interculturalism as frameworks for political relations in a context of cultural diversity. To do this satisfactorily we need first to elaborate something of our understanding of the intellectual character of multiculturalism, and it is to this that we now turn.

Liberalism and multiculturalism

To some commentators the staple issues that multiculturalism seeks to address, such as the rights of ethnic and national minorities, group representation, and perhaps even the political claims-making of 'new' social movements, are in fact 'familiar long-standing problems of political theory and practice' (Kelly 2002: 1). Indeed, some hold this view to the point of frustration:

> If we take a very broad definition of multiculturalism so that it simply corresponds to the demand that cultural diversity be accommodated, there is no necessary conflict between it and liberalism. . . . But most multiculturalists boast that they are innovators in political philosophy by virtue of having shown that liberalism cannot adequately satisfy the requirements of equal treatment and justice under conditions of cultural diversity. (Barry 2002: 205)

The first part of Barry's statement is perhaps more conciliatory than might be anticipated from an author admired for his argumentative robustness and theoretical hostility toward multiculturalism; while the second part poses more of an empirical question. Beginning with the first part, Barry's view is by no means rejected by those engaged in the 'multicultural turn'. Modood (2007a: 8), for instance, locates the genesis of multiculturalism within a 'matrix of principles that are central to contemporary liberal democracies', in a manner that establishes multiculturalism as 'the child of liberal egalitarianism, but like any child, it is not simply a faithful reproduction of its parents'. Another way of putting this is to state that as a concept, multiculturalism is a partial outgrowth of liberalism in that it establishes 'a third generation norm of legitimacy, namely respect for reasonable cultural diversity, which needs to be considered on a par with the [first and second generation] norms of freedom and equality, and so to modify policies of "free and equal treatment" accordingly' (Tully 2002: 102).

Our interest in this chapter is the political implication of this 'third generation norm of legitimacy' for a concept of citizenship, which includes the recognition that social life consists of individuals and groups, and that both need to be provided for in the formal and informal distribution of powers; not just in law, but in representation in the offices of the state, public committees, consultative exercises, and access to public fora. This means that while individuals have rights, mediating institutions such as trade unions, churches, neighbourhoods, immigrant associations and so on may also be encouraged to be active public players and fora for political discussion (and may even have a formal representative or administrative role to play in the state). One implication of this recognition means the reforming of national identity and citizenship, and offering an emotional identity with the whole to counterbalance the emotional loyalties to ethnic and religious communities (Modood 2007a).

To what extent, then, do we have an established 'canon' of multiculturalism as an intellectual ideal – one that persuasively distinguishes it from varieties of liberalism? It is certainly the case that theoretically there are three established policy-related strands of multiculturalism. One derives from radical social theory, especially uses of Derrida, and finds ideological expression in critiques of Eurocentrism, Afrocentrism and the wars over 'the canon' in the US universities in the 1980s. Another focuses on popular culture, everyday cultural interaction and the resulting hybridity and mixedness (Gilroy 2000), though the policy implications of such 'multiculture' are usually elusive (Meer and Modood 2009a). It is the third strand, however, which is the focus of our interest, and which grows out of policy developments, with Canada supplying one of the maturest examples, and, pioneered by Will Kymlicka, it is best expressed in engagements with liberal political theory.

This relationship to liberalism of this third strand of multiculturalism is a pertinent issue because it compels us to explore something of the provenance of multiculturalism as an intellectual tradition, with a view to assessing the extent to which its origins continue to shape its contemporary public 'identity'. We might reasonably ask this to identify the extent to which some of the criticism of multiculturalism is rooted in an objection to earlier formulations that displayed precisely those elements deemed unsatisfactory when compared with interculturalism, such as the fact that multiculturalism is more likely to be essentialist, illiberal, less agency-oriented, and less concerned with unity.

Before proceeding with this line of inquiry, it seems only reasonable to offer the intellectual health warning that multiculturalism as a concept is – like very many others – 'polysemic', such that multiculturalist authors cannot be held entirely responsible for the variety of ways in which the term is interpreted. This is something noted by Bhabha (1998: 31), who points to the tendency for multiculturalism to be appropriated as a 'portmanteau term', one that encapsulates a variety of sometimes contested meanings (cf. Meer and Modood 2011). In this respect the *idea* of multiculturalism might be said to have a 'chameleonic' quality that facilitates its simultaneous adoption and rejection in the critique or defence of a position (Smith 2010).

One illustration of this is the manner in which multiculturalism is simultaneously used as a label to describe both the fact of pluralism or diversity in any given society *and* a moral stance that cultural diversity is a desirable feature of a given society (as well as the different types of ways in which the state could recognise and support it). Moreover, in both theoretical and policy discourses, multiculturalism means different things in different places. In North America, for example, multiculturalism encompasses discrete groups with territorial claims, such as the native peoples and the Quebecers, even though these groups want to be treated as 'nations' within a multinational state, rather than merely as ethno-cultural groups in a mononational state (Kymlicka 1995). Indeed, in Europe, while groups with such claims, like the Catalans and the Scots, are thought of as nations, multiculturalism has a more limited meaning, referring to a post-immigration urban melange and the politics it gives rise to. One outcome is that while in North America language-based ethnicity is seen as the major political challenge, in Western Europe the conjunction of the terms 'immigration' and 'culture' now nearly always invokes the large, newly settled Muslim populations. Sometimes, usually in America, political terms such as 'multiculturalism' and 'rainbow coalition' are meant to include all groups marked by 'difference' and historic exclusion, such as women and gays (Young 1990).

Some have turned to this variety in meaning and usage of the term as an explanation of the allegedly 'widely divergent assessments of the short history and potential future of multiculturalism' (Kivisto and Faist 2007: 35), and it is to these different meanings and the contexts that generated them to which we now turn.

Forging multicultural citizenship

The term 'multiculturalism' emerged in the 1960s and 1970s in countries like Canada and Australia, and to a lesser extent in Britain and the United States (where it was initially limited to the field of education). As we have already noted, in the case of Canada the focus was from the start on constitutional and land issues, in a way that informed definitions of nationhood and related to unresolved legal questions concerning the entitlements and status of indigenous peoples, not to mention the further issue of the rise of a nationalist and secessionist movement in French-speaking Quebec.

At the outset in both Canada and Australia, multiculturalism was often presented as an application of 'liberal values' in that multiculturalism in these countries extended individual freedoms and substantiated the promise of equal citizenship. As evidence of this position, Kymlicka (2005a) points to the then Canadian Prime Minister Pierre Elliot Trudeau's 1971 speech on the implementation of a bilingual framework (a precursor to the later Multiculturalism Act). In this Trudeau promised that 'a policy of multiculturalism within a bilingual framework is basically the conscious support of individual freedom of choice. We are free to be ourselves' (Trudeau, quoted in Cardinal and Couture 1998: 249–50). In Kymlicka's (2005a: 2) reading this statement reflected the natural outgrowth of the liberalisation of Canadian social legislation in the period between the Bill of Rights (1960) and the Charter of Rights and Freedoms (1982), because 'the fundamental impulses behind the policy were the liberal values of individual freedom and equal citizenship on a non-discriminatory basis'.

While similar observations might be made in relation to Australia, this is only in so far as it reflected 'essentially a liberal ideology which operates within liberal institutions with the universal approval of liberal attitudes' (Jupp, quoted in Kymlicka 2005a: 2). This is because, in contrast with Canada, Australian multiculturalist policy developed more as a means to better integrate new immigrants, by easing the expectations of rapid assimilation.[2] As Levey (2008) elaborates, the policy did not include Indigenous Australians until the end of the 1970s and the Galbally Report (1978), which spoke of multiculturalism being a policy for 'all Australians' *including* Indigenous Australians.[3]

---

[2] We are very grateful to Geoff Levey for alerting us to the nuances of the inception of Australian multiculturalism.

[3] This inclusiveness was formalised in the first national multicultural policy, the National Agenda for a Multicultural Australia, under the Hawke Labor government in 1989. It has been retained in every subsequent version. However, while Indigenous Australians are formally included, the policy also states that their situation is distinct and requires its own special treatment and set of measures. As a consequence, many Indigenous leaders themselves reject multiculturalism as being irrelevant to them and, indeed, as undercutting their special status as First Peoples; see Levey 2008.

This kind of multiculturalism nevertheless simultaneously encompassed the recognition of discrete groups with territorial claims, such as the native peoples and the Quebecers, even though these groups wanted to be treated as 'nations' within a multinational state, rather than as minority groups in a mononational state. In reconciling these political claims to a political theory of liberalism, Kymlicka's (1995) own intellectual work is reflective of how an early theorisation of liberal multiculturalism was developing. This is because Kymlicka proposed group differentiated rights for three types of minorities comprising indigenous peoples, 'substate' national minorities and immigrant groups. The general principles common to each of these different types of minorities, he argued, included, firstly, that the state must be seen as belonging equally to all citizens. Secondly, individuals should be able to access state institutions, and act as full and equal citizens in political life, without having to hide or deny their cultural identity. Thirdly, the state should acknowledge the 'historic injustice' done to minority (non-dominant) groups. He interpreted these principles to mean that national and indigenous minorities were entitled to territorial autonomy and separate political representation, while migration-based groups, who were assumed to have no relationship to the country prior to migration, were entitled only to 'polyethnic rights', namely full civic integration that respected their cultural identities.

Outside of Canada, in the US, the UK and, later, the Netherlands, Kymlicka's distinction between national minority rights and polyethnic rights was not easily transposed. On the one hand, multiculturalism in these contexts mostly comprised 'polyethnicity': the policy focus was more likely to be concerned with schooling the children of Asian/black/Hispanic post-/neocolonial immigrants, and multiculturalism in these instances meant the extension of the school, both in terms of curriculum and as an institution, to include features such as 'mother-tongue' teaching, non-Christian religions and holidays, halal food, Asian dress and so on. On the other hand, the citizenship regimes in European countries included historical relationships with former colonial subjects that were distinct from the citizenship regimes of settler nations. For example, the 1948 British Nationality Act granted freedom of movement to all formerly or presently dependent – and now Commonwealth – territories (irrespective of whether their passports were issued by independent or colonial states) by creating the status of 'Citizenship of the United Kingdom and Colonies' (CUKC). Until they acquired one or other of the national citizenships in these post-colonial countries, these formerly British subjects continued to retain their British status. Thus, post-colonial migrants to Britain clearly were not historic minorities, but neither were they without historic claims upon Britain, and so they constituted a category that did not fit Kymlicka's categories of multicultural citizens.

Nevertheless, the term 'multiculturalism' in Europe came to mean – and now means throughout the English-speaking world and beyond – the political accommodation by the state and/or a dominant group of all minority cultures defined first and foremost by reference to race, ethnicity or religion, and, additionally but more controversially, by reference to other group-defining characteristics such as nationality and aboriginality. The latter is more controversial not only because it extends the range of the groups that have to be accommodated, but also because of the larger political claims made by such groups, who resist having these claims reduced to those of immigrants. Hence, despite Kymlicka's attempt to conceptualise multiculturalism-as-multinationalism, the dominant meaning of multiculturalism in politics relates to the claims of post-immigration groups.

This provenance of multiculturalism has bequeathed to its contemporary instantiations the importance of reconciling ideas of multiculturalism to ideas of citizenship, within a reciprocal balance of rights and responsibilities, assumptions of virtue and conceptions of membership or civic status (Meer 2010). While there is agreement that the membership conferred by citizenship should entail equal opportunity, dignity and confidence, different views remain about the proper ways, in culturally diverse societies, to confer this civic status. Those engaged in the 'multicultural turn' still maintain that conceptions of citizenship can frequently ignore the sensibilities of minorities marked by social, cultural and political differences (May, Modood and Squires 2004).

Hence the *political* multiculturalism of Modood, for example, insists that 'when new groups enter a society, there has to be some education and refinement of . . . sensitivities in the light of changing circumstances and the specific vulnerabilities of new entrants' (2006: 61). As such, a widely accepted *contemporary* thrust of what multiculturalism denotes includes a critique of 'the myth of homogeneous and monocultural nation-states', and an advocacy of the right of minority 'cultural maintenance and community formation, linking these to social equality and protection from discrimination' (Castles 2000: 5).

Beyond multicultural co-existence, towards intercultural dialogue and communication

Outside of Canada and North America more broadly, the idea of interculturalism has hitherto more commonly featured in Dutch and German accounts of integration, as well as in Spanish and Greek discussion of migrant diversity in the arena of education (Gundara 2000). Until relatively recently it has been less present in British discourses because concepts of race-relations, anti-racism, race-equality and multiculturalism have been more prominent (Gundara and Jacobs 2000). While its current advocates conceive it as something societal and therefore of much broader appeal than in the specific commercial usage found in some American formulations (in terms of facilitating 'communication' across transnational business and commerce) (Bennett 1998), what its present formulation perhaps retains from such incarnations is an emphasis upon communication. Indeed, according to Wood, Landry and Bloomfield (2006: 9) 'communication' is the defining characteristic and the central means through which 'an intercultural approach aims to facilitate dialogue, exchange and reciprocal understanding between people of different backgrounds'. The question is to what extent this can be claimed as either a unique or a distinguishing quality of interculturalism, when dialogue and reciprocity are also foundational to most, if not all, accounts of multiculturalism. To put it another way, what makes communication unique for interculturalism in a manner that diverges from multiculturalism? According to some advocates, a difference is perceptible in the social or convivial 'openness' in which communication is facilitated. As Wood, Landry and Bloomfield maintain,

Multiculturalism has been founded on the belief in tolerance between cultures but it is not always the case that multicultural places are open places. Interculturalism on the other hand requires openness as a prerequisite and, while openness in itself is not the guarantee of interculturalism, it provides the setting for interculturalism to develop. (2006: 7)

The 'openness' or 'closedness' that the authors have in mind is not an ethical or a moral but a sociological concern related to – if not derived from – a spatial sense of community and settlement as discussed further below. But it is also an openness of another kind that is not more than a few steps away from what Smith (2004) characterises as models of inter-religious dialogue. These models come from the North American context, including the 'Dialogue as Information Sharing' and 'Dialogue to Come Closer' models, which encourage religious groups to focus on commonalities in a way that seeks to eschew differences in order to elevate mutuality and sharing. What is striking, however, is the extent to which Wood, Landry and Bloomfield's characterisation ignores how central the notions of dialogue and communication are to multiculturalism. This might easily be illustrated with reference to some canonical contributions that have provided a great deal of intellectual impetus to the advocacy of multiculturalism as a political or public policy movement.

Our first example could be Charles Taylor's essay from 1992, widely considered to be a founding statement of multiculturalism in political theory and in which he characterises the emergence of a modern politics of identity premised upon an idea of 'recognition'. The notion of recognition, and its relationship to multiculturalism, can be abstract but is located for Taylor as something that has developed out of a move away from conceiving historically defined or inherited hierarchies as the sole provenance of social status (in the French sense of *préférence*), toward a notion of dignity more congruent with the ideals of a democratic society or polity, one that is more likely to confer political equality and a full or unimpaired civic status upon all its citizens.[4]

Drawing upon his previous, densely catalogued account of the emergence of the modern self (Taylor 1989), Taylor mapped the political implications of this move onto two cases of equality. The first is the most familiar and is characterised as a rights-based politics of universalism, which offers the prospect of affording equal dignity to all citizens in a polity. The second denotes a politics of

---

[4] Thus making equal recognition an essential part of democratic culture, a point not lost on Habermas (1994: 113), who argues that 'a correctly understood theory of [citizenship] rights requires a politics of recognition that protects the individual and the life contexts in which his or her identity is formed'.

difference where the uniqueness of context, history and identity are salient and potentially ascendant. For Taylor, this coupling crystallises the way in which the idea of recognition has given rise to a search for 'authenticity'. This is characterised as a move away from the prescriptive universalisms that have historically under-written ideas of the Just or the Right, in favour of the fulfilment and realisation of one's true self, originality or worth. According to Taylor, therefore, people can no longer be recognised on the basis of identities determined from their positions in social hierar-chies alone but, rather, through taking account of the real manner in which people form their identities. That is to say that Taylor emphasises the importance of 'dialogical' relationships to argue that it is a mistake to suggest that people form their identities 'monologically' or without an intrinsic dependence upon dialogue with others (see Meer 2010: 31–56). As such, he maintains that we are 'always in dialogue with, sometimes in struggle against, the things our significant others want to see in us' (Taylor 1992: 33).

In this formulation Taylor is openly drawing upon both Hegel and Mead, each of whom maintained that our idea of ourselves, what we claim to be, and what we really think we are, is depend-ent upon how others come to view us to the extent that our sense of *self* is developed in a continuing dialogue. Self-consciousness exists only by being acknowledged or recognised, and the related implication for Taylor is that a sense of socio-cultural self-esteem emerges not only from personal identity, but also in relation to the group in which this identity is developed. This is expressed in Taylor's account as follows:

> [O]ur identity is partly shaped by recognition or its absence, often by the *mis*recognition of others, and so a person or group of people can suffer real damage, real distortion, if the people or society around them mirror back a confining or demeaning or contemptible picture of them-selves. Non recognition or misrecognition can inflict harm, can be a form of oppression, imprisoning some in a false, distorted, and reduced mode of being. (1992: 25–6)

This is therefore one illustration of how central a concern with dialogue and communication is to multiculturalism too. Let us consider another landmark text on this topic: Bhikhu Parekh's

Rethinking Multiculturalism (2000). The central argument here is that cultural diversity and social pluralism are of an intrinsic value precisely because they challenge people to evaluate the strengths and weaknesses of their own cultures and ways of life. Parekh explicitly distinguishes his multiculturalism from various liberal and communitarian positions. Some of the latter recognise that cultures can play an important role in making choices meaningful for their members (Kymlicka 1995), or play host to the development of the self for the members of that culture (Sandel 1982). Their argument that culture is important for individual group members is well made but they are less successful in explaining why cultural diversity is necessary in itself. For this Parekh offers the following explanation:

> Since human capacities and values conflict, every culture realizes a limited range of them and neglects, marginalizes and suppresses others. However rich it may be, no culture embodies all that is valuable in human life and develops the full range of human possibilities. Different cultures thus correct and complement each other, expand each other's horizon of thought and alert each other to new forms of human fulfillment. The value of other cultures is independent of whether or not they are options for us ... inassimilable otherness challenges us intellectually and morally, stretches our imagination, and compels us to recognize the limits of our categories of thought. (Parekh 2000: 167)

His argument that cultures other than one's own have something to teach us, and that therefore members of minority cultures should be encouraged to cultivate their moral and aesthetic insights for humanity as a whole, is largely built upon a prescription of intercultural dialogue. Indeed, for both Taylor and Parekh communication and dialogue are in different ways integral features of their intellectual and political advocacy of multiculturalism, and by implication must necessarily be considered so by those drawing upon their work unless a different reading is offered. The point is that to consider multiculturalists who draw upon these and similar formulations as being unconcerned with matters of dialogue and communication is to profoundly misread and mischaracterise their positions.

Moreover, even amongst those theorists who do not elaborate a philosophical concept of dialogical multiculturalism, dialogue is important at a political level. Whatever their varying views about the importance of, say, entrenched rights, democratic majoritarianism, special forms of representation and so on, they all see multiculturalism as the giving of 'voice' in the public square to marginalised groups (Young 1990; Kymlicka 1995; Modood 2007a). Specifically, these authors also argue that dialogue is the way to handle difficult cases of cultural practices such as clitoridectomy, hate speech, religious dress, gender relations and so on (see also Eisenberg (2009) on public assessment of identity claims). So, whether it is at a philosophical or a political level, the leading theorists of multiculturalism give dialogue a centrality missing in liberal nationalist or human rights or class-based approaches – and missed by interculturalist critics of multiculturalism. The multiculturalists assume, however, that there is a sense in which the participants to a dialogue are 'groups' or 'cultures', and this leads us to a second point of alleged contrast with interculturalists.

Less groupist and culture bound: More synthesised and interactive

A related means through which the concern with 'closed' communities or groupings that advocates of interculturalism conceive multiculturalism as giving rise to takes us to our next characterisation of interculturalism contra multiculturalism. This is found in the assertion that 'one of the implications of an intercultural framework, as opposed to a multicultural one . . . is that culture is acting in a multi-directional manner' (Hammer 2004). This depiction of interculturalism as facilitating an interactive and dynamic cultural 'exchange' informs a consistent line of distinction, as the following two portrayals make clear:

> Multiculturalism tends to *preserve* a cultural heritage, while interculturalism acknowledges and enables cultures to have currency, to be exchanged, to circulate, to be modified and evolve. (Powell and Sze 2004: 1)

> [Interculturalism] is concerned with the task of developing cohesive civil societies by turning notions of singular identities into those of multiple ones, and by developing a shared and common value system

and public culture. In building from a deep sharing of differences of culture and experience it encourages the formation of interdependencies which structure personal identities that go beyond nations or simplified ethnicities. (Booth 2003: 432)

This emphasis is warranted for advocates of interculturalism who maintain that the diversity of the locations from where migrants and ethnic minorities herald gives rise not to a creation of communities or groups but to a churning mass of languages, ethnicities and religions all cutting across each other and creating a 'super-diversity' (Vertovec 2007). An intercultural perspective is better served to facilitate management of these sociological realities, it is argued, in a way that can be positively contrasted with a multiculturalism that emphasises strong ethnic or cultural identities at the expense of wider cultural exchanges.

Notwithstanding this problematic description of how groups feature in multiculturalism, which is challenged in other readings (cf. Modood 2007a), what such characterisations of interculturalism ignore are the alternative ways in which political interculturalism is itself conceptualised. As stated at the outset, by political interculturalism we refer to ways in which interculturalism is appropriated in the critique of multiculturalism (Booth 2003; Powell and Sze 2004; Wood, Landry and Bloomfield 2006), in a way that may not necessarily be endorsed by interculturalism's advocates.

Writing in the Quebec context, Gagnon and Iacovino (2007) are one example of authors who contrast interculturalism positively with multiculturalism. The interesting aspect for our discussion is that they do so in a way that relies upon a formulation of groups. They proceed by arguing that Quebec has developed a distinctive intercultural political approach to diversity that is explicitly in opposition to federal Canadian multiculturalism. Their starting point is that two broad considerations are accepted by a variety of political positions, including liberal nationalists, republicans and multiculturalists; indeed, by most positions except liberal individualism, which they critique and leave to one side. These two considerations are that, firstly, 'full citizenship status requires that all cultural identities be allowed to participate in democratic life equally, without the necessity of reducing conceptions of identity to the level of the individual' (2007: 96). Secondly, with respect to unity, 'the key element is a sense of common purpose in public matters', 'a *centre* which also serves as a marker of identity in the larger society and denotes in itself a pole of allegiance for all citizens' (2007: 96).

For Gagnon and Iacovino, however, Canadian multiculturalism has two fatal flaws, which means that it is de facto liberal individualist in practice if not in theory. Firstly, it privileges an individualist approach to culture: as individuals or their choices change, the collective culture must change; in contrast, Quebec's policy states clearly the need to recognise the French language as a collective good that requires protection and encouragement (Rocher et al., quoted in Gagnon and Iacovino 2007: 99). Secondly, Canadian multiculturalism locates itself not in democratic public culture but rather '[p]ublic space is based on individual participation via a bill of rights' (2007: 110–11); judges and individual choices, not citizens debating and negotiating with each other, become the locus of cultural interaction and public multiculturalism.

Gagnon and Iacovino's positive argument for interculturalism can therefore be expressed in the following five stages. First, there should be a public space and identity that is not merely about individual constitutional or legal rights. Second, this public space is an important identity for those who share it and so qualifies and counterbalances other identities that citizens value. Third, this public space is created and shared through participation, interaction, debate and common endeavour. Fourth, this public space is not culture-less but neither is it merely the 'majority culture'; all can participate in its synthesis and evolution, and while it has an inescapable historical character, it is always being remade and ought to be remade to include new groups. Fifth, and finally, Quebec, and not merely federal Canada, is such a public space and therefore an object immigrants need to have identification with and integrate into in order to maintain Quebec as a nation and not just a federal province (the same point may apply in other multinational states, but there are different degrees and variations of 'multinationalism').

This characterisation, then, is very different to that proposed by Booth (2003), Hammer (2004) or Powell and Sze (2004) because it makes a moral and policy case for the recognition of relatively distinct substate nationalisms. As such it is less concerned with the diversity of the locations from where migrants and ethnic minorities herald or the 'super-diversity' that this is alleged to cultivate. Its emphasis on multinationalism does distinguish it from post-immigration multiculturalism (and post-immigration inter-culturalism) but not multiculturalism per se (cf. Kymlicka 1995). Alternative, less macro-level interculturalism which focuses on neighbourhoods, classroom pedagogy, the funding of the arts and so on, on the other hand, seems apolitical. As such they are not critiques of multiculturalism but a different exercise.

Committed to a stronger sense of whole: National identity and social cohesion

A third related charge is that far from being a system that speaks to the whole of society, multiculturalism, unlike interculturalism, speaks only to and for the minorities within it and, therefore, also fails to appreciate the necessary wider framework for its success. As Goodhart (2004) has protested, multiculturalism is asymmetrical in that it not only places too great an emphasis upon difference and diversity, upon what divides us more than what unites us, but also ignores the needs of majorities. It thus encourages resentment, fragmentation and disunity. This can be prevented or overcome, as Alev (2007) and other commentators put it, through invocations of interculturalism that promote community cohesion on a local level, and more broadly through an interculturalism that encourages the subscription to national citizenship identities as forms of meta-membership. It is argued that European societies and states have been too laissez-faire in promoting commonality and this must now be remedied (Joppke 2004), hence the introduction of measures such as the swearing of oaths of allegiance at naturalisation ceremonies, language proficiency requirements when seeking citizenship, and citizenship education in schools, amongst other things. What such sentiment ignores is how all forms of prescribed unity, including civic unity, usually retain a majoritarian bias that places the burden of adaptation upon the minority, and so are inconsistent with interculturalism's alleged commitment to 'mutual integration' as put forward in Alev's account.

As Viet Bader (2005: 169), reminds us, 'all civic and democratic cultures are inevitably embedded into specific ethno-national and religious histories'. Were we to assess the normative premise of this view, however, we would inevitably encounter a dense literature elaborating the continuing disputes over the interactions between the civic, political and ethnic dimensions in the creation of nations, national identities and their relationship to each other and to non-rational 'intuitive' and 'emotional' pulls of ancestries and cultures and so forth. Chief amongst these is whether or not 'nations' are social and political formations developed in the proliferation of modern nation-states from the eighteenth century onwards, or whether they constitute social and political formations – or 'ethnies' – bearing an older pedigree that may be obscured by a modernist focus. What is most relevant to our discussion, however, is not the debate between different camps of 'modernist', 'ethno-symbolist' and 'primordialist' protagonists, amongst others, but the ways in which minorities' differences are conceived in contemporary forms of meta-unity.[5]

It is perhaps telling, however, that much of the literature on national identity in particular has tended to be retrospective to the extent that such contemporary concerns do not enjoy a widespread appeal in scholarly accounts of national identity (while the opposite could be said to be true of the literature on citizenship). This tendency is not limited to academic arenas, and one of the curiosities in popular articulations of national identity is the purchase that these accounts garner from a recourse to tradition, history and the idea of a common past (Calhoun 1994). One implication is that national identities can frequently reflect desires to authenticate the past, 'to select from all that has gone before that which is distinctive, "truly ours", and thereby to mark out a unique, shared destiny' (Smith 1998: 43).

It was this very assessment which, at the turn of the millennium, informed the Commission on Multi-Ethnic Britain's (CMEB) characterisation of British national identity as potentially 'based on generalisations [that] involve a selective and simplified account of a complex history'. Chaired by Bhikhu Parekh, it feared such an account would be one in which '[m]any complicated strands are reduced to a simple tale of essential and enduring national unity' (2000: 2.9, 16). It was precisely this tendency that informed the

---

[5] Though this concern perhaps relies on something from the cultural-imaginary form of 'modernist' argument most associated with Anderson (1983). Moreover, for a study of how this is happening in non-political urban contexts, see Kyrikiades, Virdee and Modood 2009.

CMEB's alarm at how invocations of national identity potentially force ethnic minorities into a predicament not of their making: one in which majorities are conflated with the nation and where national identity is promoted as a reflection of this state of affairs (because national identities are assumed to be cognates of monistic nations). Not easily fitting into a majoritarian account of national identity, or being either unable or unwilling to be reduced to or assimilated into a prescribed public culture, minority 'differences' may therefore become variously negatively conceived. Such concerns have not been limited to the UK, however, and may be observed in the Intercultural Dialogue Commission (2005) set up by the federal government in Belgium to facilitate a transition in the federal-level emphasis from integration to cultural diversity. This identified several historical tendencies, concerning (1) a political pluralism that facilitated working-class emancipation and wider political consultation; (2) philosophical pluralism that incrementally led to the official recognition of various public religions (Catholic, Protestant, Jewish, Islamic and Anglican) and non-religion; and (3) community pluralism as stemming from Flemish and Walloon movements that created the current federal state of Belgium. Importantly, the Commissioners underscored a further form of pluralism as the next step: (4) cultural pluralism. More precisely, they insisted that integration issues should take into account relevant cultural dimensions and that it no longer makes sense to qualify the descendants of migrants as 'migrant' or 'allochtone', used in the Walloon and Flemish regions respectively; instead 'cultural minorities' would be a much more relevant definition. The report on the whole focused its conclusions on the lack of cultural recognition in a manner that invited the criticism that the Commission had been highly influenced by communitarian theories 'trying to develop civic responsibility and common citizenship rather than thinking about an increasing space for cultural communities' (La Libre, 6 June 2005).

One scholarly intervention in this vein can be found in Modood's (2007a) restatement of multiculturalism as a civic idea that can be tied to an inclusive national identity, and some of the responses this has elicited (see Modood 2007b) help cast light upon this debate. This concern was present in his Not Easy Being British: Colour, Culture and Citizenship, first published in 1992, where, not unusually among advocates of multiculturalism, Modood emphasised the role of citizenship in fostering commonality across differences, before recasting part of this civic inclusion as proceeding through claims-making upon, and therefore reformulating, national identities. In his more contemporary formulation he puts this thus:

> [I]t does not make sense to encourage strong multicultural or minority identities and weak common or national identities; strong multicultural identities are a good thing – they are not intrinsically divisive, reactionary or subversive – but they need the complement of a framework of vibrant, dynamic, national narratives and the ceremonies and rituals which give expression to a national identity. It is clear that minority identities are capable of exerting an emotional pull for the individuals for whom they are important. Multicultural citizenship, if it is to be equally attractive to the same individuals, requires a comparable counterbalancing emotional pull. (Modood 2007b)

This restatement contains at least two key points that are central to the preceding discussion. The first concerns an advocacy and continuity of earlier forms of multiculturalism that have sought to accommodate collective identities and incorporate differences into the mainstream. These differences are not only tolerated but respected, and include the turning of a 'negative' difference into a 'positive' difference in a way that is presented in the ethnic pride currents as elements of racial equality. The second is to place a greater emphasis upon the unifying potential of an affirmation of a renegotiated and inclusive national identity. While the latter point is welcomed by some commentators who had previously formed part of the pluralistic left, the bringing of previously marginalised groups into the societal mainstream is, at best, greeted more ambivalently.

Illiberalism and culture

The fourth charge is that multiculturalism lends itself to illiberality and relativism, such that there is often 'uncertainty surrounding the tackling of culturally specific practices that infringe people's rights such as forced marriage' (BRAP 2012: 63). Interculturalism has the capacity to criticise and censure culture (as part of a process of intercultural dialogue), and so is more likely to emphasise the protection of individual rights. In Bouchard's terms,

Interculturalism is built on the basic wager of democracy, that is, a capacity to reach consensus on forms of peaceful co-existence that preserve basic values and make room for the future of all citizens. (2011: 467)

In Europe this charge clearly assumed a role in the backlash against multiculturalism since, as Kymlicka (2005b: 83) describes, 'it is very difficult to get support for multiculturalism policies if the groups that are the main beneficiaries of these policies are perceived as carriers of illiberal cultural practices that violate norms of human rights'. This view is particularly evident in the debates concerning the accommodation of religious minorities, especially when the religion in question is perceived to take a conservative line on issues of gender equality, sexual orientation and progressive politics generally (something that has arguably led some commentators who may otherwise sympathise with religious minorities to argue that it is difficult to view them as victims when they may themselves be potential oppressors (see Meer and Modood 2009b)).

Kymlicka (2005b: 83) narrows down this observation further in his conclusion that 'if we put Western democracies on a continuum in terms of the proportion of immigrants who are Muslim, I think this would provide a good indicator of public opposition to multiculturalism'. As Bhikhu Parekh (2006: 180–1) notes, this can be traced to a perception that Muslims are 'collectivist, intolerant, authoritarian, illiberal and theocratic', and that they use their faith as 'a self-conscious public statement, not quietly held personal faith but a matter of identity which they must jealously guard and loudly and repeatedly proclaim ... not only to remind them of who they are but also to announce to others what they stand for'. It is thus unsurprising to learn that some attitude surveys in Britain report that 77 per cent of people are convinced that 'Islam has a lot of fanatical followers', 68 per cent consider it 'to have more to do with the middle ages than the modern world', and 64 per cent believe that Islam 'treats women badly' (Field 2007: 453).

For these reasons Muslim claims-making has been characterised as specifically ambitious and difficult to accommodate (Joppke 2004; Moore 2006; Policy Exchange 2007). This is particularly the case when Muslims are perceived to be – often uniquely – in contravention of liberal discourses of individual rights and secularism (Hansen 2006) and is exemplified by the way in which visible Muslim practices such as veiling have in public discourses been reduced to and conflated with alleged Muslim practices such as forced marriages, female genital mutilation, a rejection of positive law in favour of criminal sharia law, and so on. This suggests a radical 'otherness' about Muslims and an illiberality about multiculturalism, since the latter is alleged to license these practices.

It is difficult, however, not to view this as a knee-jerk reaction that condemns religious identities per se rather than examining them on a case-by-case basis, while on the other hand assuming that ethnic identities are free of illiberalism. This is empirically problematic given that some of the problematic practices are not religious but cultural. Clitoridectomy, for example, is often cited as an illiberal practice in the discussions we are referring to. It is, however, a cultural practice among various ethnic groups, yet has little support from any religion. So to favour ethnicity and problematise religion is a reflection of a secularist bias that has alienated many religionists, especially Muslims, from multiculturalism. It is much better to acknowledge that the 'multi' in multiculturalism will encompass different kinds of groups and does not itself privilege any one kind, but that 'recognition' should be given to the identities that marginalised groups themselves value and find strength in, whether these be racial, religious or ethnic (Modood 2007b).

Conclusions

This chapter provides an entry point in developing a discussion on the relationship between interculturalism and multiculturalism. The question it raises is to what extent the present criteria proposed by advocates of interculturalism, in positively contrasting it with multiculturalism, are persuasive. In addressing this we maintain that whilst interculturalism and multiculturalism share much as approaches concerned with recognising cultural diversity, the answer to Lentin's (2005: 394) question – is interculturalism merely an 'updated version' of multiculturalism? – is, in the main, 'no'. That is to say that while advocates of interculturalism wish to emphasise its positive qualities in terms of encouraging communication, recognising dynamic identities, promoting unity, and challenging illiberality, each of these qualities already features (and is on occasion foundational) in multiculturalism. Moreover, multiculturalism presently surpasses interculturalism as a political orientation that is able to recognise that social life consists of individuals and groups, and that both need to be provided for in the formal and informal distribution of powers, as well as reflected in an ethical conception of citizenship, not just an instrumental one. As such we conclude that until interculturalism as a political discourse is able to offer an original perspective, one that can speak to a variety of concerns emanating from complex identities and matters of equality and diversity in a more persuasive manner than at present, it cannot, intellectually at least, eclipse multiculturalism.

References

Alev, F. (2007), 'Europe's Future: Make Yourselves at Home', *The Guardian*, 5 June, <http://www.theguardian.com/commentisfree/2007/jun/05/europesfuturemakeyourselvesathome> (last accessed 18 June 2015).

Anderson, B. (1983), *Imagined Communities*, London: Verso.

Bader, V. (2005), 'Ethnic and Religious State Neutrality: Utopia or Myth?', in H. G. Sicakkan and Y. Lithman (eds), *Changing the Basis of Citizenship in the Modern State*, Lewiston: The Edwin Mellen Press, pp. 161–98.

Barry, B. (2001), *Culture and Equality: An Egalitarian Critique of Equality*, London: Polity Press.

Barry, B. (2002), 'Second Thoughts: Some First Thoughts Revived', in P. Kelly (ed.), *Multiculturalism Reconsidered*, Cambridge: Polity, pp. 204–38.

Bennett, M. J. (1998), *Basic Concepts of Intercultural Communication*, Boston, MA: Intercultural Press.

Bhabha, H. K. (1998), 'Culture's In Between', in D. Bennet (ed.), *Multicultural States: Rethinking Difference and Identity*, London: Routledge, pp. 29–36.

Booth, T. (2003), Review of *Interculturalism, Education and Inclusion*, British *Journal of Educational Studies*, 51 (4), 432–3.

Bouchard, G. (2011), 'What Is Interculturalism?', *McGill Law Journal*, 56 (2), 435–68.

BRAP (2012), *Interculturalism: A Breakdown of Thinking and the Practice: Lessons from the Field*, London: The Baring Foundation.

Brubaker, R. (2001), 'The Return of Assimilation? Changing Perspectives on Immigration and its Sequels in France, Germany, and the United States', *Ethnic and Racial Studies*, 24 (4), 531–48.

Caldwell, C. (2009), *Reflections on the Revolution in Europe: Immigration, Islam and the West*, London: Penguin Books.

Calhoun, C. (ed.) (1994), *Social Theory and Politics of Identity*, Oxford: Blackwell.

Cantle, T. (2012), *Interculturalism: The New Era of Cohesion and Diversity*, Basingstoke: Palgrave Macmillan.

Cardinal, L., and C. Couture (1998), 'L'Immigration et le multiculturalisme au Canada: la genèse d'une problématique', in M. Tremblay (ed.), *Les Politiques publiques canadiennes*, Sainte-Foy: Les Presses de l'Université Laval, pp. 239–64.

Castles, S. (2000), *Ethnicity and Globalization: From Migrant Worker to Transnational Citizen*, London: Sage.

Commission on Multi-Ethnic Britain (CMEB) (2000), *The Future of Multi-Ethnic Britain*, London: Profile Books.

Dobbernack, J. (2010), '"Things Fall Apart": Social Imaginaries and the Politics of Cohesion', *Critical Policy Studies*, 4 (2), 146–63.

Eisenberg, A. (2009), *Reasons of Identity: A Normative Guide to the Political and Legal Assessment of Identity Claims*, Oxford: Oxford University Press.

Field, C. D. (2007), 'Islamophobia in Contemporary Britain: The Evidence of the Opinion Polls, 1988–2006', *Islam and Christian-Muslim Relations*, 18 (4), 447–77.

Froumin, I. (2003), 'Citizenship Education and Ethnic Issues in Russia', in J. A. Banks (ed.), *Diversity and Citizenship Education: Global Perspectives*, San Francisco: Jossey-Bass, pp. 273–98.

Gagnon, A.-G., and R. Iacovino (2007), *Federalism, Citizenship and Quebec: Debating Multinationalism*, Toronto: University of Toronto Press.

Gilroy, P. (2000), *Between Camps*, London: Routledge.

Goodhart, D. (2004), 'Too Diverse?', *Prospect Magazine*, February, <http://www.prospectmagazine.co.uk/features/too-diverse-david-goodhart-multiculturalism-britain-immigration-globalisation> (last accessed 23 June 2015).

Gove, M. (2006), *Celsius 7/7*, London: Weidenfeld and Nicolson.

Gundara, J. S. (2000), *Interculturalism, Education and Inclusion*, London: Paul Chapman.

Gundara, J. S., and S. Jacobs (eds) (2000), *Intercultural Europe: Diversity and Social Policy*, Aldershot: Ashgate.

Habermas, J. (1994), 'Struggles for Recognition in the Democratic Constitutional State', in A. Gutmann (ed.), *Multiculturalism: Examining the Politics of Recognition*, Princeton: Princeton University Press, pp. 107–48.

Hammer, L. (2004), 'Foreword', in D. Powell and F. Sze (eds), *Interculturalism: Exploring Critical Issues*, Oxford: Interdisciplinary Press, pp. i–ii.

Hansen, R. (2006), 'The Danish Cartoon Controversy: A Defence of Liberal Freedom', *International Migration*, 44 (5), 7–16.

Jacobs, D., and A. Rea (2007), 'The End of National Models? Integration Courses and Citizenship Trajectories in Europe', *International Journal on Multicultural Societies*, 9 (2), 264–83.

Joppke, C. (2004), 'The Retreat of Multiculturalism in the Liberal State: Theory and Policy', *British Journal of Sociology*, 55 (2), 237–57.

Joppke, C. (2008), 'Immigration and the Identity of Citizenship: The Paradox of Universalism', *Citizenship Studies*, 12 (6), 533–46.

Kelly, P. (2002), 'Between Culture and Equality', in P. Kelly (ed.), *Multiculturalism Reconsidered*, Cambridge: Polity, pp. 1–17.

Kivisto, P., and T. Faist (2007), *Citizenship: Discourse, Theory, and Transnational Prospects*, London: Blackwell.

Kohls, L. R., and J. M. Knight (1994), *Developing Intercultural Awareness*, Boston, MA: Intercultural Press.

Kymlicka, W. (1995), *Multicultural Citizenship: A Liberal Theory of Minority Rights*, Oxford: Clarendon Press.

Kymlicka, W. (2003), 'Multicultural States and Intercultural Citizens', *Theory and Research in Education*, 1, 147–69.

Kymlicka, W. (2005a), 'Testing the Bounds of Liberal Multiculturalism', draft paper presented at Toronto, 9 April.

Kymlicka, W. (2005b), 'The Uncertain Futures of Multiculturalism', *Canadian Diversity*, 4 (1), 82–5.

Kymlicka,W. (2007), 'The New Debate on Minority Rights (and Postscript)', in A. S. Laden and D. Owen (eds), *Multiculturalism and Political Theory*, Cambridge: Cambridge University Press, pp. 25–59.

Kyrikiades, C., S. Virdee and T. Modood (2009), 'Racism, Muslims and the National Imagination', *Journal of Ethnic and Migration Studies*, 35 (2), 289–308.

Lentin, A. (2005), 'Replacing "Race": Historizing the "Culture" in Multiculturalism', *Patterns of Prejudice*, 39 (4), 379–96.

Levey, G. B. (ed.) (2008), *Political Theory and Australian Multiculturalism*, New York: Berghahn Books.

Luchtenberg, S. (2003), 'Citizenship Education and Diversity in Germany', in J. A. Banks (ed.), *Diversity and Citizenship Education: Global Perspectives*, San Francisco: Jossey-Bass, pp. 40–63.

McGhee, D. (2008), *The End of Multiculturalism? Terrorism, Integration and Human Rights*, Milton Keynes: Open University Press and McGraw-Hill Education.

Malik, M. (2008), 'Modernising Discrimination Law: Proposals for a Single Equality Act for Britain', *International Journal of Discrimination and the Law*, 9 (2), 73–94.

Maxwell, B., D. I. Waddington, K. McDonough, A.-A. Cormier and M. Schwimmer (2012), 'Interculturalism, Multiculturalism, and the State Funding and Regulation of Conservative Religious Schools', *Educational Theory*, 62 (4), 427–47.

May, S., T. Modood and J. Squires (2004), *Ethnicity, Nationalism, and Minority Rights*, Cambridge: Cambridge University Press.

Meer, N. (2010/2015), *Citizenship, Identity and the Politics of Multiculturalism*, Basingstoke: Palgrave.

Meer, N., and T. Modood (2009a), 'The Multicultural State We Are In: Muslims, "Multiculture" and the "Civic Re-balancing" of British Multiculturalism', *Political Studies*, 57 (3), 473–97.

Meer, N., and T. Modood (2009b), 'Refutations of Racism in the "Muslim Question"', *Patterns of Prejudice*, 43 (3–4), 332–51.

Meer, N., and T. Modood (2011), 'Diversity, Identity, and Multiculturalism in the Media', in G. Cheney, S. May and D. Munshi (eds), *Handbook of Communication Ethics*, London: Routledge.

Meer, N., and T. Modood (2012), 'How Does Interculturalism Contrast with Multiculturalism?', *Journal of Intercultural Studies*, 33 (2), 175–96.

Modood, T. (1992), *Not Easy Being British: Colour, Culture and Citizenship*, London: Runnymede Trust/Trentham Books.

Modood, T. (2005), *Multicultural Politics*, Edinburgh: Edinburgh University Press.

Modood, T. (2006), 'Obstacles to Multicultural Integration', *International Migration*, 44 (5), 51–62.

Modood, T. (2007a), *Multiculturalism: A Civic Idea*, Cambridge: Polity Press.

Modood, T. (2007b), 'Multiculturalism's Civic Future: A Response', *Open Democracy*, 20 June, <http://www.opendemocracy.net/faith_ideas/Europe_islam/multiculturalism_future> (last accessed 18 June 2015).

Modood, T., and N. Meer (2011), 'Characterizing Contemporary Political Orientations in the Study of Citizenship', in A. Triandafyllidou, T. Modood and N. Meer (eds), *European Multiculturalism(s): Cultural, Religious and Ethnic Challenges*, Edinburgh: Edinburgh University Press, pp. 33–60.

Moller Okin, S. (1999), *Is Multiculturalism Bad for Women?*, Princeton: Princeton University Press.

Moore, C. (2006), 'How Cromwell Gave Us Joan Collins and Other Luminaries', *Daily Telegraph*, 17 June, <http://www.telegraph.co.uk/comment/personal-view/3625765/How-Cromwell-gave-us-Joan-Collins-and-other-luminaries.html> (last accessed 19 June 2015).

Mouritsen, P. (2008), 'Political Responses to Cultural Conflict: Reflections on the Ambiguities of the Civic Turn', in P. Mouritsen and K. E. Jørgensen (eds), *Constituting Communities: Political Solutions to Cultural Conflict*, London: Palgrave, pp. 1–30.

Orgad, L. (2009), '"Cultural Defense" of Nations: Cultural Citizenship in France, Germany and the Netherlands', *European Law Journal*, 15 (6), 719–37.

Parekh, B. (2000), *Rethinking Multiculturalism: Cultural Diversity and Political Theory*, Basingstoke: Macmillan.

Parekh, B. (2006), 'Europe, Liberalism and the "Muslim Question"', in T. Modood, A. Triandafyllidou and R. Zapata-Barrero (eds), *Multiculturalism, Muslims and Citizenship: A European Approach*, London: Routledge, pp. 179–203.

Phillips, A. (2007), *Multiculturalism without Culture*, Princeton: Princeton University Press.

Phillips, M. (2006), *Londonistan: How Britain Created a Terror State Within*, London: Gibson Square Books.

Policy Exchange (2007), *Living Apart Together: British Muslims and the Paradox of Multiculturalism*, London: Policy Exchange.

Powell, D., and F. Sze (eds) (2004), *Interculturalism: Exploring Critical Issues*, Oxford: Interdisciplinary Press.

Prins, G., and R. Salisbury (2008), 'Risk, Threat and Security: The Case of the United Kingdom', *RUSI Journal*, 153 (1), 22–7.

Sandel, M. (1982), *Liberalism and the Limits of Justice*, Cambridge: Cambridge University Press.

Serwer, S. (2009), 'The '00s: Goodbye (at Last) to the Decade from Hell', *Time Magazine*, 24 November, <http://content.time.com/time/magazine/article/0,9171,1942973,00.html> (last accessed 19 June 2015).

Smith, A. D. (1998), *Nationalism and Modernism: A Critical Survey of Recent Theories of Nations and Nationalism*, London: Routledge.

Smith, J. I. (2004), 'Muslims as Partners in Interfaith Encounter: Models for Dialogue', in Z. H. Bukhari, S. S. Nyang, M. Ahmad and J. L. Esposito (eds), *Muslims' Place in the American Public Square: Hope, Fears, and Aspirations*, New York: Altamira Press, pp. 165–97.

Smith, K. E. (2010), 'Academic Treadmills and the Squeeze on Imaginative Spaces', *British Journal of Sociology*, 61, 176–5.

Storti, C. (1994), *Cross-Cultural Dialogues*, Boston, MA: Intercultural Press.

Taylor, C. (1989), *Sources of the Self: The Making of the Modern Identity*, Cambridge, MA: Harvard University Press.

Taylor, C. (1992), 'The Politics of Recognition', in A. Gutmann (ed.), *Multiculturalism and 'The Politics of Recognition'*, Princeton: Princeton University Press, pp. 25–73.

Tully, J. (2002), 'The Illiberal Liberal', in P. Kelly (ed.) (2002), *Multiculturalism Reconsidered*, Cambridge: Polity.

Vertovec, S. (2007), 'Super-Diversity and its Implications', *Ethnic and Racial Studies*, 30 (6), 1,024–54.

Vertovec, S., and S. Wessendorf (2005), 'Migration and Cultural, Religious and Linguistic Diversity in Europe: An Overview of Issues and Trends', Centre on Migration, Policy and Society (COMPAS), Working Paper No. 18, University of Oxford, <https://www.compas.ox.ac.uk/fileadmin/files/Publications/working_papers/WP_2005/Vertovec%20Wessendorf%20WP0518.pdf> (last accessed 19 June 2015).

Wood, P., C. Landry and J. Bloomfield (2006), *Cultural Diversity in Britain: A Toolkit for Cross-Cultural Co-Operation*, York: Joseph Rowntree Foundation.

Young, I. M. (1990), *Justice and the Politics of Difference*, Princeton: Princeton University Press.

3

Theorising Intercultural Citizenship

Ricard Zapata-Barrero

Introduction: Framing the intercultural/multicultural divide

The emergent controversy over multiculturalism/interculturalism (MC/IC) resides in the logic of the necessary requirements for managing a society that recognises itself as diverse. The great multicultural debates of the late twentieth century, and even the early twenty-first century, followed a cultural rights-based approach to diversity. They were centred on questions such as the rights of cultural recognition in the public sphere and how to reassess equality and cultural rights of non-national citizens with different languages, religions and cultural practices. This approach characterised multicultural citizenship studies until the emergence of a new paradigm that is taking shape in this second decade of the twenty-first century: intercultural citizenship.

This new European trend has been promoted in part by the Council of Europe since 2008, first with some seminal urban and social management literature,[1] and has penetrated normative and policy debates on diversity and immigration studies only very recently.[2] It certainly arises in a context where MC is in its lowest moments, under suspicion of having promoted segregation rather

---

[1] See, among others, Blommaert and Verschueren 1998, Gundara and Jacobs 2000, Zachary 2003, Bloomfield and Bianchini 2004, Sandercock 2004, Powell and Sze 2004, Wood 2004, Festenstein 2005, Brecknock 2006, Khan 2006, Hussain, Law and Haq 2006, Page 2007, Wood and Landry 2008.
[2] See Lüken-Klaßen and Heckmann 2010, Clarijs et al. 2011, Cantle 2012, Meer and Modood 2012, Taylor 2012, Barrett 2013, Zapata-Barrero 2015b, d.

than union, of giving rise to ethnic conflicts rather than a common public culture, of having difficulties in grounding community cohesion (Cantle 2008) and social capital (Putnam 2007), and even of grounding affirmative actions. Political leaders such as Merkel in Germany in October 2010 and Cameron in the United Kingdom in February 2011 – with even Sarkozy joining this view – have promoted this argument of crisis, backlash or even the 'death' of the multicultural paradigm, initiating a great European public discussion (*Daily Mail* reporter 2011). This essentially illustrates how super-diverse societies have difficulties in connecting public discourse, policies and practices (see, among others, Vertovec and Wessendorf 2010).

IC enters into this negative diagnosis of MC, offering a lifeline. The epicentre of the debate in Europe is that MC has neglected intergroup relations and interpersonal contact among people with different origins and cultures. IC positions itself in contrast to both MC and assimilationism, based on substantial insights on the view of ethnicity and collective identity, as self-ascribed, flexible and dynamic, and emphasising the need for contact among culturally defined enclaves (which foster neither mutual identification nor interaction). This is why its primary normative force is that it is viewed as a set of arguments sharing one basic idea: that interaction among people from different backgrounds matters.

But it is also true that even if we are in an 'intercultural turn' (Zapata-Barrero 2015a), there is still no political theory founding this turn. It is within this framework that I want to explore the building blocks of a preliminary theory, having Europe as the main contextual framework. In Europe, IC has entered the diversity debate only recently. It attracts academics who feel we need to react to increasing diversity following an inclusion strand, but who are dissatisfied with the multicultural paradigm. IC has a number of key attributes that make it well suited to addressing some of the shortcomings of the multicultural citizenship approach, maintaining the importance of the difference rather than sameness, as criteria driving policy legitimation (Parekh 2000).

I am inclined to agree with those scholars, basically coming from the multiculturalist front, who argue that the two paradigms are complementary (Meer and Modood 2012), but instead of only focusing on similarities, my interest will be to identify the dividing lines. How the paradigms can work together and how they can influence one another offers potentially interesting questions for further research, but that goes beyond the scope of this chapter, which will be strictly foundational. My final purpose, then, is to address what I consider to be the distinctive features of intercultural citizenship.

To look for the foundation, I will go so far as to contend that IC manages to channel the majority of the substantial criticisms of MC that have been deployed during the last decade. I will enter into this discussion by taking citizenship as the main focus, following two argumentative steps. First, I will address the key distinctions of MC/IC, arguing that this framework of discussion represents an important shift in the conceptualisation of citizenship in super-diverse societies. As a consequent second step, and against certain initial simplistic views of IC, I will argue that there is not just one way in which IC can make a difference in relation to MC, but that there are in fact at least three, based on how interaction is promoted. The chapter will conclude by highlighting some additional key features of IC, perhaps going beyond the normative focus of this chapter, but this is paramount for any effort to theorise intercultural citizenship. The fact that IC illustrates a certain pragmatic turn in how to deal with diversity dynamics, and the empirical evidence that IC is more attractive than MC in the eyes of policy-makers, are outcomes, I will argue, of its following a mainstreaming public philosophy.

Markers of difference between multicultural and intercultural citizenship

I will focus the MC/IC framework of discussion on how the politics conceptualises relations of citizenship. Multicultural citizenship follows a cultural rights-based approach, attributing to people certain cultural ascriptions, and having left concerns for interactions among people of whatever origin, even national citizens, in the background. Intercultural citizenship tries to uncover interpersonal relations, making them visible to understand the 'intercultural lens'. Its core concept is interaction – that is, acting together, sharing a public sphere and working for some common purpose. Contrary to multicultural citizenship, which focuses on people's cultural rights and thus has an initial understanding of interpersonal comparisons centred in what is different rather than similar, the clue to grasping IC is that it is not based on an individual or a group agent, but is rather a strategy to manage a dynamic process of interaction between individuals or even between groups. And by covering interaction, IC is much more concerned with prioritising what is common between two people of different backgrounds. With this, it emphasises what is (or can be) shared between people or groups, rather than exhibiting what is different and 'must be recognised and respected' among people who see each other in terms of otherness. It is due to this initial focus that IC points to the common humanity that emerges from interactions. IC not only suggests the acceptance of principles of equal rights, values and abilities, but also supports the development of policies to promote interaction, collaboration and exchange with people of different cultures, languages, ethnicities or religions living in the same territory. Furthermore, IC is an approach that sees difference as a positive resource that can enrich a society (Titley 2012, quoted by Farrar 2012).

To deepen this framework of discussion, I will collect much of the criticism that MC has received from a position of respect for difference. I will articulate this section following three markers of difference to allow comparisons: (1) the intercultural approach has a view of the public sphere as a contact zone, and it is based on everyday personal experiences in diversity settings, concentrating on the barriers of interaction; (2) the intercultural view of diversity is based on bridging differences and rejects preconceived categorisations of diversity; (3) IC is a more appropriate framework for dealing with the complexity of current super-diverse societies.

1. THE INTERCULTURAL APPROACH HAS A VIEW OF THE PUBLIC SPHERE AS A CONTACT ZONE, AND IT IS BASED ON EVERYDAY PERSONAL EXPERIENCES IN DIVERSITY SETTINGS, CONCENTRATING ON THE BARRIERS OF INTERACTION

Considering public space as the point of departure, we can say that MC tends to problematise the public sphere, interpreted as being the institutionalisation of sameness (for instance, Young 1990, Parekh 2000). IC manages a dynamic process of encounters, based on everyday personal experiences in public spaces (Wood 2015), and then promotes a process of individualisation of intercultural experience. It is also crucial to highlight that interaction is not forced, but promoted. This is why most intercultural citizenship policies aim at facilitating the conditions for interaction and then formulate a diagnosis regarding the inequalities of distribution of rights, along with other factors (cognitive, structural, institutional, personal) that constrain contact (see the Intercultural Cities network, and chapters such as Wood 2015 and Guidikova 2015).

We might say that IC is a technique of bridging differences, bonding and promoting social capital in public spheres of people's everyday lives (neighbourhoods, schools, market places, playgrounds, public libraries and other cultural public spaces of interaction, etc.). That is, it promotes contact zones among people who share certain characteristics (reinforcing bonds) and facilitates relations between individuals from different backgrounds (building bridges), such as when it promotes interaction between people across different religions, languages, and so on (Gruescu and Menne 2010: 10). Rather than claiming recognition of cultural rights, as MC does, IC claims rights to address the obstacles that prevent interaction. It is here that IC governance claims representation of diversity in public administration, participation of immigrants in public institutions, and even voting rights. This is because these issues are obstacles to ensuring an equitable interaction in the public sphere, and may even be used as an argument by national citizens to justify the lack of trust or interest in people from different backgrounds. It is in this building and facilitating of public contexts of interaction that IC has its focus, because it is also convinced that through interaction some of the arguments driving racist and xenophobic political discourses can be reduced (Zapata-Barrero 2011).

In contrast, the basic concern of the multicultural citizenship approach is marginalisation, segregation, cultural isolation from mainstream society, and the misrecognition of minority cultural citizens (see, for instance, Kymlicka 1995 and Triandafyllidou, Modood and Zapata-Barrero 2006). This has been put forward by Kymlicka as 'state multiculturalism', which recognises that citizens are different in their language and culture, and so will relate to the state in different ways, with different forms of membership (2003: 153). The normative dimension of the MC literature always attempts to rectify the consequences of this increasing marginalisation coming from social and political structures, and focuses on the principle of equality, understood as redistribution of wealth and recognition of cultural rights (Frazer and Honneth 2003).

IC gives rise to the possibility that individuals change their identities autonomously, even though the boundary between two groups is maintained in terms of some other differences. It rests on the core idea that through positive interaction, prejudice reduction and knowledge promotion is assured. Taking the work of Kymlicka on intercultural citizenship, we can say he misses precisely this preliminary question when he argues that people tend to be much more intercultural globally rather than locally. Namely, he states that individuals seek to interact more with people from other countries and civilisations when travelling than they do with their own different neighbours. It is true that examining certain aspects of current reality may confirm this diagnosis, but I see no critical argument being formulated against this situation. There are certainly educational and social-class factors and even religious preconceptions that have been dominant factors in this lack of interaction. Kymlicka's view is, then, too narrow, though his diagnosis confirms the importance of fostering a favourable context for intercultural promotion.

2. The intercultural view of diversity is focused on bridging differences and on rejecting any preconceived categorisations of diversity

IC does not approach differences in terms of what the cultural needs of people are, but rather is concerned with interactions and, as a corollary, with ensuring an equitable context for their promotion. IC rejects categorising people according to pre-social attributions. It incorporates all people (without exception, including nationals), without any view of society based on group and ethnic division. For IC, difference is based on various categories of diversity that are not necessarily linked to ethnicity, nationality or even race (this is one of the key criticisms of MC put forward by Cantle 2012). From its starting premise, it criticises, then, the ethnicity-based and rights-based approaches of multicultural citizenship. From this perspective, intercultural citizenship's main concerns are to do with ensuring the basis of contact, communication and interaction. This is why it is much more exclusively concerned with anti-discriminatory programmes and anti-racist practices than MC.

In essence, IC illustrates a different way of thinking about diversity, without even sharing the system of categorising diversity that MC follows. Following Faist's (2009) suggestive analysis of diversity categorisation, this involves people being considered not only in terms of their rights, but in terms of what they can do and are able to achieve, given current cognitive, social and even legal and institutional barriers. As Castles (2000: 5) pointed out well over a decade ago, conventional MC generally 'does not question the territory principle' and 'maintains the idea of a primary belonging to one society and a loyalty to just one nation-state'. Newer approaches to MC – despite their conscious anti-essentialism (Modood 1998) – also perpetuate the model of nation-state-as-territorial-container. The view of culture as personal identity in everyday life, as national identity and as a sense of belonging to a collective cultural and/or political identity has been rightly criticised when used in a conservative manner. This gets critiqued as an attempt to align culture with genetics, as though it were hereditary like skin colour (Bloomfield and Bianchini 2001: 104), or even with the presumption that culture is rooted in territory, in the sense also already signalled by the liberal Will Kymlicka (1995: 84) in his seminal book. There, he criticised the communitarian view, according to which 'one cannot choose to belong'. We can also include here Phillips's (2007) 'multiculturalism without culture' argument, in which she claims that it is time to elaborate a version of MC that dispenses with reified notions of culture, one that engages more ruthlessly with cultural stereotypes. A central part of her theory rests on the idea that people in minority cultures have autonomy. This recognition that people need to be treated as free to choose (and to rank) their multiple identities is also the driving argument of Sen's recent reflections on identity, culture and violence (2006). This particular understanding of the autonomy principle is at the core of IC. But IC is not a simple view of multiple identities as an aggregation of multiple, static identities; but displays, rather, an awareness of people having identities that are always open to change and to processes of autonomous hybridisation.[3]

IC shares, then, the premise that from a policy point of view, we cannot force people to self-identify with a fixed category of cultural

---

[3] We can say that the new edition (2015) of the debate on cultural hybridity proposed by Werbner and Modood nearly two decades ago falls within this IC dimension, in spite of calling it MC.

identity according to their nationalities and cultures of origin. This is the most flagrant evidence that the concept of diversity itself is a construction and is not politically neutral. As I highlighted in my work on multiple diversities in Spain (Zapata-Barrero 2013a: Introduction), the concept of diversity is not set in stone, and there is something 'magical' that happens when those who define diversity never include themselves within the category. IC expresses the challenge that we need to break this epistemological barrier of the diversity concept. Blommaert and Verschueren assume this epistemological propriety of the diversity concept, for instance, when they state that 'the discourse on diversity is an instrument for the reproduction of social problems, forms of inequality and majority power' (1998: 4). They also argue that the problem of diversity is ideologically constructed, since it seems that the definition is dominated and controlled by the majority, and that even a tendency to 'abnormalize the other' (1998: 19–20) can be observed.

3. IC IS A MORE APPROPRIATE FRAMEWORK FOR DEALING WITH THE COMPLEXITY OF CURRENT SUPER-DIVERSE SOCIETIES

From the above section, it follows that MC is becoming out of tune with complex new diversity dynamics that demand a focus on interpersonal relations, rather than on agents (whether individual or group) or cultural identity-right claims. I also think that the rise of interest in IC is connected to new trends of migration studies such as transnationalism or the fact that people have multiple identities without really being willing to rank them in a decontextualised manner. This is connected to the framing of the globalisation process, as Cantle rightly views it (2012). The fact is that there is not a universal ranking of identities. Identities arise in given practices and according to determinate contexts. If I go to see a football match, my supportive identity will come first, but in other contexts, other identities would emerge first. To rank identities without taking context into account is what certain multiculturalists seem to promote, as if there were primary identities that are permanently active in any given context.[4] In the same

---

[4] It is true that some multiculturalists recognise that some identities are more salient or pervasive than others and more important to their bearers (see Modood 2007: 108–10).

vein, a diversity of loyalties amidst growing global mobility and increasing cross-border human movement is becoming the rule. MC has difficulties incorporating this political, transnational social dynamic. The new debate on super-diversity also belongs to this track of incorporating complexity into diversity studies (Vertovec 2014), as does the literature on network societies arising from the seminal work of Castells (1996, 1997), showing that the question of personal identity is much more connected to how people relate to each other, rather than the traditional 'Who am I?' based on where I was born (territory) or who my parents are (descent). We can even add some generational arguments of intercultural conflict. People already socialised into diverse societies are facing the challenge of reconciling national and city identities, on the one hand, with different cultural strands and multiple identities in everyday social life (Crul, Schneider and Lelie 2012). The multicultural citizenship debate has difficulties here with incorporating the practical implications of these new trends first academically articulated by sociologists and demographers.

Taking this perspective, it seems to me that MC has more in common with assimilationist and homogeneous minds, returning to the logic that Castles critiques. They share interpretative frameworks of diversity, namely in the way they similarly categorise attributes such as nationality, race, religion and community. MC, to my knowledge, has never formulated a critical interpretative framework regarding the way homogeneous cultural and national states categorise diversity dynamics. My main argument is that we cannot impose our diversity categories on others. This also involves putting into doubt the glue of most of the multicultural debates between ethnicity and nationality. Ethnicity is self-ascribed, flexible and cannot be imposed by those with the power to define diversity categories. Ethnicity, understood as self-identification, concerns the categories of ascription. Ethnic boundaries are also places of social interactions. IC reacts against the process of political ethnicisation of people, and against considering ethnicity a given notion in categorising groups.

This substantial criticism of the multicultural citizenship approach in the domains of ethnicity, nationalism and race is very close to what Brubaker calls 'groupism', namely 'the tendency to treat ethnic groups, nations and races as substantial entities to which interests and agency can be attributed' (2002:

164), or even Sen's 'solitarism' (2006: xii–xiii), criticising this tendency to reduce people to singular, differentiated identity affiliations, to 'miniaturise' people into one dimension of their multiple identities.

IC is a better tool for dealing with the complexity of our super-diverse societies, with transnational and multiple identities and cultural affiliations. It has a much more dynamic view of ethnicity and assumes the interactive nature of culture, instead of a simplistic, ready-made view of current diverse societies, as multiculturalists illustrate. Culture is interactive, following again Brubaker's statement:

> Ethnicity, race and nation should be conceptualized not as substances or things or entities or organisms or collective individuals—as the imagery of discrete, concrete, tangible, bounded and enduring 'groups' encourages us to do—but rather in relational, processual, dynamic, eventful and disaggregated terms. (2002: 167)

This also means that a category of diversity does not entail a group. A category of diversity, such as religion, language and so on, can be a potential basis for group formation or 'groupness', but it must be initially treated from above as a set of individuals, without any entailed generalisation. For instance, a Moroccan person is not necessarily Muslim. In essence, the multicultural citizenship paradox is that it tends to view groups in terms of nationality, and from there assumes a culture and a religion, without asking people about personal religious or cultural experiences in their everyday lives in a context that has not been constructed with this assumption. IC is about asking first how people sense their identities, and it then respects their self-identification. Its premise is that we cannot impose our ethnic categories onto others. This also includes a respect for the diversity of identities within the same national-cultural category. I am thinking, for instance, that even if Morocco does not recognise cultural diversity among its own nationals (for instance, Amazigh or Berber culture), multicultural citizenship contributes to this homogenisation of Moroccan culture by being too national-dependent in ascribing the cultural identities of people of Moroccan origin. Reality seems again to contradict some assumptions of MC.

A pluralistic view of intercultural citizenship: Normative building blocks

As happens with MC (in, for instance, Crowder 2013), we cannot assume a generalised view of intercultural citizenship. There is not a unique way of understanding IC. Things are, again, more complex than multiculturalists seem to admit (see Kymlicka 2003, which is, in my view, a simplistic narrative promoting dialogue). In this second stage of my argumentation, I present IC as having three basic premises, as being founded with three main hypotheses and as following three main normative drivers, against the tendency to reduce intercultural citizenship to just one simplistic view of 'dialogue among people from different backgrounds'.

As far as I have argued, the core of intercultural citizenship is essentially one basic idea: that the interaction among people from different diversity attributions matters, and that this has been overlooked by the multicultural citizenship paradigm, which has mainly concentrated on ensuring the cultural rights of diverse groups. Currently, the strategy based on the promotion of interaction, community-building and prejudice reduction is one of the approaches most widely recognised by international institutions – especially European ones.

Intercultural citizenship is, then, the answer to this common concern. Roughly stated from a policy point of view, IC is a real change of focus. The lenses are now placed on citizens' relations rather than on individuals and/or groups. From this point of view, summarising the recent literature on IC, we can say that it focuses on three basic premises promoting intercultural citizenship:

1. *(Positive) interaction*: The concern is not only with the promotion of interpersonal contact as such, but also with the resulting disconfirmation of stereotypes and reduction in prejudice towards 'others'. In this sense, it is a means to an end, through an ongoing process, intended to develop and maintain relational competences. In other words, it tries to ensure that the contact zones between people are areas of (positive) interaction, rather than areas of conflict.
2. *Anti-discrimination*: This is a fundamental element of intercultural citizenship promotion, since it focuses on the factors that hinder or support intercultural relations. There are contextual,

legal, institutional and structural factors that reduce people's motivations to interact and that even produce walls of separation between people, due to misinterpretations of their differences. Here, we take into account legal frameworks concerning voting rights for foreigners and naturalisation policies, along with gaps in socio-economic opportunities among citizens when differences become the explanatory factor for reduced contact.

3. *Diversity advantage*: This means redesigning institutions and policies in all fields to treat diversity as a potential resource and a public good, and not as a nuisance to be contained. In practice, this diversity management is great in terms of equal opportunities for education, employment, entrepreneurship, holding civil office and so on (Wood and Landry 2008; Guidikova 2015).

These three premises cover different spheres of interaction in practice. We can identify three empirical hypotheses emerging from the literature, which focus on the potential impacts of diversity and require the promotion of intercultural citizenship. I will also assess how each hypothesis develops a theory that informs the three main normative drivers of IC.

Understood from the beginning as positive interaction, anti-discrimination and diversity advantage (the three dimensions defining intercultural citizenship), the first key question is how to justify these promotions. Three hypotheses found IC.[5]

1. The *social hypothesis* says that diversity tends, at the beginning of the process, to provoke segregation and exclusion, and it reduces social capital and the sense of belonging to society, either through social inequality or through interference of information and knowledge among immigrants and citizens (see, for instance, Putnam 2007). Intercultural citizenship seeks to restore social cohesion, trust and feelings of belonging through social equality policies, in addition to policies that try to promote knowledge formation and prejudice reduction.

2. The *political hypothesis* argues that diversity tends to alter the traditional expression of national identities, threatening traditional values and the system of relations of rights and duties,

[5] I just follow some previous version of this comprehensive view (Zapata-Barrero 2015d).

which ensure a common sense of loyalty and stability between citizens and the basic structure of society. In this case, the three types of promotion seek to maintain control of any justified change in traditional national values, maintaining equilibrium between the loyalty of citizens and the rights of immigrants (see, for instance, Bouchard 2011).

3. The *cultural hypothesis* rests on the notion that citizens' cultural capabilities are not fully developed in a diverse society. Here, I mean not only nationality-based culture, but also cultural citizenship in general. Left alone, diversity tends to close off the cultural opportunities of diverse people. IC, as three means of promotion, seeks to develop the creative and innovative potentiality of cultures in diverse societies (see, for instance, Bennett 2001).

Each hypothesis develops a theory that informs each strand. Answering the social hypothesis requires the development of a *social theory of diversity*, grounded on Allport's (1954) well-known contact theory (which, roughly speaking, holds that contact reduces prejudice and promotes knowledge formation), and based on Cantle's (2008) view of IC as community cohesion and community-building. We can mention here the class perspective and its relation to intercultural relationships in diverse and often physically segregated societies.

Hence, supporting positive interaction involves transforming initial conflict zones into areas of positive contact, in order to ensure an optimal living situation and social inclusion. Its basic aim is social conflict reduction, as diversity becomes an explanatory factor in social disturbances. Moreover, conflict is a broader notion, encompassing racism, poverty and social exclusion (Cantle 2012: 102). The promotion of participation and representation in intercultural citizenship and the incorporation of IC into the main social networks of society are also main priorities in fostering cohesion.

To react to the political hypothesis, we need to develop a *political theory of diversity*. I can take as a most recent illustration of this view the work of Bouchard (2012), centred primarily on managing the relationship between immigrants and the basic structures of society, ensuring what he calls 'the survival of national identity', avoiding dualism in society between traditional social values and diversity.[6] It seeks to provide the most appropriate spaces for motivating agreements between national tradition, which accepts unavoidable changes, and the context of diversity, through participative policy channels and other means of vertical communication. Its purposes are to manage the potential impact that changes can have on tradition, to regulate the behaviour of nationals, and to minimise impacts on the loyalty of citizens and the rights/duties of immigrants (especially equal opportunities).

Lastly, if we want to formulate policy reactions to the cultural hypothesis, we need to frame a *cultural theory of diversity*, based on promoting the cultural capabilities of people, which is to be understood in terms of the cultural goods and resources needed to develop creative and innovative capacities in society. This theory rests on a particular application of the democratisation of culture and cultural citizenship (see the recent work on cultural citizenship, R. Zapata-Barrero 2015c). There already exists some recent initial literature on this, albeit without taking diversity contexts into account too explicitly (see, for instance, Turner 2001 and Stanley 2005). IC is a way to produce something new as a product of interaction, which helps the cultural development of persons qua citizens.

Generally speaking, each theory brings about its own way of justifying the need to promote intercultural citizenship, and each pursues specific goals and establishes its own limits to diversity. The social theory of diversity shapes a cohesion strand of IC and has social inclusion and trust as normative drivers, with social conflict as its basic 'diversity limit'. The political theory of diversity seeks to legitimate a contractual strand of IC, with stability (of tradition and rights/duties) as its normative driver and with the loss of national identity as its basic 'diversity limit'. Finally, the cultural theory of diversity is grounded in a constructivist strand of IC. It has the development of capabilities, innovation and creativity as its normative driver, and the lack of equal cultural capabilities (personal and social) as its basic 'diversity limit'. Let me look further at each of these angles.

1. *Social inclusion/cohesion/diversity nexus*: When speaking of 'social inclusion' or, as Cantle categorises it, 'community

---

[6] The Québécois academic stresses, 'IC is the better option to ensure Québec's survival' (Bouchard 2012: 229).

cohesion', the basic idea is to promote interpersonal contact, community-building or – as Cantle (2012: 102) again insists – a mechanism for generating trust and mutual understanding, and for breaking down prejudices, stereotypes and the misconceptions of others. We might say that it is a way of bonding, bridging differences and building social capital. It is a way, then, to avoid the confinement and segregation of citizens, which as a last resort become explanatory variables of social exclusion and social inequalities. Social cohesion is the horizon, as well, in the sense of encouraging interaction to overcome social and cultural barriers among people, especially in neighbourhoods (Cantle 2012: 103). Cantle also draws a link between programmes of interaction and those of belonging that cannot be dismissed, in that in order to ensure the permanence of cohesion, it is necessary to promote a minimal sense of belonging.

The *cohesion strand* addresses power relations as well, particularly in terms of tackling inequalities, both in opportunities and in outcomes. The purpose here is to work on the preconditions of mutual respect prior to intercultural dialogue, such that 'contact' is more likely to be effective (Allport 1954; Hewstone et al. 2007).

Therefore, in contrast to the *contractual strand*, it promotes better face-to-face relations, step by step, in a proximal context. Cantle explicitly speaks about local identity and belonging campaigns that aim to garner a sense of solidarity. We might say that, whereas feelings of common values were the cement of past periods, Cantle highlights (quoting Kymlicka 2003) that it is now necessary to focus on a common space of interaction and common citizenship. From the perspective of the cohesion view, IC tends to bridge the tension between being 'too diverse' (Goodhart 2004) and being cohesive.

2. *Tradition/stability/diversity nexus*: The contractual strand understands intercultural citizenship as a function for enhancing stability in a diverse society, with tradition expressing itself through collective routines and socially acceptable behaviour. It designates a set of established values and beliefs transmitted from generation to generation (Friedrich 1972: 18), which can be interpreted as jeopardised by diversity dynamics, or as Weber conceptualised with the suggestive expression 'what has always existed' (1964: 29). It also requires no rational justification,

since it is better transmitted through (national) emotions. The word 'tradition' derives from the Latin *tradere*, which means to transfer or to deliver. Tradition plays, then, a vital role for the political body, as the purpose for maintaining social stability. In politics, tradition is also a framework for the unity of a community of citizens, and it is a tool for promoting a sense of loyalty.

This variant of the contractual approach can be associated with Bouchard (2012), when he claims that there are two constant concerns in the intercultural view: the survival of the national identity and respect for the rights of minorities. The basic pillar of Bouchard's contractual view as equilibrium rests on this point. When tradition becomes social action, it defines the minimum level of unity necessary for structuring a stable society. What this view fears is that leaving diversity alone (without promoting positive interaction) can give rise to an element of cultural division and instability in society.

3. *Innovation/development/diversity nexus*: The constructivist view basically enhances the proactive nature of intercultural citizenship, in the sense that it is not grounded on a reaction against any particular negative outcome of diversity, but is instead concentrated on producing an innovative outcome from the interaction. It is, then, creativity-based. This view highlights the fact that, through interaction, something new is potentially generated, which can drive individual and social development. This idea of development is its distinguishing characteristic. Both the earlier contractual and cohesion strands miss this added value of intercultural citizenship promotion. Expressing itself in the form of innovation and creativity, this constructivist approach also has a different view of diversity. Diversity is basically considered an asset and an opportunity. From this viewpoint, IC can then be considered a strategy that promotes a context of mutual development. It follows a bonding/bridging strategy, in the sense that it tries to promote interaction between people with common interests but with different backgrounds. In this way, it can campaign for the sense of cohesion and belonging from the cohesion strand. But this *constructivist* view, in my opinion, takes a step forward, in that it promotes the *capabilities of people*.

In this pluralistic view of intercultural citizenship, we have three angles within the same triangle, which has positive interaction, anti-discrimination and diversity advantage at its conceptual core. These three strands become the basic normative drivers of intercultural citizenship. They involve policies, behaviours, cultural practices, institutional routines and management programmes that help create bridges between 'what has always existed' (tradition), 'what has potential for social conflict' (in broader terms) and 'what is new' (innovation). Although this goes beyond the scope of this chapter, we can highlight that the real challenge of intercultural citizenship is not in deciding which of these three views is right or wrong, but in balancing them in a comprehensive way (Zapata-Barrero 2015b). These three normative drivers show that promoting intercultural citizenship is not a simple task of putting two agents into contact (for it does not follow an agent-based approach), but is rather a matter of managing the process of interaction towards normative ends.

Concluding remarks: Policy implications of IC – the pragmatic turn and mainstream public philosophy

IC has to be interpreted as the most pragmatic answer to concrete concerns and to policy agenda related to diversity dynamic contexts. Such a change in perspective is certainly related to a broad shift in focus that took place in the realm of political theory during the last decade, as different scholars called for a 'contextualised' political theory engaged with existing practices (Carens 2000 and 2004, Favell and Modood 2003, Kukathas 2004, Zapata-Barrero 2004, Triandafyllidou, Modood and Zapata-Barrero 2006).

With this pragmatic logic, we have also recognised that the potentialities of the intercultural citizenship approach to drive stability, cohesion and development have to incorporate socio-economic constraints as well. Here, we may find some limits to intercultural citizenship. A major challenge across European cities is precisely the lack of physical contact between different groups, and it is hard to draw a sharp line between class and ethnic/immigrant status as determining social disadvantage. Poor national and immigrant-origin citizens typically cohabit the least attractive housing areas; this points to some degree of 'interaction' in this kind of dwelling. Thus, we could legitimately ask, why would interaction necessarily lead to better relationships, especially in times of financial crisis and increased competition over jobs? Despite our having argued that promoting interaction is important, it is also crucial to problematise this question and the significance of the context in which these intercultural contacts would take place. This is a significant point, since it highlights something important: IC is a proximate policy, always performance-oriented, with the aim of inverting diversity's negative impact and of promoting a view of diversity as an opportunity and advantage for personal and social development.

This problem-solving approach is in the very nature of intercultural citizenship. This is the case, for instance, of Gérard Bouchard himself, who recognises that his last book (2012) tries to summarise his own position after the much-discussed practical and public debate of the Bouchard-Taylor Commission (Bouchard and Taylor 2008). Ted Cantle, meanwhile, has been a key player in policy orientations surrounding the British government's concern for local social disturbances in northern towns in August 2011. These events directly linked social conflicts with the failure of British multicultural policy. His book *Community Cohesion* (2008) – based on an approach first presented in a previous report (the so-called 'Cantle Report', 2001) – proposes reducing tension in local communities by promoting cross-cultural contact and by developing support for diversity and promoting unity. This work has had a direct influence in changing state behaviour and policy focus in Britain. Wood (2004) and other interculturalists connected, to different degrees, to the Intercultural Cities programme, offered by the Council of Europe since 2008, are policy-oriented practitioners.[7] To my knowledge, MC has not shown such policy-oriented attractiveness at the city level in such a relatively short time. There is empirical evidence that we are seeing an interculturalist wave, but we cannot say that there is a multiculturalist wave in cities. I would even contend that cities opting for the intercultural approach are aware, as has been so brilliantly illustrated by one of the foundational documents of the Intercultural Cities programme, that 'one of the defining factors that will determine, over coming years, which cities flourish and which decline will be the extent to which they allow their diversity to be their asset, or their handicap. Whilst national and supra-national bodies will continue to wield an influence it will

[7] See footnotes 1 and 2 for references.

increasingly be the choices that cities themselves make which will seal their future' (Council of Europe 2008: 22).

So, even if interculturalism is a newcomer in the debates over citizenship and diversity, it has shown a power of seduction for policy-makers, who basically understand that this approach does not force them to target explicit groups, since they interpret affirmative action as being one of the factors of negative public opinion, the rise of xenophobia and anti-immigrant discourses (Zapata-Barrero 2011). This 'attraction' is then connected with its differentiated policy implications in contrast to MC. If I may confess, in policy circles, sometimes the debate touches on how and why IC is so 'sexy' for policy-makers.

In exploring some explanations for this fact, I suggest that this rests in its practical application. I argue that IC is much more inclined toward the mainstream, since one of its most important assets is that it does not request specific policies or affirmative action (which was founded by the multicultural citizenship approach). Rather, it follows a *mainstreaming public philosophy*, which could be defined as an effort to address diversity questions by catering to the entire population, and not only a sector of it, based on some categorisation of difference, and without encapsulating them within a given conception of culture, ethnicity or group. Mainstreaming refers to an amalgam of efforts to abandon target-group-specific policy measures (Collett and Petrovic 2014: 2) and to incorporate IC as an integral part of generic policies in public domains (Scholten, Collett and Petrovic 2014). Mainstreaming strategies involve intercultural policy approaches that speak to the entire diverse population and that involve multiple policy stakeholders besides the nation-state, including other levels of government and NGOs (Zapata-Barrero 2015e). As intercultural citizenship is not agent-based, but focuses on interaction, the specificity of its policies separated from the mainstream is simply non-posed. Specific policies, when they exist within IC, are always placed with the aim of diversifying mainstream services and institutions, and then via mainstream policies at the end. Here lies what may be a concrete, visible point of departure from the policy of multicultural citizenship.

We cannot deny that IC has already attracted many cities and local policy-makers. From the point of view of governance, it has even reached a level of consensus between society and politics that did not occur in most cities with other paradigms, such as assimilation and MC (see the Barcelona case-study analysis in Zapata-Barrero 2015e). This agreement in policy strategy on what, for many years, had been a matter of social dispute and political cleavage is perhaps the basic argument that supports the need to better articulate this intercultural expansion. The question of 'how to focus diversity policy' becomes more easily accepted politically, then, when the answer is IC. It is also my view that this initial political support for the tasks of policy-makers belongs to the first phase of implementing intercultural policy. Now, however, it probably needs to offer distinctive arguments, not necessarily built against other approaches, which fight to occupy the space of being a reference framework in the diversity management debate. Conceptual reflection and empirical studies dealing with policy definition and implementation are now a necessary step complementing this one, which is basically centred on the foundations. I think, too, that this foundational debate can become nonsense without contextual analysis and theorisation of intercultural practice, already identifying most European cities and even urban projects. A theory of IC would certainly benefit from empirically based and informed conceptual reflection. The already existing policy attraction of IC certainly needs academic attention as well. We particularly need input from those still inside some sort of 'multicultural bunker', who are still willing to apply their interpretative frameworks to a diversity dynamics that is becoming more and more complex, and is thus difficult to grasp with old-fashioned ethnic categories.

References

Allport, G. W. (1954), *The Nature of Prejudice*, Cambridge, MA: Addison Wesley.

Barrett, M. (ed.) (2013), *Interculturalism and Multiculturalism: Similarities and Differences*, Strasbourg: Council of Europe.

Bennett, T. (ed.) (2001), *Differing Diversities: Transversal Study on the Theme of Cultural Policy and Cultural Diversity*, Strasbourg: Council of Europe.

Blommaert, J., and J. Verschueren (1998), *Debating Diversity: Analyzing the Discourse of Tolerance*, London: Routledge.

Bloomfield, J., and F. Bianchini (2001), 'Cultural Citizenship and Urban Governance in Western Europe', in N. Stevenson (ed.), *Culture and Citizenship*, London: Sage, pp. 99–123.

Bloomfield, J., and F. Bianchini (2004), *Planning for the Intercultural City*, Stroud: Comedia.

Bouchard, G. (2011), 'What Is Interculturalism?', *McGill Law Journal/Revue de droit de McGill*, 56 (2), 435–68.

Bouchard, G. (2012), *L'interculturalisme. Un point de vue québécois*, Montreal: Boréal.

Bouchard, G., and C. Taylor (2008), *Building the Future: A Time for Reconciliation*, Report of the Consultation Commission on Accommodation Practices Related to Cultural Difference, Quebec City: Government of Quebec.

Brecknock, R. (2006), *Planning and Designing Culturally: More Than Just a Bridge*, London: Comedia.

Brubaker, R. (2002), 'Ethnicity without Groups', *European Journal of Sociology*, 43, 163–89.

Cantle, T. (2001), *Community Cohesion: A Report of the Independent Review Team* (The 'Cantle Report'), London: Home Office, <http://www.tedcantle.co.uk/publications/001%20Cantle%20Report%20CCRT%202001.pdf> (last accessed 12 June 2015).

Cantle, T. (2008), *Community Cohesion: A New Framework for Race and Diversity*, Basingstoke: Palgrave Macmillan.

Cantle, T. (2012), *Interculturalism: The New Era of Cohesion and Diversity*, Basingstoke: Palgrave Macmillan.

Carens, J. (2000), *Culture, Citizenship, and Community*, New York: Oxford University Press.

Carens, J. (2004), 'A Contextual Approach to Political Theory', *Ethical Theory and Moral Practice*, 7 (2), 117–32.

Castells, M. (1996, 2nd edn 2000), *The Information Age: Economy, Society and Culture Volume 1: The Rise of the Network Society*, Malden, MA, and Oxford: Blackwell.

Castells, M. (1997, 2nd edn 2004), *The Information Age: Economy, Society and Culture Volume 2: The Power of Identity*, Malden, MA, and Oxford: Blackwell.

Castles, S. (2000), *Ethnicity and Globalization: From Migrant Worker to Transnational Citizen*, London: Sage.

Clarijs, M. A. J. L., I. Guidikova and T. Malmberg (2011), *Diversity and Community Development: An Intercultural Approach*, Amsterdam: SWP.

Collett, E., and M. Petrovic (2014), *The Future of Immigrant Integration in Europe: Mainstreaming Approaches for Inclusion*, Brussels: Migration Policy Institute.

Council of Europe, Committee of Ministers (2008), *Living Together as Equals in Dignity: White Paper on Intercultural Dialogue*, Strasbourg: Council of Europe.

Council of Europe (2011), *Intercultural Cities*, <http://www.coe.int/t/dg4/cultureheritage/culture/Cities/Default_en.asp> (last accessed 23 June 2015).

Crowder, G. (2013), *Theories of Multiculturalism: An Introduction*, Oxford: Polity.

Crul, M., J. Schneider and F. Lelie (2012), *The European Second Generation Compared: Does the Integration Context Matter?*, Amsterdam: Amsterdam University Press.

Daily Mail reporter (2011), 'Nicolas Sarkozy Joins David Cameron and Angela Merkel View that Multiculturalism Has Failed', *Daily Mail* online, 11 February, <http://www.dailymail.co.uk/news/article-1355961/Nicolas-Sarkozy-joins-David-Cameron-Angela-Merkel-view-multiculturalism-failed.html> (last accessed 12 June 2015).

Emerson, M. (ed.) (2011), *Interculturalism: Europe and its Muslims in Search of Sound Societal Models*, Brussels: Centre for European Policy Studies.

Faist, T. (2009), 'Diversity – A New Mode of Incorporation?', *Ethnic and Racial Studies*, 32 (1), 171–90.

Farrar, M. (2012), '"Interculturalism" or "Critical Multiculturalism": Which Discourse Works Best?', in M. Farrar, S. Robinson and O. Sener (eds), *Unedited Workshop Proceedings: Debating Multiculturalism 1*, London: The Dialogue Society, <http://maxfarrar.org.uk/max-blog//wp-content/uploads/2014/05/DebatingMultiCulturalism1-copy.pdf> (last accessed 12 June 2015).

Farrar, M., S. Robinson and O. Sener (2012), 'Interculturalism in Europe: Fact, Fad or Fiction – The Deconstruction of a Theoretical Idea', in M. Farrar, S. Robinson and O. Sener (eds), *Unedited Workshop Proceedings: Debating Multiculturalism 1*, London: The Dialogue Society, <http://maxfarrar.org.uk/max-blog//wp-content/uploads/2014/05/DebatingMultiCulturalism1-copy.pdf> (last accessed 12 June 2015).

Favell, A., and T. Modood (2003), 'The Philosophy of Multiculturalism: The Theory and Practice of Normative Political Theory', in A. Finlayson (ed.) *Contemporary Political Thought: A Reader and Guide*, Edinburgh: Edinburgh University Press, pp. 484–95.

Festenstein, M. (2005), *Negotiating Diversity: Culture, Deliberation, Trust*, Cambridge: Polity.

Frazer, N., and A. Honneth (2003), *Redistribution or Recognition? A Political-Philosophical Exchange*, London: Verso Books.

Friedrich, K. (1972), *Tradition and Authority*, London: Macmillan.

Goodhart, D. (2004), 'Too Diverse', *Prospects Magazine*, 20 February, <http://www.prospectmagazine.co.uk/magazine/too-diverse-david-goodhart-multiculturalism-britain-immigration-globalisation/> (last accessed 12 June 2015).

Gruescu, S., and V. Menne (2010), *Bridging Differences: What Communities and Government Can Do to Foster Social Capital*, London: The Social Market Foundation.

Guidikova, I. (2015), 'Intercultural Integration: A New Paradigm for Managing Diversity as an Advantage', in R. Zapata-Barrero (ed.), *Interculturalism in Cities: Concept, Policy and Implementation*, Cheltenham: Edward Elgar Publishing, pp. 136–51.

Gundara, J. S., and S. Jacobs (eds) (2000), *Intercultural Europe: Diversity and Social Policy*, Aldershot: Ashgate.

Hewstone, M., N. Tausch, J. Hughes and E. Cairns (2007), 'Prejudice, Intergroup Contact and Identity: Do Neighbourhoods Matter?', in M. Wetherell, M. Lafleche and R. Berkeley (eds), *Identity, Ethnic Diversity and Community Cohesion*, London: Sage, pp. 102–13.

Hussain, A., B. Law and T. Haq (2006), 'Engagement with Culture: From Diversity to Interculturalism', *Vaughan Papers*, 41, Leicester: University of Leicester.

Khan, N. (2006), *The Road to Interculturalism: Tracking the Arts in a Changing World*, London: Comedia.

Kukathas, C. (2004), 'Contextualism Reconsidered: Some Skeptical Reflections', *Ethical Theory and Moral Practice*, 7 (2), 215–25.

Kymlicka, W. (1995), *Multicultural Citizenship: A Liberal Theory of Minority Rights*, Oxford: Clarendon Press.

Kymlicka, W. (2003), 'Multicultural States and Intercultural Citizens', in *Theory and Research in Education*, 1 (2), 147–69.

Lüken-Klaßen, D., and F. Heckmann (2010), *Intercultural Policies in European Cities*, report, European network of cities for local integration policies for migrants (CLIP), <http://dare.uva.nl/record/1/329855> (last accessed 12 June 2015).

Meer, N., and T. Modood (2012), 'How Does Interculturalism Contrast with Multiculturalism?', *Journal of Intercultural Studies*, 33 (2), 175–96.

Modood, T. (1998), 'Anti-Essentialism, Multiculturalism and the "Recognition" of Religious Groups', *The Journal of Political Philosophy*, 6 (4), 378–99.

Modood, T. (2007), *Multiculturalism: A Civic Idea*, Cambridge: Polity Press.

Page, S. E. (2007), *The Difference: How the Power of Diversity Creates Better Groups, Firms, Schools and Societies*, Princeton: Princeton University Press.

Parekh, B. (2000), *Rethinking Multiculturalism: Cultural Diversity and Political Theory*, Basingstoke: Macmillan.

Phillips, A. (2007), *Multiculturalism without Culture*, Princeton: Princeton University Press.

Powell, D., and F. Sze (eds) (2004), *Interculturalism: Exploring Critical Issues*, Oxford: Interdisciplinary Press.

Putnam, R. (2007), 'E Pluribus Unum: Diversity and Community in the Twenty-First Century', *Scandinavian Political Studies Journal*, 30 (2), 137–74.

Sandercock, L. (2004), 'Reconsidering Multiculturalism: Towards an Intercultural Project', in P. Wood (ed.), *Intercultural City Reader*, London: Comedia, pp. 16–21.

Scholten, P., E. Collett and M. Petrovic (2014), 'Mainstreaming Migrant Integration: Beyond the Assimilationist Turn in European Policies', unpublished manuscript.

Sen, A. (2006), *Identity and Violence: The Illusion of Destiny*, New York: W. W. Norton & Co.

Stanley, D. (2005), *Recondita armonia – A Reflection on the Function of Culture in Building Citizenship Capacity*, a study prepared for the Council of Europe in the framework of the European Year of Citizenship 2005, Policy Note 10, <http://www.coe.int/t/dg4/cultureheritage/culture/resources/Publications/Recondita_armonia_EN.pdf> (last accessed 12 June 2015).

Taylor, C. (2012), 'Interculturalism or Multiculturalism?', *Philosophy and Social Criticism*, 38 (4–5), 413–23.

Titley, G. (2012), 'After the Failed Experiment: Intercultural Learning in a Multicultural Crisis', in O. Yael and H. Otten (eds), *Where Do You Stand? Intercultural Learning and Political Education in Contemporary Europe*, Wiesbaden: VS Verlag, pp. 161–80.

Triandafyllidou, A., T. Modood and R. Zapata-Barrero (2006), 'European Challenges to Multicultural Citizenship: Muslims, Secularism and Beyond', in T. Modood, A. Triandafyllidou and R. Zapata-Barrero (eds), *Multiculturalism, Muslims and Citizenship: A European Approach*, London: Routledge, pp. 1–22.

Turner, B. (2001), 'Outline of a General Theory of Citizenship', in N. Stevenson (ed.), *Culture and Citizenship*, London: Sage, pp. 11–32.

Vertovec, S. (ed.) (2014), *Migration and Diversity*, Cheltenham: Edward Elgar Publishing.

Vertovec, S., and S. Wessendorf (eds) (2010), *The Multiculturalism Backlash: European Discourses, Policies and Practices*, London: Routledge.

Weber, M. (1964), *Economia y Sociedad*, Mexico City: Fondo de Cultura Económica.

Werbner, P., and T. Modood (eds) (2015), *Debating Cultural Hybridity: Multicultural Identities and the Politics of Anti-Racism*, London: Zed Books.

Wood, P. (2004), *The Intercultural City Reader*, Stroud: Comedia.

Wood, P. (2015), 'Meet Me on the Corner? Shaping the Conditions for Cross-Cultural Interaction in Urban Public Space', in R. Zapata-Barrero (ed.), *Interculturalism in Cities: Concept, Policy and Implementation*, Cheltenham: Edward Elgar Publishing, pp. 53–75.

Wood, P., and C. Landry (2008), *The Intercultural City: Planning for Diversity Advantage*, London: Earthscan.

Young, I. M. (1990), *Justice and the Politics of Difference*, Princeton: Princeton University Press.

Zachary, P. (2003), *The Diversity Advantage: Multicultural Identity in the New World Economy*, Boulder: Westview.

Zapata-Barrero, R. (2004), 'Political Theory Today: Political Innovation and the Management of Structural Change', *European Political Science*, 3 (3), 39–50.

Zapata-Barrero, R. (2011), 'Anti-Immigration Populism: Can Local Intercultural Policies Close the Space?', Discussion Paper, London: Policy Network, <http://www.policy-network.net/uploads/media/160/7726.pdf > (last accessed 23 June 2015).

Zapata-Barrero, R. (2013), *Diversity Management in Spain*, Manchester: Manchester University Press.

Zapata-Barrero, R. (2015a), 'Introduction: Framing the Intercultural Turn', in R. Zapata-Barrero (ed.), *Interculturalism in Cities: Concept, Policy and Implementation*, Cheltenham: Edward Elgar Publishing, pp. vii–xvi.

Zapata-Barrero, R. (ed.) (2015b), *Interculturalism in Cities: Concept, Policy and Implementation*, Cheltenham: Edward Elgar Publishing.

Zapata-Barrero, R. (2015c), 'Diversity and Cultural Policy: Cultural Citizenship as a Tool for Inclusion', *International Journal of Cultural Policy* (online first), DOI:10.1080/10286632.2015.1015533

Zapata-Barrero, R. (2015d), 'Exploring the Foundations of the Intercultural Policy Paradigm: A Comprehensive Approach', *Identities: Global Studies in Culture and Power* (online first), DOI:10.1080/1070289X.2015.1006523

Zapata-Barrero, R. (2015e), 'Multi-Level Intercultural Governance in Barcelona: Mainstreaming Comprehensive Approach', unpublished manuscript.

4

Quebec Interculturalism and Canadian Multiculturalism

Gérard Bouchard

What I intend to do in this chapter is to come back to the book I have recently published on Quebec interculturalism (Bouchard 2012) in order to foreground a few points, to offer some clarifications, and also to address additional issues.

Interculturalism viewed from Quebec

A BRAND OF PLURALISM

First of all, interculturalism is a form of pluralism. This background philosophy, as we know, is shared by other models, each of them offering a specific application.[1] Thus, I would say that multiculturalism and interculturalism are two different incarnations of pluralism. This goes against a common view that makes pluralism the prerogative, even a synonym of multiculturalism.

Accordingly, the interculturalist model promotes:

- the protection of civil rights, especially minority rights, and the practice of reasonable accommodations;
- a vision of minority cultures as fluid so that their members can choose and negotiate their identity and belonging;
- the free expression of religions in the public sphere (including the rights for state employees to wear religious signs);

---

[1] This also holds for the European Union, as shown in the policy statement adopted in 2004: integration as a two-way process, access to job market, basic knowledge of the host society, freedom of religion, civic participation, etc.

- the necessity of various forms of support to minorities (for example, the teaching of their language) so that their culture can be perpetuated if their members wish to do so;
- the construction of a national memory that reflects the diversity of the whole society;
- the formation of a national identity as 'a work in progress' feeding on the majority and minority cultures, and so forth.

THE NATIONAL FRAMEWORK

I have also inscribed my conception of interculturalism within the framework of the nation-state (without excluding the relevance of subnational or transnational configurations). This is the case with most models of diversity management. The choice is justified on the grounds that, in Quebec, like in most countries of the world, the mechanisms that govern the management of diversity operate at the level of or within the nation-state: just think of immigration and integration policies, school curriculum, acquisition of citizenship, protection of civil rights, promotion of a common language, identity and memory building, choice of a secularist regime, and the whole judicial process that litigates conflicts generated by cultural encounters. Even within the European Union, the member states still wield important powers in these areas.

MORE DISTINCTIVE TRAITS

More specifically, through Bill 101 (a measure whose legitimacy has been acknowledged by the supreme court of Canada), Quebec interculturalism establishes French as the official language of public life. The model also places an emphasis on integration (not to be confused with assimilation), particularly the integration of newcomers, as a two-way, reciprocal process that confers a joint responsibility to the majority and the minorities, making sure that (a) immigrants are included politically, socially and economically (especially in the job market), and (b) they are provided with the means to learn the public language and to embrace the basic values of the host society, as they are enshrined in the Charter of Human Rights and Freedoms. In the case of Quebec, we are talking primarily of civic and social equality (including gender equality), democracy, freedom of speech, social justice and non-violence.

At the micro level, which is the sphere of interculturality, the model calls for exchange and interactions as a way to facilitate integration, to activate diversity as a resource, to foster mutual trust, but also to fight stereotypes which, as we know, breed racism, exclusion and discrimination. And, in so doing, interactions help make ethno-cultural boundaries more porous. They are also instrumental in the development of a common culture in the civic place, that is, a common language and a body of shared values, cultural codes and symbols.

The enactment of interculturalism is a collective responsibility and, as such (as I make clear in my book), it must be implemented at various levels: the state, the major public and private institutions, the municipalities, and the neighbourhood or community level.

Finally, a central part of the model is to take into account a majority/minority relationship. This duality feature is uppermost in Quebec, where it is deeply rooted in the national imaginary. One reason is that the French majority culture is itself a minority in North America. A collective feeling of cultural fragility is a constant in the history of Quebec, along with the sense of a duty to fight for the future of the francophone culture. As a consequence, the presence of non-francophones in Quebec feeds a vivid majority/minority consciousness. Another reason is that for a long time Quebec has been a colony of Great Britain, and since the second half of the eighteenth century it has harboured a powerful English minority.[2] Recent history has shown that any model that would not build on this duality is doomed to fail. That explains, for instance, why Canadian multiculturalism was a non-starter in Quebec.

It is important to stress that interculturalism, by itself, does not create nor stimulate the growth of the majority/minority relationship. The model is only designed in such a way as to manage this duality once it has taken shape. If and when this structure happens to disappear, then the model must adjust, but it can survive at the level of interculturality. The goal of interculturalism is to ensure that duality is lived in a decent way, in keeping with the requirements of pluralism, with a view to preventing tension and conflict.

[2] Nowadays, Quebecers who have French as their mother tongue account for 80 per cent of Quebec's population, which represents 2 per cent of the North American population.

From the foregoing, one could conclude that interculturalism should also establish as a priority the suppression of the majority/minority relationship on the grounds that the latter is likely to feed and to harden an us/them cleavage detrimental to minorities. Actually, this issue is more complicated than it may appear. Undoubtedly, in a number of cases, minorities are created by majorities as part of a strategy of domination and exclusion, such that, to a large extent, the minorities can be said to be instrumentally invented. Then, the duality is clearly harmful and it should be destroyed. But in many cases, the majority and minorities exist because of the willingness of their respective members to perpetuate their culture and identity. And this is a choice that must be respected for the sake of pluralism.

Of course, one should not preclude various forms of intense exchange and hybridisation. For instance, it is expected that in the long run, the dual relationship will lose some of its grip if a common culture develops. But, again, it will survive if this is the choice of the citizens. That's what I call the paradox of pluralism, which at once attempts to eliminate and to preserve the duality. This is the first paradox – or should I say conundrum? – of diversity management.

This being said, interculturalism, quite consistently, shows a concern for power relation. It is obvious that the duality dynamic harbours a potential for social inequality and domination by the majority. This may seem to be a drawback of interculturalism, but it is just the opposite. In all societies, overtly or covertly, majorities find ways to wield their power at the expense of minorities. So, it is a merit of the model in so far as it puts the power relations at the forefront, rather than concealing them.

The issue of state cultural neutrality: The case for controlled interventionism

I certainly agree that democratic, liberal societies should be culturally neutral. It is unquestionably a lofty ideal. As we know, this radical principle, which forbids government from intervening in the definition and promotion of a public morality or a conception of the 'good life', takes its roots in the liberal philosophy of John Locke, John Stuart Mill and Immanuel Kant. During the 1970s and 1980s, authors such as Rawls (1971), Ackerman (1980) and Dworkin (1985) were among its main proponents. According to this theory, it is solely up to free, autonomous individuals to cultivate the values of their choice, protected from the interference of the state or its substitutes.

However, in reality, there is no such thing as a culturally neutral state. A state should be as neutral culturally as possible,[3] but I do not believe that, practically, a state can be neutral and I do not believe that it should be. First, let's start with the undisputed fact that even the most so-called 'civic' states are not neutral. They constantly intervene in a biased way in the cultural life. Here are a few examples drawn from the religious sphere:

- Switzerland maintains a reference to God in its constitution.
- There is a reference to the supremacy of God in the preamble of the Canadian constitution.
- Every year, the Canadian government enacts the ritual of the 'Prayer Breakfast', attended by elected officials, Senate members, judges of the Supreme Court and ministers of the cabinet, in order to call upon 'Almighty God', to 'ask the Most High for strength and wisdom, to show our faith and renew our devotion and that of our nation to God and to His works', all 'in the spirit of Jesus Christ'.[4]
- In Ireland, the Catholic Church controls the national public school system.
- In the United States, religion, and more specifically Protestantism, is a major part of the state discourse and rituals.
- France, ignoring its own law, refuses to officially recognise Islam as it does other denominations, even though this religion is the second largest in the country.
- Belgium funds Catholic schools but is less enthusiastic about funding Muslim schools.
- The Church of England is still the official religion of that country, and in April 2014 Prime Minister David Cameron asserted the Christian character of Britain.
- Besides England, a number of democratic countries maintain a state religion or acknowledge in their constitution a dominant religion (e.g. Denmark, Greece, Ireland, Poland).

---

[3] This is, more or less, the view expressed by Weinstock 2003.

[4] According to the text of the invitation card. See also <http://www.canadaprayer breakfast.ca> (last accessed 4 June 2015).

Those cases should be seen as illegitimate forms of state interventionism (or non-neutrality, also called 'perfectionism' in political philosophy literature) since one can see no compelling motive
to accord a precedence to or to discriminate against one religion. By contrast, other forms of cultural interventionism are not
only acceptable but necessary. For example, I imagine that few
people, at least in the Western world, will question the right for
a host society to promote a national language or a set of basic
liberal values that will be imposed upon immigrants and minorities (freedom of speech, equality, democracy, non-violence and so
forth). Yet, in these two cases, it is clear that the violation of strict
neutrality serves the views of the majority. In other words, in some
circumstances, it can be legitimate to break the neutrality rule in
favour of the majority, at least indirectly.

Another telling example is the case of the language law in Quebec
(known as Bill 101). In 1977, when the bill was adopted, the francophones accounted for 82 per cent of the Quebec population. But
the future of the francophone culture in Quebec was threatened
by a radical fertility decline and a growing wave of immigration
from all parts of the world. By making French the official language
of public life, the bill obviously catered to the needs of the majority culture. However, it also helped minorities and immigrants by
allowing them an equal opportunity to be socially integrated, to
find a job and get ahead, to participate in public life, and so on.
Moreover, it contributed to restoring social order by putting an end
to old conflicts on the verge of lapsing into violence. Interestingly,
this example shows that interventionism can serve both the majority and the minorities.

In the same vein, many democratic countries, in order to protect
their culture, adopt laws that suppress the right to buy and sell
cultural goods (because of their heritage value) or restrict the circulation of foreign products (movies, magazines, radio and television broadcasts and so on). They also orient the construction of
memory and collective identity, determine the educational curriculum, select immigrants, and define the rituals of civic life.

What is the criterion that would allow one to distinguish legitimate from illegitimate forms of interventionism? The answer lies
primarily in a sociological requirement. I believe that legitimate
forms are those which are meant to protect or to restore the
symbolic foundation of a society or a nation when it is seriously

threatened. I am referring here to cultural resources and conditions deemed necessary for a society to function and to develop: world-views, basic values, ideals and beliefs, memory, traditions, sense of belonging, common language or languages, public institutions that provide essential services, some level of social order and solidarity, and so forth. This is one of the oldest basic lessons taught by socio-logical and anthropological tradition: no collective action without a social bond, and no social bond without a symbolic support.

Especially in a context of tensions, rapid change or crisis, only the existence of broadly shared references – that is, a specific culture and identity – makes possible the elements of affiliations and solidarity that provide the basis of any form of collective mobi-lisation for the pursuit of the common good (reduction of inequali-ties, improvement of healthcare, environmental policies and so on). These are the conditions that make possible democracy, civic participation, social justice and a sense of mutual responsibility, and they should never be taken for granted. It is therefore desir-able for liberal states to support – as all of them actually do – the symbolic foundation in which institutions and, more generally, the social bond are rooted.[5] However, it should be understood that this symbolic foundation must be construed as minimalist, lest it erodes minority cultures.

In other words, there must be a civic or a societal purpose[6] driving the interventionism and not only a strategy to bolster the majority culture. Practically, this means that sometimes the state can bestow some privilege to the majority culture when it is closely associated with the formation or the preservation of the symbolic foundation. Thus, for Maclure and Taylor (2010: 86), 'it is only natural that certain public norms should be rooted in the attributes and interests of the majority'. And, according to Weinstock (2014: 195), another liberal political philosopher, '[w]hile citizens of diverse cultural origins have a right to be treated as equal citizens, they do not have a right to be immunized from the natural cultural bias that might be the natural concomitant of the particular history that the community that they are now a part of has undergone'.[7]

---

[5] One understands that a symbolic foundation matters at the individual level as well (Kraus 2011: 17–18).

[6] I use the word 'societal' in its usual sociological meaning as referring to the whole of a social structure.

[7] See also Maclure 2006: 155. A similar idea is expressed in Poole 1999: 128–9.

Consistently, the same logic applies to minority cultures that have been established very early in the past of a society and have contributed to its development and continuity. In doing so, they have become part of its symbolic foundation and they deserve a similar treatment. Thus, in keeping with a tradition in Quebec, the Montreal Council does not convene on Jewish holidays out of regard for some of its members who are then free to perform their religious duties.

One understands that, in any society, the maintenance of a symbolic foundation requires a continuity that, inevitably, is provided to a very large extent by the majority (or the founding) culture and the values that are forged in its history. For a society to maintain some control over its destiny, it needs to endorse orientations and ideals that are based on both heritage and goals for the future. While the latter aspect is indisputably the responsibility of all citizens, the former is mainly associated with the path of the founding culture. These remarks highlight the particular situation of the majority culture as the major support for the societal or national culture. In this sense, interventionism is therefore not only a tool serving the majority.

One can see here the always ambiguous status of the majority culture: on the one hand, it has to be restrained because of the relationship of domination that it tends to establish with minorities; on the other hand, it has to be preserved in the interest of the symbolic societal foundation of the collective life. This is the second paradox of diversity management.

In a sense, the objection could be made that, through interventionism, the majority is unjustifiably appropriating the public space for itself. Part of the answer to this criticism lies in the principle of double recognition, already mentioned, and the reciprocity that it entails: cultural interventionism can be seen as a reasonable accommodation, this time in favour of the majority rather than minorities. Again, this arrangement is justified by the fact that the maintenance of the majority culture, by ensuring the reproduction of the symbolic foundation, will also serve the minorities. Here we are very much in the spirit of interculturalism, which advocates a logic of harmonisation through mutual adjustments.

However, isn't there a danger of abuse on the part of the majority? What are the limits of interventionism? Since, by definition, the latter usually operates in grey areas not covered by existing laws, the limits lie with the judgements of the court. Any form of interventionism should be able to pass the test of the tribunal. This ensures that no undue hardship is inflicted on citizens and that encroachments on cultural neutrality remain within the margin of tolerance. Besides, one should not preclude the fact that various forms of interventionism can be implemented thanks to a consensus built through public debate.

I take special care to specify that contextual, controlled interventionism, by virtue of its ad hoc nature, does not come down to decreeing an a priori or formal precedence for the majority, which would result in establishing a hierarchy and creating two classes of citizens. Similarly, the report of the Bouchard-Taylor Commission also refers to a 'de facto precedence' as opposed to a 'precedence of law'.[8] The reader will understand that this distinction is paramount. Again, controlled interventionism does not at all lead to the institution of a legal hierarchy. On this point, it should be noted that interculturalism distinguishes itself from certain republican regimes that, directly or not, under the pretext of universalism, grant systematic, a priori precedence to what I call the majority or founding culture. In summary, by explicitly recognising the existence of a majority/minority relationship where this structure exists, interculturalism does a better job in doing justice to both the majority and the minorities, in protecting the rights of all citizens, in ensuring the preservation of the societal symbolic foundation, and in projecting in the open the power relation, always active in societies, between a silent majority and (often) silenced minorities.

It might be useful to offer concrete examples – drawn from the Quebec scene – of forms of interventionism that I would consider legitimate or excessive. First, a few examples of the former:

1. the institution of French as the common public language;
2. allocating a reasonably prominent place to the teaching of the francophone past in history courses, or, in other words, a national memory that is inclusive but gives some predominance to the majority narrative;
3. the current priority (in terms of time) given to the presentation of Christian religions in the new course on ethics and religious culture;

---

[8] See Bouchard and Taylor 2008: 214.

4. the official burials of heads of state in Catholic churches;
5. keeping the cross on the Quebec flag (it has already been subject to some challenges);
6. displaying some Christmas decorations (such as trees and lights) in public squares or buildings;
7. maintaining the old crosses along rural roads;
8. the sounding of bells in Catholic churches at various moments of the day;
9. a priority given to French knowledge in the weighting system used in the selection of immigrants.

On the other hand, I consider the following examples to be abusive extensions of the principle of controlled interventionism:

1. keeping a cross on the wall of the National Assembly and in public courtrooms;
2. the recitation of prayers at municipal council meetings;
3. the funding of chaplain or Catholic pastoral care positions in public hospitals with state funds, to the exclusion of other religions;
4. the general prohibition against wearing religious signs for all state and state-run companies' employees;
5. the reference to the supremacy of God in the preamble of the Canadian Charter of Rights and Freedoms;
6. including articles or clauses in a charter that establish a formal hierarchy between the majority and minority cultures;
7. the prohibition against wearing a burka in streets and public places (except for security or other compelling reasons);
8. restricting the number of moques in a city;
9. forbidding separate cemeteries for non-Christian burials.[9]

I conclude this part with four brief comments. First, I believe that, as useful and even necessary as I think it is, cultural interven-

---

[9] Just so that the reader knows exactly where I stand on this matter, I disagree with Miller 2014 on the minarets issue in Switzerland. I would allow the construction of minarets with a possibility of restrictions on the size and the sites. But Miller's blunt statement to the effect that 'there is no direct contradiction between religious precedence and equal citizenship' (2014: 16) should obviously be qualifed. Likewise, I distance myself from the allegation that the building of minarets should not be considered as part of religious freedom.

tionism is presently uncontrolled in most democratic societies and it should be reined in since this extensive practice flies in the face of pluralism. But in the present state, this area is like a blind spot of the liberal thought. Relying on a sociological argumentation, my goal here was to make the case for interventionism. But at the same time, I think that we should be more concerned about the necessity of defining criteria and setting limits to it. Second, I do not list controlled interventionism among the specific components of interculturalism, simply because it is a widespread practice, irrespective of the prevailing model of diversity management.

Third, as many authors have pointed out, the position of prohibitionists (opponents to interventionism) is fundamentally contradictory. On the one hand, they argue for the cultural neutrality of the government in the name of liberty and autonomy of individuals, while, on the other hand, they expect the government to protect these fundamental values of liberal society. And, finally, I expect that my thesis about controlled interventionalism will be met with contrasted feelings since a number of majority cultures have a troubled past and deserve some level of distrust.

Reasonable accommodations

If we acknowledge that liberal states have no obligation to strict cultural neutrality and that majorities have a right to some forms of interventionism, in return we must recognise for minorities the right to a corrective mechanism to protect themselves against potential abuses by majorities. This argument is particularly well-founded in the case of interculturalism because of the principle of double recognition, which is a lynchpin of the model.

The function of these accommodations – or collaborative adjustments – is to permit certain citizens who are victims of discrimination or serious disadvantages (because they are culturally different) to exercise their fundamental rights, unless there are compelling reasons to restrict them. In this sense, accommodations indeed derive from a legal obligation.

Quebec interculturalism: A form of nationalism?

In the light of the foregoing, one could suspect Quebec interculturalism of being mainly motivated by nationalism and lapsing into a form of majoritarianism (Pathak 2008). I reject this criticism. First of all, inscribing interculturalism within the nation-state is dictated by practical constraints, as happens in English Canada with multi-culturalism and all other nation-states. In Quebec, the government already detains major legislative powers over the mechanisms that I have mentioned before, in order to manage diversity. So, there is no 'nationalist' claim, no demand whatsoever, implicit or other-wise, inherent in the model as characterised here. And there is no provision whatsoever in the model designed to advance the Quebec nation on the Canadian political arena.

We are far from nationalism, understood as a spirited celebra-tion of the nation, as a crusade to praise its uniqueness and excep-tional values, to foster an awareness of its unique mission in the world, and to develop a strong, exclusive emotional attachment along with an overarching agenda that overrides all others.

Sources and forms of duality

Let's come back briefly to the majority/minority relationship. The nature of the factors that have triggered the emergence of this duality is paramount. There are several possibilities:

- The relationship can involve two ethno-cultural groups of uneven size who share an old past of difference and peaceful co-existence on the basis of mutual respect.
- I have already mentioned another form where a society strategi-cally creates its minorities.
- There is also the case where a majority takes shape because (rightly or not) it feels threatened by minorities.

I won't list every possible scenario. I am particularly interested by the last, since I think it is a growing feature in Western countries nowadays, mostly because of the Muslim minorities. In Europe, as elsewhere, this cleavage has been made more and more visible lately by various polls attesting to the fear that Muslims might be a factor of disruption because of their values and their inability to integrate into the host societies. It follows that interculturalism, at least the way I define it, could find a favourable ground in these countries – the cases of France, Italy, Germany and Greece, in par-ticular, come to mind, although in the light of the last European election, this list could be expanded. This would bear practical consequences in so far as the duality structure calls for specific policies designed to smooth over the relationship between the majority and the minorities.

In a wider perspective, beyond interculturalism, I think that we should be concerned about the growing rift that is opposing pluralist elites and a fair number of reluctant citizens in various societies or nations. Again, this can be observed in Europe with the rise of rightist political populism.

Interculturalism and multiculturalism: Similarities and differences

In the Quebec context, it is not possible to talk about interculturalism without broaching the subject of Canadian multiculturalism. From a sociological point of view, it is obvious that this model has been designed for anglophone Canada. Concern for national language is practically absent and, except for a few authors, the questions related to the national minority status have received little attention. It therefore closes the door on a bi- or multinational conception of Canada. Finally, I recall that this model does not recognise any national or majority culture. The idea of interculturalism in Quebec is born out of the rejection of multiculturalism in 1971[10] and the desire to develop a model that would be more suited to the reality and the needs of Quebec society, in particular the need to better protect the characteristics of francophone culture. However, Quebec researchers are regularly called upon to explain the differences between these two models. For various reasons, there is no simple answer to this question.

One of these reasons is the fact that Canadian multiculturalism is a moving target. It has evolved considerably since its introduction in 1971; this is an important fact that is not always taken into account, particularly in Quebec. Another reason is related to the highly polysemic nature of this concept, which assumes different meanings from one author, one school of thought or one country to another (see Meer and Modood 2012). We need therefore to ensure that we carefully select the standard of comparison.

---

[10] By the then Premier Robert Bourassa who was heading the liberal, federalist party in Quebec.

First, I will refer to the most widespread perception of multiculturalism currently in the West, which commonly defines it (and criticises it) with reference to five main features:

1. a definition of the nation as made up of individuals and groups, which does not recognise the existence of a national culture or a majority culture;
2. an openness to diversity to the point that it can jeopardise integration, going as far as to expose a society to the danger of fragmentation;
3. a wide practice of pluralism that tends toward relativism, to the detriment of fundamental, universal values;
4. a promotion of ethno-cultural minorities that confines those of its members who would like to distance themselves from their allegiance;
5. little concern for the establishment of a shared culture that would secure for the nation or society an essential symbolic foundation, a rallying point that is a source of cohesiveness and solidarity.

It is obvious that interculturalism, as presented above, is distinct from this version of multiculturalism. It could even be said that, on all these points, it advocates orientations that are diametrically opposed. But is it appropriate to identify Canadian multiculturalism with the configuration that I have just outlined?

The answer to this question has to be negative because of the changes that the model has gone through in the course of its history[11] and because of the characteristics that it has come to exhibit (Kymlicka 2010, 2012). In the 1970s, for example, the preservation and promotion of the diversity of languages and cultures were key elements of the Canadian model. Starting in the 1980s, the social dimension (the fight against inequalities and exclusion) became salient, along with the legal dimension expressed, among other things, in the fight against racism and discrimination. At the same time, the programmes designed to perpetuate the folk traditions of minorities were gradually abandoned.

With the 1990s and the beginning of the 2000s there emerged an increasing concern for collective cohesiveness, for integration and

---

[11] See, for example, Kymlicka 1998, Helly 2000, Abu-Laban and Gabriel 2002.

shared values, for the formation (or consolidation) of a Canadian sense of belonging and identity. An analysis of polls taken since 1983 shows an increase in support for a policy aimed at the integration of immigrants into a Canadian culture. This statement was endorsed by 26 per cent of respondents in 1995 and 32 per cent in 2005.[12]

Among intellectuals, we also saw a few pleas for a redefinition of multiculturalism, which, concretely, was moving towards interculturalism (for example, Tully 1995). Even more recently, the model provided more room for concepts of interactions ('interactive pluralism'), exchanges, Canadian values and participation. It should be noted that the idea of exchanges between ethno-cultural groups was already mentioned in the text of the 1971 motion, but it was barely applied and did not get much attention. Some major pioneers of multiculturalism such as Charles Taylor and Bhikhu Parekh have strongly emphasised dialogue and interaction. But again, the policies and programmes did not really follow suit. Nevertheless, according to Meer and Modood (2012), this dimension is at the very heart of multiculturalism – a statement that goes against the common perception.

Other recent calls for increased 'connections', harmonious relations and intercultural dialogue demonstrate the need for a shared culture. According to Minister Jason Kenney, it is time for Canada to build bridges rather than silos.[13] It is also hoped that all the components of the Canadian mosaic will become part of a whole. Finally, the Canadian government has recently launched a new programme (Inter-Action) intended to promote intercultural exchanges (Canada 2010). It appears that this evolution is far from over. According to Kymlicka (2011), after having overcome the challenges of ethnicity and discrimination, Canadian multiculturalism now has to face the problem of secularism, which, again according to this author, will require another expansion of the model.

From the above, readers may be interested to note that in recent years Canadian multiculturalism has seemed to come closer to duality. At the same time, it has also come closer to Quebec interculturalism. If we add to all this the persistent feeling in anglophone Canada that 'Canadian' culture is constantly under

---

[12] See <http://www.crop.ca/en/blog/2011/55> (last accessed 4 June 2015).
[13] Statement reported in *Le Devoir*, 11 February 2009, p. A3.

threat from the expansion of American culture, then it is getting even closer to the situation that prevails in Quebec. I will refrain, however, from making any judgement on the strength or intensity of these movements and I will not venture to speculate on their future (polls conducted over the last ten or fifteen years show that multiculturalism still enjoys strong support outside Quebec). But they are worthy of mentioning and Canadians will definitely have to be attentive to them in the years to come.

In the same vein, we note that the duality structure also manifests itself in the Official Languages Act (which established the rule of bilingualism in the public service) or when all francophones are considered as a minority within Canada. These elements are not peripheral; according to Kymlicka (2011), the duality created by bilingualism policy constitutes the only possible basis for the survival of Canada as a country. There is also the ambiguous status of aboriginal peoples or the recognition of Quebec as a nation by the Canadian Parliament in 2006 (although it has not been constitutionalised). From this, Canadian multiculturalism emerges as a hybrid, unsettled system (more on this below). However, the model remains significantly different from Quebec interculturalism, for the following reasons.

1. The first element is strictly contextual but it is worth mentioning. Interculturalism is concerned with the Quebec nation as a host society, a nation whose historical, sociological and institutional roots are deep and whose existence is the subject of a very broad consensus. By contrast, multiculturalism recognises Quebecers of French-Canadian origin only as forming an ethnic group (or a 'community') among all the others that make up the Canadian mosaic; more generally, it rejects a pluri-national concept of Canada.

2. The federal government still endorses the idea that there is no majority culture in Canada. Diversity is said to characterise this country. Accordingly, the idea of an us/them relationship has no explicit existence in anglophone Canada. As for Quebec, the reflection on diversity was traditionally structured, as we have seen, through the duality lens, placing in the forefront the majority/minority relationship. This choice is consequential with regard to the vision of nationhood, identity and a national sense of belonging.

I have explained elsewhere (Bouchard 2011) that the two models do not belong to the same families. It might be useful here to highlight this point by outlining the paradigms that support the major models of diversity management. Five of them can be identified:

i.   A first paradigm is that of *diversity*. The guiding premise is that the nation is composed of individuals and ethno-cultural groups placed on equal footing and protected by the same laws. There is no recognition of a majority culture and, as a corollary, no minorities per se.

ii. Secondly, there is the paradigm of *homogeneity* which fundamentally asserts an ethno-cultural similarity in public life and sometimes in private life as well.

iii. The third paradigm I call *bi- or multipolarity*. It refers to societies made up of two or more national groups or sub-groups, sometimes officially recognised as such and granted a kind of permanence. Therefore, none of them fears for its future.

iv. The fourth paradigm is that of *duality*. It can be observed where diversity is conceived of and managed as a relationship between a cultural majority that could be described as *foundational* and minorities born from a recent or distant period of immigration.

v.   The fifth paradigm is rooted in *mixity*. It is predicated on the idea that, through miscegenation and intense cultural exchange, the ethno-cultural diversity of a nation will be progressively reduced, eventually creating a new culture different from (and superior to) its original constituents.[14]

Obviously, multiculturalism and interculturalism belong respectively to the first and the fourth paradigm. It follows from this that the main challenges are not the same for the two sides. In one case, the existence of a majority culture is recognised and the development of a shared culture feeding on the majority and the minority cultures is emphasised. Therefore what matters here is to manage in a pluralist spirit the relationship between the majority and the minorities. In the other case, this relationship is not formalised since the existence of a majority culture is not recognised. In addition, the concept

[14] More on this in Bouchard 2011: 441–4.

of a common, national culture is problematic. The challenge consists, then, in implementing a symbolic foundation for the social bond.

Clarification is necessary, however, about the absence of a majority culture in Canada. Without going into an extended critique of this postulate, I will point out that, in various regions of the country, significant segments of the anglophone population (if the media are to be believed) maintain a feeling that there is a real Canadian culture inherited from the past and that this culture is not sufficiently expressed within the framework of multiculturalism. According to many, it is threatened by the diversification brought about by immigration. The common-place opposition, sometimes explicit, between 'real' Canadian values and the 'others' follows the same lines (Tolley 2004). Finally, the concerns regularly expressed with respect to the growing influence of American culture highlight the feeling that there is a national culture to be preserved.

From a different perspective, it has also been shown that English Canada, like any other society, is not exempt from the dynamics of power that inevitably operates between a cultural majority, which is supposed to embody continuity and symbolic 'normality', and minorities (Winter 2011).

3. Because they themselves constitute a minority, Quebec franco-phones instinctively fear forms of socio-cultural fragmentation, marginalisation and ghettoisation likely to weaken the nation. This accounts for the particular emphasis that Quebec intercul-turalism places on integration and more specially on interac-tions, rapprochement between cultures, the development of a sense of belonging and the emergence of a shared culture along with respect for minorities. Traditionally, Canadian multicul-turalism does not cultivate this concern to the same degree. The idea of multiculturalism was put forward in the 1960s at the initiative and in the interest mainly of minorities coming from Eastern Europe, for a long time established in Western Canada and very well integrated, but looking for official recognition beside anglophones and francophones. Accordingly, the model lays more emphasis on valuing difference and ethnic groups.

4. Another distinctive trait arises from the fact that, as mentioned before, Canadian multiculturalism pays little attention to the protection of a national language. This is because inevitably, for

sheer reasons of survival, immigrants who settle in anglophone Canada will always want, sooner or later, to learn the language of the continent. It is very different with French in Quebec, which is always struggling to ensure its survival in a lopsided competition with English. This concern is obviously rooted in a cultural motivation but also in the fact that the language plays a key role in social integration, collective cohesiveness and civic life.

5. More generally, in all Western nations, the advancement of pluralism is accompanied by a concern for values and even for the cultural future of the host society (or, where applicable, of the majority culture). This concern is felt more intensely in minority nations worried about their future, in which respect for diversity assumes an entirely different dimension. In other words, the issues arising from the practice of pluralism are more sensitive and give rise to tensions that are not known by more powerful nations firmly established culturally and politically. This is a constraint that inevitably permeates Quebec interculturalism, much more than Canadian multiculturalism.

6. Another element of differentiation relates to collective memory. Because of the political struggles that the Quebec francophones have had to carry out in the course of their history as a colony, an intense memory as a small, fragile, combative nation has naturally developed. For many francophones, this memory carries a strong message that inspires a feeling of loyalty if not a duty for present and future generations. Reference to this past lies at the heart of the imaginary of the founding majority, which can be another source of tension: in a context marked by the growing presence of immigrants and minorities, how can this memory of the majority be transmitted without diluting its symbolic content, without stripping it of its psychological resiliency, all the while making room for minority narratives?[15] These kinds of challenges, again, do not have the same resonance from a multiculturalist perspective, where the issue of a majority culture is absent.

7. The differences that have just been mentioned manifest themselves in various ways, for instance how the principle

---

[15] It is worth noting that, despite these constraints, the Quebec record in matters of diversity management has been really good up until the cusp of this century. The recent years have been marked by an increased fear for its values and identity.

of recognition and the management of accommodations are applied. In the latter case, as I have indicated, requests for accommodations in Quebec will have more chance of being granted if they favour integration. For example, allowing the wearing of the hijab in the classroom encourages Muslim students to continue attending public schools and to be more open to the values of Quebec society. The same is true for the offering of special menus in school cafeterias, a reasonable adaptation of exam schedules in accordance with the dates of religious activities, a flexible policy for certain educational activities where this does not violate the Education Act, and so on.

8. In the opposite direction, Quebec interculturalism also has to make room for the particular relationship to religion that has developed in the course of Quebec history. Abuses of power committed by the Catholic clergy have resulted in suspicion toward churches and clergy that is expressed today through a great sensitivity to the separation of state and religion of which we find no equivalent either in anglophone Canada or in Canadian multiculturalism.

One could be tempted to see another difference in the fact that Canadian multiculturalism, unlike Quebec interculturalism, is characterised by its commitment to the cultural neutrality of the state. But, as I noted above, that claim is baseless since no state, including Canada, practises such a hands-off approach. Likewise, I do not agree with an analysis by Kymlicka (2003) according to which the two models are distinguished by the fact that multiculturalism operates at the macro-social level, in particular as a government policy, while interculturalism works at the micro-social level (interpersonal relations). This is a reductive vision of interculturalism, which operates fully at these two levels.

On the whole, if we try to single out how the two models differ essentially, beyond Canadian and Quebec realities or contexts, four elements stand out: the recognition (or non-recognition) of duality, the uneven emphasis on integration, common culture and what I have called interculturality. However, the first element trumps the others. As we have seen, interculturalism is sensitive to the problems and needs of the majority culture and the challenge of reconciling majority and minority rights and expectations. Multiculturalism does not show these concerns, once again because it does not recognise the existence of the duality.[16] However, the two models are adaptable and evolving, in keeping with the different requirements of specific contexts and moving challenges. As a result, trying to contrast them *in abstracto* is likely to become a tricky business – and perhaps not that relevant. What matters is, for every society, to make the right choices and carve out the package of goals, ways and means most likely to meet its needs.

This being said, if we compare the policies actually implemented over the past few decades by the Canadian and Quebec governments in the area of ethnic diversity, significant similarities can be observed despite the differences that I have mentioned at a more theoretical level (see McAndrew 1995, 2005; Juteau 1994; Juteau et al. 1998; Nugent 2006). How to explain this paradox? Apart from the already mentioned recent evolution of multiculturalism in the direction of interculturalism, I believe that these similarities are due in part to the fact that the two models fundamentally share the same pluralist orientation as well as the major objectives that define it (equality, respect for diversity, non-discrimination, civic and political participation, rejection of assimilation and exclusion, and so on), an orientation of which, however, they propose different versions in order to fit specific realities.

But the similarities also result from the fact that successive governments in Quebec have not sufficiently aligned their policies with the interculturalist model. A gap has developed between the philosophy of reference and the policies actually in place. This is a deficiency that has been criticised for a long time, and an important effort needs to be made to remedy this anomaly in Quebec. It is urgent to design projects and policies that will give real substance to the spirit and distinctive goals of interculturalism.

Daniel Weinstock has expressed a different view on this issue. In two papers (Weinstock 2013, 2014), he asserts that, fundamentally, the two models are not that different. According to him, they differ less on the basic principles than on the kind of policy goals that each pursues. While the requirements of social justice are presented as central to multiculturalism, interculturalism is said to be built on an untenable position, since it pursues the out-of-

---

[16] On this topic, see also Gagnon 2010, in particular pp. 258–9 and p. 261, and Gagnon and Iacovino 2007, chapter 4.

GÉRARD BOUCHARD

reach goal of combining the merits of both multiculturalism and assimilationism while rejecting their deficiencies. For my part, I do believe that the quest for such a compromise is actually at the heart of interculturalism and, although a difficult challenge, it can be implemented, Quebec being a case in point in the 1980s and the 1990s.

At the same time, Weinstock asserts that with regard to the kind of society to promote, multiculturalism is rather 'agnostic', contrary to interculturalism. This comes as a bit of a surprise since Canadian multiculturalism is clearly built on a set of liberal values enshrined in the Charter of Rights and Freedoms. The author also believes that the philosophical and normative aspirations inherent in interculturalism cannot be translated into policies without encroaching on individual freedom. But what about incentives policies? Weinstock does not believe that policies can change 'people's minds and hearts', a statement which sounds to me strangely pessimistic and sociologically doubtful. Finally, the central fact that, as opposed to interculturalism, multiculturalism does not recognise the existence of a majority culture is barely mentioned in these papers.

On the same side of the issue but from a different angle, Meer and Modood (2012) argue that multiculturalism, just like interculturalism, (a) is very open to interaction, (b) avoids 'groupism', (c) is committed to a strong sense of a whole and to social cohesion, and (d) rejects relativism. If they are right, this should put an end to this debate – which, I believe, is not going to happen soon. The authors also conclude that interculturalism has not proven itself yet, which is quite true given its newness, and that it should not be construed as superior to or a substitute for multiculturalism, about which again I agree – but does it have to be? One should not see it as a competition; let's see what the future holds for these models.

Overall, these authors give short shrift to the major fact that both models are evolving, they are the source of various interpretations where they prevail, and they have assumed different guises from one society and one author to another. This should be front and central in a comparative analysis. Moreover, as a result of late changes, the two models significantly overlap, which makes the matter even more complex. At the end of the day, having to adopt a model, each society carves out its own configuration according to its needs, choices and constraints. Sometimes, it becomes very tricky to put the 'right' name to it.

Canadian multiculturalism: A hybrid, shifting model

I return, by way of a conclusion, to the hybrid, shifting nature of Canadian multiculturalism to point out an interesting paradox. Kymlicka (2007) presents this model as being made up of three 'silos'. This refers to an interplay of relationships of the host society (one would be tempted to say the majority) with (a) immigrants and ethnic groups, (b) national minorities ('substate national groups'), and (c) aboriginal populations. He also asserts that each of these subsets or silos has followed its own course in the past and has generated different policies belonging to specific processes. The paradox comes from the fact that the 1971 motion that introduced multiculturalism actually contained a formal warning against this kind of tripartite definition of Canada ('there cannot be one cultural policy for Canadians of British and French origin, another for the original peoples and yet a third for all others'). From this perspective, the vision of multiculturalism put forward by Kymlicka is therefore in direct contradiction with the founding vision of the model.

This contradiction also leads to an ambivalence that can be summarised as follows:

- According to a broad representation of Canadian multiculturalism, all three silos must be considered. But then this is a break with the most common representation of the model (in Europe in particular), which is centred on a single silo, namely the relations with immigrants and ethnic groups.
- If we endorse this restricted vision, Canada can no longer be identified only with multiculturalism since two main components are excluded.

In summary, from the perspective of the restricted definition, Canadian multiculturalism appears as different from but, as I have said, slowly evolving towards Quebec interculturalism. On the other hand, in the hypothesis of the broad vision (the three silos), the model becomes at best hybrid and at worst contradictory. From one meaning to another, what is gained in scope is lost in consistency. This being said, the model has definitely experienced significant failures, specially regarding the struggle against discrimination, the aboriginal question and the relationship with Quebec.

Nevertheless, it is fair to say that, all things considered, within the framework of anglophone Canada, the model has been quite successful. One only has to compare the situation of inter-ethnic relationships in anglophone Canada with those in other Western countries (Kymlicka 2012). Beyond that, it is a model that is obviously based more on pragmatism than on any intrinsic theoretical cohesiveness. In addition, it is a model that has been constantly evolving since its introduction and that is perhaps about to undergo further changes.

Finally, the heterogeneous, ambivalent character of Canadian multiculturalism is not limited to the elements that have just been mentioned. Analysing the content of two major Canadian newspapers (the *Globe and Mail* and the *Toronto Star*) during the 1990s, Winter (2011: 184–5 and *passim*) was able to identify three competing visions of the model, which she calls 'republicanism', 'liberal-pluralism' and 'liberal-multiculturalism'. We can also see another important ambivalence in the fact that, according to many authors, multiculturalism defines the Canadian nation as being made up of a set of ethnic groups of which the distinctive natures need to be protected and promoted, while for others, this model emphasises individuals and their rights, in accordance with liberalism. From this last perspective, ethnic groups are only involved indirectly, to the extent that citizens can feel a legitimate need to cultivate a more or less close affiliation or identification with their cultures of origin, hence the need to protect them; this is the very foundation of the policy of recognition. Thus these two competing visions (communitarian and individualist) of Canadian multiculturalism may be the source of another point of confusion.

To recapitulate, multiculturalism is the site of four types of ambiguity:

- confusion between the stereotype that has been established at the international level, especially in Europe, and the Canadian model;
- the original, unitary definition of Canadian multiculturalism (1971) and the thesis of the three silos;
- a perception of the model centred on the protection of the rights either of individuals (in the spirit of classic liberalism) or of ethnic groups (in the spirit of communitarianism);
- a static vision of the model as opposed to a dynamic vision that

takes into account the various changes that it has undergone since 1971.

References

Abu-Laban, Y., and C. Gabriel (2002), *Selling Diversity: Immigration, Multiculturalism, Employment Equity and Globalization*, Peterborough, Ontario: Broadview Press.

Ackerman, B. A. (1980), *Social Justice in the Liberal State*, New Haven: Yale University Press.

Bouchard, G. (2011), 'What Is Interculturalism?', *McGill Law Journal/Revue de droit de McGill*, 56 (2), 435–68.

Bouchard, G. (2012), *L'Interculturalisme. Un point de vue québécois*, Montreal: Boréal; English translation at University of Toronto Press, 2015, Japanese translation underway.

Bouchard, G. (2014), *Raison et déraison du mythe*, Montreal: Boréal.

Bouchard, G., and C. Taylor (2008), *Building the Future: A Time for Reconciliation*, Report of the Consultation Commission on Accommodation Practices Related to Cultural Differences, Quebec City: Government of Quebec.

Canada (2010), *Inter-Action: Canada's New Multiculturalism Grants & Contributions Program*, Ottawa: Citizenship and Immigration Canada.

Dworkin, R. (1985), 'Liberalism', in *A Matter of Principle*, Cambridge, MA: Harvard University Press, pp. 181–204.

Gagnon, A.-G. (2010), 'La diversité et la place du Québec au sein de la fédération canadienne', in B. Gagnon (ed.), *La Diversité québécoise en débat. Bouchard, Taylor et les autres*, Montreal: Québec Amérique, pp. 247–61.

Gagnon, A.-G., and R. Iacovino (2007), *De la nation à la multination. Les rapports Québec-Canada*, Montreal: Boréal.

Helly, D. (2000), 'Le multiculturalisme canadien: de la promotion des cultures immigrées à la cohésion sociale, 1971–1999', *Cahiers de l'URMIS*, 6, 7–20.

Juteau, D. (1994), 'Essai – Multiples francophonies minoritaires: multiples citoyennetés', *Sociologie et sociétés*, 26 (1), 33–45.

Juteau, D., M. McAndrew and L. Pietrantonio (1998), 'Multiculturalism à la Canadian and Intégration à la Québécoise: Transcending their Limits', in R. Baubock and J. Rundell (eds), *Blurred Boundaries: Migration, Ethnicity, Citizenship*, Vienna: Ashgate, pp. 23–95.

Kraus, P. A. (2011), 'The Politics of Complex Diversity', *Ethnicities*, 12 (1), 3–25.

Kymlicka, W. (1998), *Finding Our Way: Rethinking Ethnocultural Relations in Canada*, New York: Oxford University Press.

Kymlicka, W. (2003), 'Multicultural States and Intercultural Citizens', *Theory and Research in Education*, 1 (2), 147–69.

Kymlicka, W. (2007), 'Ethnocultural Diversity in a Liberal State: Making Sense of the Canadian Model(s)', in K. Banting, T. J. Courchene and F. L. Seidle (eds), *Belonging? Diversity, Recognition and Shared Citizenship in Canada*, Montreal: Institute for Research on Public Policy, pp. 39–86.

Kymlicka, W. (2010), *The Current State of Multiculturalism in Canada and Research Themes on Canadian Multiculturalism 2008–2010*, Ottawa: Citizenship and Immigration Canada.

Kymlicka, W. (2011), 'The Evolving Canadian Experiment with Multiculturalism', in G. Bouchard et al. (eds), *L'Interculturalisme. Dialogue Québec-Europe*,

Actes du Symposium international sur l'interculturalisme, Montreal, 25–27 May 2011; available at <http://www.symposium-interculturalisme.com> (last accessed 5 June 2015).

Kymlicka, W. (2012), *Multiculturalism: Success, Failure, and the Future*, Washington, DC: Migration Policy Institute.

McAndrew, M. (1995), 'Multiculturalisme canadien et interculturalisme québécois: mythes et réalités', in M. McAndrew, R. Toussaint and O. Galatanu (eds), *Pluralisme et éducation. Politiques et pratiques au Canada, en Europe et dans les pays du Sud. L'apport de l'éducation compare*, Montreal/Paris: Faculté des sciences de l'éducation/Association francophone d'éducation compare, pp. 22–51.

McAndrew, M. (2005), 'Québec Immigration, Integration and Intercultural Policy: A Critical Assessment', paper given at the International Conference on Multiculturalism, Public Policy and Problem Areas in Canada and India, New Delhi, 5–7 December 2005.

Maclure, J. (2006), 'Politique linguistique ou politique d'intégration? La promotion de la langue dans une communauté politique libérale, Démocratique et pluraliste', in M. Pagé and P. Georgeault (eds), *Le Français, langue de la diversité québécoise. Une réflexion*, Montreal: Québec Amérique, pp. 153–70.

Maclure, J., and C.-H. Taylor (2010), *Laïcité et liberté de conscience*, Montreal: Boréal; available in English as *Secularism and Freedom of Conscience*, Cambridge, MA: Harvard University Press, 2011.

Meer, N., and T. Modood (2012), 'How Does Interculturalism Contrast with Multiculturalism?', *Journal of Intercultural Studies*, 33 (2), 175–96; available at <http://www.tandfonline.com/doi/abs/10.1080/07256868.2011.618266> (last accessed 5 June 2015).

Miller, D. (2014), 'Majorities and Minarets: Religious Freedom and Public Space', *British Journal of Political Science*, published online 5 June, <http://journals.cambridge.org/action/displayAbstract?fromPage=online&aid=9278509&fileId=S0007123414000131> (last accessed 23 June 2015).

Nugent, A. (2006), 'Demography, National Myths, and Political Origins: Perceiving Official Multiculturalism in Quebec', *Canadian Ethnic Studies*, 38 (3), 21–36.

Pathak, P. (2008), 'The Rise of the Majority', *The Journal*, 10, 2 October; available at <http://www.journal-online.co.uk/article/3222-the-rise-of-the-majority> (last accessed 5 June 2015).

Poole, R. (1999), *Nation and Identity*, London: Routledge.

Rawls, J. (1971), *A Theory of Justice*, Cambridge, MA: Belknap Press (Harvard University Press).

Tolley, E. (2004), 'National Identity and the "Canadian Way": Values, Connections and Culture', *Canadian Diversity*, 3 (2), 11–15.

Tully, J. (1995), *Strange Multiplicity: Constitutionalism in an Age of Diversity*, Cambridge: Cambridge University Press.

Weinstock, D. (2003), 'La neutralité de l'État en matière culturelle est-elle possible?', in R. Le Coadic (ed.), *Identités et Démocratie. Diversité culturelle et mondialisation. Repenser la démocratie*, Rennes: Presses universitaires de Rennes, pp. 365–80.

Weinstock, D. (2013), 'Interculturalism and Multiculturalism in Canada and Quebec: Situating the Debate', in P. Balint and S. Guérard de Latour (eds), *Liberal Multiculturalism and the Fair Terms of Integration*, Basingstoke: Palgrave Macmillan, pp. 91–108.

Weinstock, D. (2014), 'What Is Really at Stake in the Multiculturalism/ Interculturalism Debate?', in J. Jedwab (ed.), *The Multiculturalism Question: Debating Identity in 21st Century Canada*, Montreal and Kingston: McGill-Queen's University Press, pp. 187–201.

Winter, E. (2011), *Us, Them, and Others: Pluralism and National Identity in Diverse Societies*, Toronto: University of Toronto Press.

5

Interculturalism and Multiculturalism:
Similarities and Differences

Alain-G. Gagnon and Raffaele Iacovino

Introduction

This chapter addresses the formative projects undertaken by states
that aim to delineate the terms of belonging in a given political
community in the context of growing ethno-cultural diversity.[1]
What are the socio-political 'anchors' that frame and define the
terms of belonging[2] in a democratic polity? How do we evaluate
such criteria in light of the challenge of ethno-cultural diversity?
Such questions will be explored through a comparative conceptual assessment of the Canadian policy of multiculturalism
and Quebec's model of interculturalism. Both of these liberal
political communities have indeed responded to the challenge of
ethno-cultural diversity by formulating models of integration that
embrace cultural pluralism as a central norm. A comparison of
two distinct approaches will thus serve to shed light on some of
the challenges confronting culturally heterogeneous liberal democracies, as well as indicating the inherently political nature of such
actions.

Indeed, the idea of a 'revival of citizenship' coincides with an

---

[1] It is adapted from chapter 4 of A.-G. Gagnon and R. Iacovino (2007), *Federalism,
Citizenship and Quebec: Debating Multinationalism*, Toronto: University of
Toronto Press.

[2] We employ the broad category 'terms of belonging' rather than 'citizenship' due to
the presence of national communities whose initiatives with regard to social and
political integration are not supported by the constitutive capacity to formally grant
citizenship status, yet who develop a project for national integration and establish
themselves as distinct host societies through a wide array of powers in immigration
and integration.

unravelling of the linear relationship between national identity, territory and citizenship. Contemporary theorists of citizenship have pointed to a diffusion of governance to regions and subnational governments, where identities, powers and rights are distributed across multiple levels (Hepburn 2001), shifting the 'governments that make citizenship rights real' (Greer and Mätzke 2009: 12) and thus ultimately making substantive claims on shaping the bundle of rights and responsibilities projected by citizenship status. As such, a waning of the relative certainty associated with a clear linkage between sovereign states and their capacity to steer citizenship to desired ends inevitably provokes fears over sectarian pressures. While these observations rest largely on functional considerations associated with neoliberal models of governance, grounded in administrative reorganisation, this chapter contends that the process of formulating a set of policies to address the terms of belonging in Quebec was well under way prior to the structural transformations of the neoliberal age. Rather, initiatives in Quebec are best captured by revealing an unfinished constitutive project for national integration – or the 'citizenship-nation building nexus' (Dupré 2012: 227). Assessing these 'national models' of integration, in conceptual terms, reveals much about the bases of citizenship in distinct political contexts – an important empirical development that has forced theorists of citizenship to look more closely at particular 'hard cases' in which states must explicitly define the normative criteria in establishing the terms of belonging, while rejecting appeals to more traditional assimilationist approaches as morally excessive and outside of the liberal-pluralist mainstream.

This chapter will proceed, in the first section, to briefly outline the main tenets of multiculturalism as a theoretical posture, and attempt to develop normative criteria with which to evaluate current models of cultural pluralism in Canada and Quebec. The second section will offer a conceptualisation of Quebec's model of interculturalism as a distinct pattern of identity building and belonging. A third section will provide an overview of the Canadian policy of multiculturalism. Finally, the chapter will conclude with an assessment of the models in terms of their normative contribution to cultural pluralism and their place in Quebec-Canada relations.

The idea of multiculturalism

The fundamental premise of multiculturalism, at a minimum, is that cultural pluralism is a necessary corrective to the ethical individualism of traditional liberal thought which fails to account for the salience of cultural identity in an individual's exercise of autonomy. Any stifling of particular cultural expressions by way of the symbolic construction of a larger socio-cultural identity limits the individual's capacity for self-realisation, thus negating the liberal democratic ideal that individuals, as members of the larger society, be given the means by which to explore their own life chances and fully accomplish themselves. According to Christian Joppke, multiculturalism is an intellectual movement premised around the concepts of equality and emancipation. Its appeal lies in the defence of particularistic group identities that reject Western universalism as the basis for allegiance to a given community, which is depicted as 'falsely homogenizing and a smokescreen for power' (Joppke 1996: 449). Iris Marion Young argues that if one conceptualises such cultural differences as 'relationally constituted structural differentiations', then the supposed link between citizenship and the common good is upheld, because

> [i]t becomes clear that socially situated interests, proposals, claims and expressions of experience are often an important resource for democratic discussion and decision-making. Such situated knowledges can both pluralize and relativize hegemonic discourses, and offer otherwise unspoken knowledge to contribute to wise decisions. (Young 2000: 7)

As such, multiculturalism implies the salience of multiple cultures co-existing within a limited state-bounded territory, rejecting the modern Jacobin view of the monist nation-state and the homogenisation of identities. The key issue is that historically rooted cultures are said to regulate not only specific aspects but the entire life conduct and sources of meaning of the individual (see Sandel 1982; Raz 1986; Taylor 1994). Yet cultural pluralism has resulted in a widespread debate around its practical application as a normative guidepost for liberal democracies. Liberal societies[3] have

---

[3] For more on multiculturalism's challenge to liberal models of citizenship, see Semprini 1997.

largely adapted to the imperative of cultural pluralism by widening the public space for cultural identity, yet are now confronted with the task of delineating appropriate 'markers' (*balises*) in order to address the thorny and highly charged issue of determining and fixing the limits of collective rights attributed to culture.

Perhaps the most polished defence of the role that culture plays in providing a propitious context for the exercise of individual autonomy remains Will Kymlicka's groundbreaking work *Multicultural Citizenship*. While emphasising the normative primacy of individual autonomy as a basis for justice, Kymlicka transposed multiculturalism into a liberal framework by noting that rather than fall prey to atomistic conceptions of the individual citizen, ethical individualism must be complemented by the sociological contention that individuals require historical communities and cultures in order to flourish.[4] Indeed, as a testament to the seemingly ontological status of multiculturalism, radical cultural pluralists and liberal nationalists have converged around the notion that cultures matter and states need to accommodate them if they are serious about establishing just citizenship. The ends of citizenship are thus reversed – no longer is citizenship meant to transcend cultural differences; it is now meant to facilitate the arduous task of negotiating particularistic identities as a public exercise.

Indeed, the shared sentiments associated with equal citizenship status have long been regarded by liberal theorists as integral to democratic political communities, for fostering the civic spiritedness, mutual trust and allegiance required for meaningful self-government, self-realisation and political stability. Kymlicka notes that the classic liberal response to cultural diversity has been to develop common (undifferentiated) bases of citizenship in a universal vein. In this view, the integrative function of citizenship requires that cultural differences be treated with 'benign neglect', so that a shared civic identity is forged regardless of collective or group-based identity differences. Iris Marion Young notes that proponents of such arguments view any particular demands based on sociological 'differences' as detrimental to the functioning of democracy due to the contention that citizens concern themselves

---

[4] This point was made by André Laurendeau as far back as 1965, in the Blue Pages of the Preliminary Report of the Bilingualism and Biculturalism Commission. See Bickerton et al. 2006.

less with the common good and more with their own group-based or 'special' interests.[5] Kymlicka aptly summarises this view:

> Citizenship is by definition a matter of treating people as individuals with equal rights under the law. . . . [If it is group differentiated], nothing will bind the various groups in society together, and prevent the spread of mutual mistrust or conflict. If citizenship is differentiated, it no longer provides a shared experience or common status. Citizenship would yet be another force for disunity, rather than a way of cultivating unity in the face of increasing social diversity. Citizenship should be a force where people transcend their differences, and think about the common good of all citizens. (Kymlicka 1995: 174–5)

In short, culture, like religion as a tangible comprehensive doctrine, should be left to the private sphere and should not be mediated by the state. The political community ought to be predicated on universal terms of belonging which are civic, neutral and conducive to bridging rather than recognising differences.

For defenders of multiculturalism, however, the notion of 'benign neglect' is in itself infused with cultural meaning. It simply represents a preservation of the status quo in many established nation-states, which themselves exhibit varying degrees of adherence to the dictates of a dominant cultural group which has constructed the public sphere in its image. State inactivity and a strict emphasis on neutrality thus reflect a failure to adapt to contemporary rejections of cultural assimilation as morally excessive. Minority cultures are rendered unequal participants and second-class citizens if their sources of meaning are neglected in the public realm. As such, the ideal of equality cannot be achieved if citizens are forced to conform to a civic denial of cultural identity. Wsevolod Isajiw notes that the force of multiculturalism arises out of a particular sentiment in which citizen dignity is tied to the collective dignity of one's cultural and ethnic community. Multiculturalism represents a set of values whereby the recognition of identity needs is linked to the instrumental power of members of ethno-cultural communi-

---

[5] See Young 2000, in particular chapter 3, where she provides a review of arguments which construct group-specific justice claims as an assertion of group identity, and argues that the claims endanger democratic communication because they only divide the polity into selfish interest groups.

ties (Isajiw 1981, quoted in Kallen 1982: 52). The recognition of cultural pluralism by the state is thus a call for increased citizen empowerment, without resorting to national integration initiatives based on cultural assimilation or liberal neutrality. How are citizens in a culturally diverse society to be equally empowered to share and participate in the affairs of the polity, without sacrificing self-fulfilling 'modes of being'? How have states adapted to such challenges?

The theoretical contours outlined above reveal that normative evaluations of integration rest on two broad considerations. The first is that full citizenship status requires that all cultural identities be allowed to participate in public life equally, without reducing conceptions of identity to the level of individual preference. This applies for cultural pluralists as well as liberal nationalists. Empowerment implies that citizens are permitted to maintain their cultural differences when participating in debates around constitutive orientations of a given host society or, more generally, a constituted political community. The second concerns the salience of unity and social cohesion in any society. Here the key element is a sense of common purpose in public matters in order that deliberation is not confined to pockets of self-contained, fragmented collectivities in juxtaposition. These two broad poles are at issue in any model of integration and subsequent conceptualisations of citizenship status. In short, a balance must be struck between the *equal empowerment of group identities* as active constituents of the larger community and the need for a *common ground for dialogue*, for the purposes of unity – a *centre* which also serves as a marker of identity in the larger society and defines a pole of allegiance for all citizens.

'Interculturalism': Quebec's model of cultural pluralism

Quebec's ongoing initiatives to establish itself as a constituted host society can be traced back to the Quiet Revolution, where the state began to assume greater control of matters associated with social policy, education and even integration. This 'road' towards Quebec citizenship cannot be divorced from the larger issue of Quebec's national affirmation in the face of pan-Canadian attempts at nation-building. In this sense, the concept of 'two founding peoples' is not merely symbolic, but constitutes a political conflict

109

over the right to establish the terms of belonging for newcomers. In constructing its own model for integration and social cohesion, Quebec has in effect formulated a response to the Canadian policy of multiculturalism – a position that affirms the primacy of the Quebec state in the area of national integration and collective identity and challenges the reductionist notion that Quebec's place in the larger associative community is defined in terms of monolithic ethno-cultural minority. The treatment of diversity, when placed in a larger historical context, can be seen as but one of the many areas of contention between opposing visions regarding Canada's constituent political communities, or national groupings.

Historically, the main impetus for the growing appeal of Quebec citizenship has been language – where French as a public good came to represent the primary vehicle for the preservation and flourishing of a Québécois identity. Language was indeed the precursor to concerns over immigration and integration. Compounded by an alarming decline of the birth rate in Quebec, state actors became concerned with the tendency of allophones[6] to gravitate linguistically towards the anglophone community. Immigration and integration thus became inextricably tied to the fate of the Quebec nation. With a Ministry of Immigration in place since 1968, successive Quebec governments gradually concluded ever more comprehensive agreements with the federal government, eventually culminating in control over most aspects of immigration and integration, with the notable exception of naturalisation, family reunification and refugees (see Iacovino 2014). Some of its more targeted initiatives included an employment search service for newly arrived immigrants, support for community groups with the aim of adaptation, and the funding of cultural and linguistic heritage programmes, including the translation of literature into French, with the hope of building bridges between the allophone and francophone communities. From 1969 to 1979–80, the Ministry's budget grew from 2.8 to 20 million dollars. The Quebec government took a wide range of measures in the areas of language acquisition and cultural adaptation, the initial steps towards a

[6] Allophones are defined as members of Quebec society whose mother tongues are neither English (anglophone) nor French (francophone). They are a significant group with regard to any discussion of citizenship in that they are, in large part, subjects of integration for the host society.

110

more fully articulated model of integration. Indeed, as a response to critics who view the legal imposition of French on individuals as an affront to liberal principles, Joseph Carens turns to this participatory aspect of the model to defend the liberal democratic merits of the Quebec model:

> The duty to learn French is intimately connected to the duty to contribute and to participate in society, which is connected, on this account, to fundamental democratic principles. Learning French is, among other things, a necessary means to participation in society so that if one can defend the duty to participate, and I think one can, one can defend the duty to learn French. (Carens 2000: 128)

As Michael Behiels argues, however, many such positive measures were overshadowed by more controversial language legislation, as perceived by anglophones and allophones, which began with the Quebec Liberal government's Official Language Law (Bill 22) in 1974, in which Quebec was formally declared a unilingual French society, and later culminated in the Charter of the French Language (Bill 101) in 1977 under René Lévesque's Parti Québécois government. Indeed, during this period, the 'Quebec consensus' was very much reflected in language legislation, as such attempts to firm up the use of the French language in Quebec extended across partisan lines. The Charter was seen by many as a hardline approach, out of line with the bridge-building measures in progress, and was generally rejected by allophones and anglophones (see Behiels 1991). With the adoption of the Charter, the PQ government established the vision of a linguistically unilingual and culturally pluralistic political community in Quebec, a vision that has nourished subsequent models of integration to this day.

As early as 1981, the Quebec model began taking shape, with a policy statement entitled *Autant de façons d'être Québécois* (Gilbert 1981). The essence of the policy was that, unlike Canadian multiculturalism, Quebec integration would stress the idea of *cultural convergence*. Indeed, this pioneering iteration of Quebec's elaboration of interculturalism emphasised cultural pluralism as a normative framework, with cultural communities formally recognised as interlocutors in Quebec democracy, yet attempted to do so without negating the historic role of the cultural majority. This initiative represented a turning point for Quebec, as

111

the document outlined the importance of establishing harmonious inter-community relations, recognising the contributions of minority cultures in Quebec's development (and sensitising the majority about this), and recommended specific measures to address accessibility to public sector employment, adequate services and resource allocation to support ethno-cultural associations.[7] The document made explicit mention of various measures previously undertaken to promote the flourishing of minority cultural groups, including programmes such as COFI and PELO.[8] Moreover, it encouraged cultural exchanges with countries of origins and minority language instruction, and proposed the creation of subsidy programmes to contribute to those objectives.

In essence, the idea of cultural convergence stressed the requirement to formally recognise the existence of many constituent cultures in Quebec yet conceded that policy initiatives ought to account for the particular dynamics associated with majority/minority relations. The thrust of the framework was thus to clearly identify that the terrain for negotiations and mediation among cultural groups would explicitly acknowledge an existing host society grounded in the political mobilisation of a cultural majority. Recently, Gérard Bouchard, in attempting to better define the main tenets of Quebec interculturalism, has reclaimed this feature of the model as perhaps its most significant feature. Bouchard claims that one of the more appealing aspects of interculturalism for internal nations is an explicit recognition of a *foundational* culture. As such, one of the main characteristics of interculturalism, in contrast to assimilation, is that the model is premised around a desire and willingness to achieve *conciliation*:

> In summary, interculturalism recognizes the status of the majority culture (its legitimacy, its right to perpetuate its traditions, its heritage, and its right to mobilize around developmental goals) within a framework designed to reduce the excesses that all majorities are capable of enacting on minorities – as ancient and recent history has taught us. (Bouchard 2011: 448)[9]

---

[7] Indeed, the Ministry of Immigration was renamed the Department of Cultural Communities and Immigration.

[8] Centres d'Orientation et de Formation des Immigrants; Programme d'Enseignement des Langues d'Origine.

[9] Charles Taylor has also recently made a similar point: 'The best antidote, perhaps

Bouchard makes one other related point which merits discussion. He engages in a discussion over what he calls 'ad hoc precedence of the majority culture'. Here Bouchard simply concedes that no model can ever perfectly operate along consistent principles, and that some contingencies will arise in which the preferences of the majority culture will hold sway. This is an important concession to the obvious criticism that any model premised on conciliation between majority and minority cultures is bound to fall prey to power imbalances. For Bouchard, the relative power of the majority culture, as well as some of its historical grievances, cannot be altogether avoided, and he argues for openness in leaving some flexibility to respond to this dynamic as long as it is properly circumscribed and openly justified. In other words, interculturalism is a model of cultural pluralism that also pays homage to the particular needs of the majority culture, while bearing in mind the potential capacity for majorities to oppress minorities. Bouchard thus rejects overly rigid republican-secular models or procedural liberal frameworks that leave little room for adaptation to historical circumstances:

> [. . .] this practice can be considered a kind of accommodation that minorities accord to majorities, under certain conditions subject to debate. This is very much in the spirit of interculturalism, which seeks harmonization through mutual adjustments according to a principle of reciprocity. In this respect, an important lesson can be drawn from recent experience in Quebec. The principal criticism leveled against the Bouchard-Taylor Commission Report came from members of the francophone majority. According to them the Report granted a great deal to minorities and immigrants but very little to the majority – a forceful reminder that because francophone Quebec was also a minority, it too needed protections; so, there was a need for balance. The elements of ad hoc precedence are conceived in this spirit. (Bouchard 2011: 454)

Of significance here is that the Quebec model explicitly challenged the Canadian framework as a primary basis for delineating

the only one is: successful enactments of the intercultural scenario. That is, leaders and members of the majority mainstream seek out leaders and members of the minority(ies), and together with them work out new ways of resolving the conflicts, then work together effectively to resolve them. . . . The ensemble of such collaborative enterprises contributes in effect to the elaboration of a new more inclusive culture of interaction' (Taylor 2012: 421).

the terms of belonging by enunciating a comprehensive model for the first time. The jurisdictional battles of the Quiet Revolution and the linguistic conflicts of the 1970s culminated in a fully articulated discourse centred on affirming Quebec as a distinct space for the expression of a distinct citizenship regime.

In 1991, the Quebec government outlined its most comprehensive elaboration of interculturalism (Government of Quebec 1991) – which contended that the incorporation of immigrants or minority cultures into the larger political community is a reciprocal endeavour – defined by a 'moral contract'[10] between the host society and particular ethno-cultural groups, with the aim of establishing a forum for the empowerment of all citizens – a 'common public culture'.[11] The moral contract involves rights and responsibilities for both immigrants and the host society, again outlining the view that successful integration practices involve contributions from society taken as a whole. Through such a framework, the objective was to foster an evolving and plural 'common public culture' that was conceptually distinct from past attempts to privilege a majority culture as a reference for integration and as a dominant pole of cultural convergence. This model would clearly outline that cultural exchange would result in a shared space for the negotiation of identities, transforming both majority and minority cultures in the process.

The moral contract was summed up as follows:

- a society in which French is the common language of public life;
- a democratic society where participation and the contribution of everyone is expected and encouraged;
- a pluralist society open to multiple contributions within the

[10] On 1 November 1999, the Minister of Citizen Relations and Immigration, Robert Perreault, attempted to recast the model by announcing a new course of action that would emphasise a 'civic contract', more broadly defined. This new approach was designed to focus less on integration as a specific policy field premised on the recognition of minority cultures, and more on the 'needs of Quebec society in its entirety'. The reciprocity implied by the moral contract was not significantly altered, yet concretely the policy resulted in a decentralisation of services of integration to more local centres in various regions. Conceptually, this policy turn towards a civic understanding of the national community was short-lived and did not significantly transform the notion that integration is a reciprocal endeavour that involves obligations and entitlements for both the host society and minorities and immigrants. See Perreault 1999.

[11] For more on the principles of the 'common public culture' as it is understood in Quebec, see Harvey 1991 and Caldwell 1988; see also Caldwell 2001.

limits imposed by the respect for fundamental democratic values, and the necessity of inter-community exchange. (Government of Quebec 1991: 15; our translation)

The Government of Quebec later reiterated the general thrust of this model:

> The 'moral contract' affirms that, in its options for society, it follows that rights and responsibilities apply as much to immigrants, on the one hand, as the receiving society itself (including Québécois of cultural communities already integrated or on their way to being integrated) and its institutions, on the other hand. Being a Québécois means being engaged in fact in Quebec's choices for society. For the immigrant established in Quebec, having chosen Quebec as an adopted land, there requires an engagement like all other citizens, and to respect these very choices of society. It is the simultaneous existence of complementary rights and obligations attributed to all parties – and to engage in solidarity in relationships of reciprocal obligation – which justifies the vocabulary of 'moral contract' to designate the general environment governing such relations with the aim of fully integrating immigrants. (Government of Quebec 1994: 11; our translation)

The common public culture in this view does not consist solely in the juridical sphere – it is not a procedural model based on formal individual rights. Instead, the basic tenets of the moral contract are such that established 'modes of being' in economic, political and socio-cultural realms are to be respected as markers of identification and citizenship status, with the institutions of democratic participation acting as a point of convergence for groups of specific collective identities in order that all may share equally in democratic life.

In establishing a model based on cultural synthesis, the French language is to serve as the common language of public life. This is seen as an essential condition for the cohesion of Quebec society. Indeed, the French language constitutes the basis for Quebec's self-definition as a distinct political community. In this view, language is not conceptualised as an individual right. Rocher et al. elaborate:

> In Quebec ... the French language is presented as a 'centre of convergence' for diverse groups which can nevertheless maintain and let

flourish their specificity. While the Canadian policy privileges an individualist approach to culture, Quebec's policy states clearly the need to recognise French as a collective good that requires protection and encouragement. (Rocher et al. 1995: 221; our translation)

The contours of 'public life' are somewhat ambiguous. Indeed, what constitutes a public exchange is often unclear and contingent. As a general rule, the confines of public space are not relegated solely to the activities of the state, but encompass the 'public space of social interaction' as well. For example, students may, as a matter of individual right, communicate in any language they wish on the playground of a francophone school. However, language use in the classroom is considered public space. More examples of what constitutes private interaction are relations with family members, friends, colleagues or anyone involved in the social circle of the individual in question in which the choice of language use is of a consensual nature.

Moreover, the host society expects, as a matter of obligation, that members of minority groups fully integrate into the larger community, anticipating that all citizens are to contribute and participate in the social fabric of the common public culture. As a democratic community, this implies that once citizenship is attained, all members are equally encouraged to 'participate in defining the general direction of our society . . . at all stages and in all sectors where the judgement of citizens can be manifested and heard' (Government of Quebec 1994: 13; our translation).

With regard to the eventuality of conflict arising between individuals or groups, the method of resolution must correspond to democratic norms. This point is crucial because it highlights a fundamentally different perspective from an emphasis on procedural legal channels. The Quebec model stresses that in the initial manifestation of conflict, deliberative measures such as mediation, compromise and direct negotiation are preferred, leaving as much initiative and autonomy as possible to the parties in question. Legalistic measures and the recourse to specified rights are to be an option of last resort. In other words, this model values deliberation, mutual understanding and, generally, dialogue as fundamental characteristics of democratic life, in the realm of civil society, and is instrumental in the aim of fostering a cohesive and participatory conception of citizenship.

The treatment of difference in this model does not imply a society built on the juxtaposition of ethno-cultural groupings, in a mosaic, nor does it reduce citizenship status simply to procedural safeguards from state intrusion through the codification of fundamental individual rights, and the assimilation of particular identities to universal principles. The idea is that cultural contact constitutes a new synthesis and a new dynamic for the community as a whole (Harvey 1991: 239). The Quebec model of cultural pluralism operates in the tradition of parliamentary democracy, with an emphasis on deliberation and representation. Within the framework of basic principles – a commitment to the peaceful resolution of conflict, a Charter of Rights and Freedoms in order to provide legal recourse for the protection of individual and group rights, equality between the sexes, a secular state, equality and universality of citizen access to social provisions (i.e. health, social services) (Government of Quebec 1993, quoted in Rocher et al. 1995: 225) – interculturalism attempts to strike a balance between individual rights and cultural relativism by emphasising a 'fusion of horizons', through dialogue and consensual agreement. Through the participation and discourse of all groups in the public sphere, the goal of this approach is to achieve the largest possible consensus regarding the limits and possibilities of the expression of collective differences based on identity, weighed against the requirements of social cohesion and individual rights in a common public context. The recognition of cultural differences is assumed in such a view – the sources of meaning accrued from cultural identity are acknowledged as an explicit feature of citizen empowerment – yet an obligation is placed on all parties to contribute to shaping the basic tenets of a common public culture.

For example, with the goal of promoting the contribution of immigrants in society, the Government of Quebec, since 1978, has directed the Programme d'Enseignement des Langues d'Origine (PELO). This initiative has contributed to a valorisation of immigrants' heritage. According to the data supplied by the Mouvement pour une école moderne et ouverte (MEMO) before the Commission of the Estates General on the Situation and Future of the French Language in Quebec, no fewer than 1,847 students of the Montreal School Board participated, in September 2000, in these classes. Moreover, for 15 per cent of these students, it consists of a third spoken language, contributing to making Montreal one of the most trilingual cities in the world.[12] Another important instrument has been a targeted hiring policy to permit members of recent communities of immigration to attain available positions within the public service. In 2000, the Government of Quebec adopted an Act Respecting Equal Access to Employment in Public Bodies as an amendment to chapter A-2.01 of the Quebec Charter of Rights and Freedoms. The Act has been in force since 1 April 2001 and obliges public authorities to develop equal access in employment programmes for women, aboriginals, visible minorities and people whose mother tongue is neither French nor English. In order to ensure that the policy is effectively enforced, the government set up the Commission des droits de la personne et des droits de la jeunesse (CDPDJ), a body mandated to assess availability in the labour force and overseeing the substance of various employment equality access programmes.

In sum, the recognition of minority cultures is built into a model where the 'moral contract' is an integrative principle whereby ethno-cultural groups are provided with the means to contribute, in a common language, and to make their mark on the basic principles of the common public culture. Difference is recognised within the limits of societal cohesion and political community, not as an essential starting point for common identification and unity.

Canadian multiculturalism

Multiculturalism as a mobilising force in Canada came into play largely as a result of a negative response to the recommendations of the Royal Commission on Biculturalism and Bilingualism (Laurendeau-Dunton) in the 1960s by a 'Third Force' – groups which represented immigrants and ethno-cultural communities. The Commission itself was spearheaded by Prime Minister Pearson as a response to the rise of a reinvigorated Quebec nationalism through the Quiet Revolution, and the subsequent questioning of Quebec's collective place in a federation dominated largely by Anglo-Canadians in economic, cultural and political affairs. Representatives of the 'Third Force' sought recognition of their

---

[12] Mouvement pour une école moderne et ouverte (MEMO), the Commission of the Estates General on the Situation and Future of the French Language in Quebec, Montreal, 23 October 2000.

cultural contributions to Canada, and felt that they would be relegated to second-class citizenship status if the country was to be formally defined as bicultural and bilingual.

Prime Minister Trudeau's response was to alter the recommendations of the B&B Commission, which called for a 'two nations' conception of the country whereby French Canada and English Canada were to be recognised equally as founding nations, with each enjoying majority status. Trudeau would opt, however, for a policy of official multiculturalism within a bilingual framework. In doing so, he argued that language could be dissociated from culture, and individuals would be free to decide whether or not to actively preserve their ethno-cultural identities. Implicit in such an approach is the primacy of individual rights – the right of all individuals to freely dissociate themselves from their ethno-cultural communities. Moreover, the language of participation in Canadian society – between French and English – was left to individual choice. The idea that language was to correspond to sociological realities, as the B&B Commission implied, was abandoned. Canada would henceforth be constructed along universal principles, language would be dissociated from culture, and multiculturalism would stress the absence of majority cultures as structuring principles for the larger encompassing community. The community for the integration of immigrants was Canada, defined as a single (officially) bilingual host society. In Trudeau's view:

> We cannot have a cultural policy for Canadians of French and British origin, another for Aboriginals, and still another for all the others. Although we will have two official languages, there will be no official culture, and no ethnic group will have priority . . . *All men will see their liberty hindered if they are continuously enclosed in a cultural compartment determined uniquely by birth or language. It is thus essential that all Canadians, regardless of their ethnic origins, be required to learn at least one of the two languages in which the country conducts its public affairs.* (Pierre Elliott Trudeau 1971, quoted in Cardinal and Couture 1998: 249–50; their emphasis; our translation)

Although the final policy outcome could be said to represent a middle ground to the 'multicultural and multilingual' vision espoused by the 'Third Force' and the 'two nations' vision, it contributed to alienating many francophone Quebecers who chose to rally the independence movement in large numbers (Kallen 1982: 54). The federal government's policy objectives were outlined as follows:[13]

1. The Government of Canada will support all of Canada's cultures and will seek to assist, resources permitting, the development of those cultural groups which have demonstrated a desire and effort to continue to develop a capacity to grow and contribute to Canada, as well as a clear need for assistance.
2. The Government will assist members of all cultural groups to overcome cultural barriers to full participation in Canadian society.
3. The Government will promote creative encounters and interchange among all Canadian cultural groups in the interest of national unity.
4. The Government will continue to assist immigrants to acquire at least one of Canada's official languages in order to become full participants in Canadian society.

New concerns over racial and ethnic equity led to a reiteration of the policy in the 1988 Canadian Multiculturalism Act by the Progressive Conservative government of Brian Mulroney. As Yasmeen Abu-Laban notes, the act accentuated the impact of multicultural policy not only by focusing on cultural maintenance, but by more explicitly emphasising concerns over discrimination. The Act now contained a provision whereby the Minister of Multiculturalism could 'assist ethnocultural minority communities to conduct activities with a view to overcoming any discriminatory barrier and, in particular, discrimination based on race or national or ethnic origin' (Abu-Laban 1994: 471). This response by the state was a result of greater concerns surrounding the changing composition of minority ethnic groups due to recent waves of immigration. The new act, however, did little to change the general thrust of the original policy, and simply refined and further strengthened the terms of recognition with respect to the contribution of cultural groups (Cardinal and Couture 1998: 251). This refinement was particularly well received by ethno-cultural groups.

[13] House of Commons Debates (8 October 1971), Statement of Prime Minister Trudeau.

While multiculturalism had been largely proceeding through federal funding of cultural projects, of more substance was the entrenchment in 1982 of multiculturalism, as a key tenet of Canadian identity, in the Canadian Charter of Rights and Freedoms. The existing policy of multiculturalism within a bilingual framework was reinforced. Under the interpretive clause in Section 27, the constitution would henceforth 'be interpreted in a manner consistent with the preservation and enhancement of the multicultural heritage of Canadians'. Multiculturalism thus became 'a visible component of the patriated constitution', leading to the perception among ethno-cultural groups that they had achieved the status of 'legitimate constitutional actors' (Abu-Laban 1994: 472).

Concurrent projects for national integration

Prior to proceeding with the comparative study, it must be emphasised that such policies cannot be assessed in the absence of a clear understanding of political processes related to the strategy of nation-building. This qualification is particularly salient in the Canadian case, where the precarious nature of a pan-Canadian identity has been in itself something of a 'national symbol' due to the persistent existential question in Quebec. Indeed, policymakers at the federal level charged with defining the terms of belonging in Canada have not only faced the challenges associated with the incorporation of diverse ethno-cultural identities, but have been confronted with a minority nation which controls established political institutions within a well-circumscribed territory.[14]

A comparison of the policies advancing Quebec's interculturalism and Canada's multiculturalism is rendered complex for a variety of reasons. First, Canada's policy of multiculturalism has evolved over time in its emphasis on the recognition of cultural pluralism. It is not a policy that has remained static. Augie Fleras, for example, has shown that the policy began with an emphasis on cultural diversity meant to stem the tide of the legacy of assimilation, yet it moved towards greater integrative efforts in subsequent iterations. He shows that the policy evolved from *ethnicity* multiculturalism, to *equity* multiculturalism, which emphasised the participatory obstacles confronting newcomers, to *civic* multiculturalism,

[14] For a longer development on this point, refer to Gagnon 2015.

and, finally, to *integrative* multiculturalism, which offers a more robust conception of Canada as a basis for identification (Fleras 2009). These shifts can in large part be explained by the fact that multiculturalism gained a lot in substance as it emulated Quebec's approach to interculturalism.

Second, with regard to Quebec interculturalism, one prominent difficulty noted by François Rocher and Micheline Labelle is that the policy has never been clearly defined in a legislative initiative (Rocher et al. 2007). It has remained a guiding principle that has taken shape through a series of policy statements and the work of intellectuals and policy practitioners. As such, the general thrust of the policy itself continues to be hotly debated. Even its actual uniqueness relative to multiculturalism continues to elicit much discussion (Taylor 2012: 413–23). Many proponents of Canadian multiculturalism as well as many 'conservative' nationalists in Quebec who seek an elevated public status for the majority culture argue forcefully that interculturalism is simply the extension of multiculturalism in Quebec, with overlapping policies and normative priorities. Indeed, this ambiguity associated with Quebec interculturalism has also resulted in disagreements around the model's primary normative objectives in defining the place of minority and majority cultures in the public sphere, alternating between convergence towards a majority culture and a more strict 'synthesis' model leading to a common public culture.

We contend, however, that at their very core the nuances of the models, and, most importantly, their objectives, are politically salient – there are political imperatives at work in such policy outcomes that cannot be dismissed as irrelevant (see Table 5.1). Thus far, this chapter has attempted to shed light on the phenomenon of multiculturalism – distinguishing between its use as a general label for an emerging tradition in political thought and the actual policy bearing its name in Canada – in order to alleviate the ambiguities surrounding the concept, particularly in applied approaches in political theory that assess hard cases and specific policies. However, an assessment of Canadian multiculturalism cannot disregard the fact that in the final analysis it is a policy and not an ontological principle devoid of contingencies and political orientations. In other words, the ideal of multiculturalism must not be confused with the Canadian policy, as this is prone to stifling debate concerning the value of the policy in framing citizenship status.

Table 5.1 Multiculturalism and Interculturalism as Conceptual Lenses.

	Canadian Multiculturalism	Quebec Interculturalism
Social fabric metaphor	Mosaic	Togetherness – we feeling
Conflict management	Procedural	Deliberate/parliamentary institutions
Perspective on pluriethnicity or plurinationality	Cultural relativism	Cultural convergence (*foyer de convergence*)
Moral foundations	Liberalism (single context of choice)	Liberalism (multiple contexts of choice)
Visions of the country	Negotiated country Canada as central focus	Permanent negotiation Quebec as a frame of reference (G. Godin)
Dynamics of power	Mainly centrifugal forces	Mainly centripetal forces

Returning to the normative backdrop for evaluating integration as developed above, it is clear that the central government's strategy is related to both the goal of unity and the fostering of citizen dignity through the recognition of particular ethno-cultural identities. First, it seeks to achieve unity through a pan-Canadian nation-building project that emphasises the primacy of individual rights in a constitutionally entrenched Charter of Rights and Freedoms, and a choice of language use – French or English – applied across the country, although this 'free' choice of language hides the fact that the English language has been able to gain a position of domination in the country, with Quebec being the only region where French is now the main language in the workplace, services and the public sector.

Superimposed on individual rights is the official recognition of all constituent cultures, equally. Such recognition, however, is largely a symbolic concession – the construction of a new identity marker. By forging a common identity throughout the country based on the 'sum of its parts',[15] it was hoped that the identity marker for unity could be universal – the equal recognition of all cultures, within a regime governed by individual rights and bilingualism. In this way, adherence to particular cultural attachments could be voluntary for all *individuals*, while at the same time claiming to empower

[15] We owe this formulation to Morton Weinfeld; Weinfeld 1981: 94.

123

citizens of minority cultures – Canada's symbolic order was to be based on the negation rather than recognition of majority cultures. Gilles Bourque and Jules Duchastel argue that the Canadian political community in this sense is predicated on a juridical conception of the regulation of social interactions, firmly ensconced within Canada's emphasis on procedural liberalism, to the detriment of the deliberative aspects of representative democracy that characterises, as we saw, interculturalism. In other words, the idea of public space for citizen participation, reflection and deliberation within the political community is reduced to a narrow forum of rights-bearers and, ultimately, preventing citizens from identifying with others in the larger society (Bourque and Duchastel 2000).

According to Will Kymlicka, the final outcome of Canadian multiculturalism as a symbol for identification is paradoxically analogous to the civic thrust of the United States in its failure to differentiate between national minorities and ethno-cultural communities. The fundamental difference between the two is that the former strive for self-determination while the latter seek inclusion. Canada's policy fails to address this distinction – multiculturalism becomes a mechanism to quell legitimate national aspirations – thus it shares with the US model a certain homogenisation of identity, albeit through cultural relativism. Again, the Canadian model is premised on the non-recognition of majority cultures. Kymlicka argues that the American reluctance to recognise minority nations is a direct result of its assimilationist model, a fear that such recognition will trickle down to its polyethnic communities and thus undermine the bases for unity (Kymlicka 1997: 240). Canada's policy stems from similar fears. However, Canada's response was to elevate the status of all cultural groups to the same level as that of a minority national – that is Quebec. Both are universal, both are bound by nation-building projects which stress unity, and both fail in any significant way to recognise territorially defined group-differentiated rights as a federal principle, contributing as a consequence to undermine trust between political communities.

As such, we contend that the Canadian model was not predicated on a genuine commitment to the ideal of multiculturalism as a pillar upon which to frame citizenship status. The goal was unity in the face of a minority nation that made demands to be recognised as a constituent host society. Quebec's national identity was placed, constitutionally, alongside every other minority cultural group as a basis for identification.

In Charles Taylor's terms, multiculturalism as such fails to appreciate 'deep diversity' in Canada, in which difference can be recognised on tiered levels in view of particular groupings' political aspirations and historical/territorial/linguistic realities. In adopting a strategy for unity similar in aims to the American approach – uniformity from coast to coast based on universal principles – the Canadian policy failed to recognise that minority nations, as opposed to ethno-cultural communities, seek to provide a 'centre' for identification, their own pole of allegiance necessary for unity and common purpose. In other words, national identity in Quebec assumes a self-determining project for society. The community of reference for all citizens under the banner of multiculturalism, however, is Canada.

As a response to critics who view multiculturalism as a divisive force in Canada, Kymlicka provides some empirical data that illustrate the success of multiculturalism in terms of the integration of minority cultures.[16] Indeed, the line of criticism in this chapter does not challenge the integrative success of the policy. The claim is that due to the imperatives of nation-building, for the purposes of unity in the face of the Quebec question, Canada chose to adopt a 'lowest common denominator' formula that rejected the recognition of culture as an aspect of belonging altogether. Trudeau's 'just society' was predicated on the notion that any emotive attachment

---

[16] Kymlicka's work is mainly directed towards the contentions of Neil Bissoondath. Bissoondath argues that in the Canadian model minority cultures are recognised, a priori, in a vacuum of time and space, which tends towards ghettoisation and fragmentation in terms of allegiance to a larger polity. Bissoondath argues this point forcefully, labelling the phenomenon 'cultural apartheid'. The contention here is that multiculturalism in effect defines culture provisionally – in a static sense – and prohibits full social interactivity. In other words, the dynamic nature of cultural sources of meaning are neglected, resulting in the stagnant 'folklorization' or 'commodification' of cultural production, reducing culture to 'a thing that can be displayed, performed, admired, bought, sold or forgotten ... [it is] a devaluation of culture, its reduction to bauble and kitsch'. As such, neither unity nor citizen dignity accrued from cultural recognition is achieved in such a context. This is the result of recognising cultures in juxtaposition without any expectation that such cultures may contribute to the overall direction of the larger society in an evolutionary interplay of ideas. The substantive elements of minority cultures, their bases of meaning, are virtually predetermined and unchanging, disregarding the very real effects of displacement into a new context. See Kymlicka 1998; Bissoondath 1994: 83.

to a given political community or nation is destructive and retrograde, and that progress requires an emphasis on reason, which is universal, to serve as a guiding principle in any citizenship regime. If we look closely at Kymlicka's indicators for integration, however, although they demonstrate that integration has been generally successful, it came at the expense of the recognition and preservation of minority nations and cultures – which in the final analysis is the defining feature of ideological multiculturalism.

The Canadian model operates along the primacy of individual rights in a constitutional bill of rights, with an interpretive clause for the recognition of diverse cultural affiliations. There is no democratic imperative for the recognition of diverse minority cultures besides a legal/procedural provision that may be invoked if the minority group in question chooses to do so. This is a key conceptual distinction between the Canadian and Quebec models and it stems from the nature of the expectations of democracy itself. The fact that Canadian identity – the way citizens relate to each other and to the state in determining societal preferences – is predicated on such terms implies the absence of a public culture on which minority cultures can make their mark. Again, multiculturalism in Canada does not reflect a recognition of minority cultures; rather, to be blunt, it rests on the denial of culture altogether in defining the limits and confines of public space. Returning to Kymlicka's assessment on the success of Canadian multiculturalism in terms of integration, we note a dearth of evidence regarding the extent to which minority cultures feel as though they have been able to persist in living according to the sources of meaning garnered by their cultural affiliations. In his defence, this undertaking would require a large-scale empirical study, and the fact that he was able to successfully operationalise 'integration' merits credit in its own right, as it deepens the conceptual discourse surrounding these models of integration. However, the success of minority groups within indicators such as 'naturalization rates', 'political participation', 'official language competence', 'intermarriage rates' and 'a lack of territorial enclaves of cultural groups' (Kymlicka 1998: 17–19) are addressed to those critics who view multiculturalism as an obstacle to forging a strong Canadian identity. They do not speak to the explicit concern for the preservation and flourishing of minority cultures within the political community – the capacity of such groups to participate in and affect the public affairs of the country without shedding their particular group identities. The debate itself thus takes place outside the imperatives of ideological multiculturalism. In other words, these criteria may very well be addressing a regime committed to full integration and even assimilation.

The virtue of Quebec's model of interculturalism is that it strikes a balance between the requirements of unity – an identity basis – and the recognition of all minority cultures. Recognition is not limited to viewing an ethno-cultural diversity as a 'problem', and treating them as static, essentialised and separate groups that require a slice of the public purse and therefore must be 'budgeted for', and vulnerable to cutbacks. Quebec's model of integration is not assimilatory, as is the American approach, nor does it conceptually fall into cultural relativism and fragmentation in its commitment to cultural pluralism. The idea of empowerment as it pertains to marginalised ethno-cultural groups is such that integration is a necessary prerequisite to full participation in the construction of a common public culture as an identity centre. Identification with and participation through a variety of cultures is not ruled out as a basis for citizenship status, yet the possibility of enclosure and ghettoisation is discouraged because the recognition of particular cultural identities is de facto the *recognition of the right and obligation to participate* in the polity, not the recognition of culture as existing in self-contained communities that are pre-political. Recognition is an *outcome* of participation, the result of contributing to the development of a common public culture and to larger consensual bases of allegiance and identification, without a rejection of the established symbolic order offered by Quebec society as it has evolved historically, that members of minority cultures can make a difference regarding their status as concrete citizens. In this sense, the unity and solidarity sought by any model of citizenship are viewed as an ongoing process, to be constructed by the various parties involved through exchange and dialogue, rather than a model that offers a pre-existing blueprint of recognition. Leading theorist Bhikhu Parekh stresses this aspect of cultural diversity (Parekh 2000).

For Parekh, a liberal framework that states simply that culture matters to individuals is not sufficient for making the case that cultural diversity in itself is a public good. While majority cultural groups may internalise the fact that members of minority cultures warrant certain cultural rights, through recognition, it fails to appreciate the value of cultural diversity in that a sense of cultural differentiation also endows individuals with a deeper understanding of their own cultures and allows for reflection about larger questions of co-existence between people. Cultural diversity is thus valuable on top of the instrumental benefits that culture contexts provide for individuals' expression and emancipation. Let's turn to Joseph Carens, who makes this point succinctly as he argues, 'In integrating immigrants, Quebec is transforming not only their identity but its own as well' (Carens 2000: 133). As such, the French language is not meant to define a static culture into which immigrants and cultural communities are expected to 'melt'. Rather, French is the conduit through which the disagreements, contentions and conflicts inherent in a culturally diverse society can be aired in a situation of normal politics. In the end, participation implies some degree of political conflict. The political community is based on a shared language, and challenges to the prevailing tenets of the national culture are not viewed as threatening, but are encouraged as a healthy and normal effect of the democratic process and deliberation.

Conclusion

The position developed in this text is not meant as a radical argument for post-national identity politics; indeed, the normative merits of political unity in any given state have been explicitly acknowledged. Nor is it meant to prescribe a formula for unity in federal democracies.[17] It seeks to demonstrate the merits of interculturalism as an alternative model for integration, and that Canadian multiculturalism has been and continues to be a product of nation-building efforts rather than a genuine commitment to the main tenets of multiculturalism as a normative framework for the promotion of cultural pluralism. It is a component of a political strategy by the central state to forge a strong commitment, by its citizens, to Canada as a single and unified political community. The main principles of Canadian citizenship are not that far off from those of the United States, or Australia and Germany, for that matter (see Boyer et al. 2004). Indeed, the place of culture in

---

[17] For more on this dimension, see Burgess and Gagnon 2010.

128

Canadian conceptions of citizenship is liberal – it is about building a nation based on universal principles. We contend that a model of cultural pluralism along the lines of Quebec interculturalism makes a more serious effort to balance the requirements of unity with the preservation, recognition and flourishing of minority cultures. The enduring problem confronting the Quebec model – one that would have to be taken into account in any future attempts at empirical verification – is the idea of competing interpretations of citizenship by those identified for integration in the first place.

It can be argued that the failure to achieve unity and common purpose is not inherent in the model of multiculturalism adopted. Rather, fragmentation is a product of federal dynamics – Canada is not a nation-state that can claim the status of a single and unified host society. As such, one can assess the policy independently of the Quebec question which, to a large extent, may explain the motivation for the policy but not its actual effects as a model for integration. If we disregard the variable of national pluralism in Canada, has multiculturalism been successful in integrating immigrants and ethnic groups? Indeed, if we begin with the assumption that Canada constitutes a single political community, or host society, we can then proceed to evaluate the success of multiculturalism without considering disunity in terms of the fragmentation of 'national allegiance'. Unity can thus be conceptualised as the extent to which minority groups feel as though they belong to a single community called Canada, and actually participate in the general affairs of the all-encompassing polity.

The Quebec model is unique in that it is embedded in a larger project for national affirmation. The fact that it can legitimately be included as a model for integration at the very least demonstrates the strides that Quebec has made in the area of citizenship, and perhaps such conceptual overviews can spark some interest in more empirically based research in the future. Whether or not such research can be undertaken in a context of competing models of citizenship, within a single territory, should not undermine efforts to conceptually include the model of interculturalism in debates about recognition and integration in liberal democracies. Indeed, Quebec intellectuals, in formulating the boundaries of the national project, have been engaged in a rich debate about the terms of belonging in Quebec.

References

Abu-Laban, Yasmeen, Y. (1994), 'The Politics of Race and Ethnicity: Multiculturalism as a Contested Arena', in J. P. Bickerton and A. -G. Gagnon, *Canadian Politics*, 3, Peterborough: Broadview Press, pp. 463–86.

Behiels, M. D. (1991), *Quebec and the Question of Immigration: From Ethnocentrism to Ethnic Pluralism 1900–1958*, Ottawa: Canadian Historical Association.

Bickerton, J. P., S. Brooks and A.-G. Gagnon (2006), 'André Laurendeau: The Search for Political Equality and Social Justice', in *Freedom, Equality, Community: The Political Philosophy of Six Influential Canadians*, Montreal: McGill-Queen's University Press, pp. 55–70.

Bissoondath, N. (1994), *Selling Illusions: The Cult of Multiculturalism in Canada*, Toronto: Penguin Books.

Bouchard, G. (2011), 'What Is Interculturalism?', *McGill Law Journal*, 56 (2), 435–68.

Bourque, G., and J. Duchastel (2000), 'Multiculturalisme, pluralisme et communauté politique: le Canada et le Québec', in M. Elbaz and D. Helly (eds), *Mondialisation, citoyenneté et multiculturalisme*, Sainte-Foy: Les Presses de l'Université Laval, pp. 147–70.

Boyer, P., L. Cardinal and D. Headon (eds) (2004), *From Subjects to Citizens: A Hundred Years of Citizenship in Australia and in Canada*, Ottawa: University of Ottawa Press.

Burgess, M., and A.-G. Gagnon (eds) (2010), *Federal Democracies*, London: Routledge.

Caldwell, G. (1988), 'Immigration et la nécessité d'une culture publique commune', *L'Action nationale*, 78 (8) (October), 705–11.

Caldwell, G. (2001), *La Culture publique commune*, Quebec City: Éditions Nota Bene.

Cardinal, L., and C. Couture (1998), 'L'Immigration et le multiculturalisme au Canada: la genèse d'une problématique', in M. Tremblay (ed.), *Les Politiques publiques canadiennes*, Sainte-Foy: Les Presses de l'Université Laval, pp. 239–64.

Carens, J. H. (2000), *Culture, Citizenship, and Community: A Contextual Exploration of Justice and Evenhandedness*, Oxford: Oxford University Press.

Dupré, J.-F. (2012), 'Intercultural Citizenship, Civic Nationalism and Nation-Building in Quebec: From Common Public Culture to *Laïcité*', *Studies in Ethnicity and Nationalism*, 12 (2), 227–48.

Fleras, A. (2009), *The Politics of Multiculturalism: Multicultural Governance in Comparative Perspective*, New York: Palgrave.

Gagnon, A.-G. (2015), *Minority Nations in an Age of Uncertainty: National Emancipation and Empowerment*, Toronto: University of Toronto Press.

Gilbert, M. (1981), *Autant de façons d'être Québécois. Plan d'action à l'intention des communautés culturelles*, Quebec City: Department of Communications/ Direction générale des publications gouvernementales.

Government of Quebec (1991), *Au Québec pour bâtir ensemble: Énoncé de politique en matière d'immigration et d'intégration*, Quebec City: Direction des communications du ministère des communautés culturelles et de l'immigration du Québec.

Government of Quebec (1993), *La Gestion de la diversité et l'accommodement raisonnable*, Montreal: Ministère des communautés culturelles et de l'immigration.

Government of Quebec (1994), Conseil des relations interculturelles, 'Culture publique commune et cohésion sociale: le contrat moral d'intégration des immigrants dans un Québec francophone, démocratique et pluraliste', in *Gérer la diversité dans un Québec francophone, démocratique et pluraliste: principes de fond et de procédure pour guider la recherche d'accommodements raisonnables*, Montreal: Conseil des communautés culturelles et de l'immigration.

Greer, S. L., and M. Mätzke (2009), 'Introduction: Devolution and Citizenship Rights', in S. L. Greer (ed.), *Devolution and Social Citizenship in the UK*, Bristol: Policy Press, pp. 1–19.

Harvey, J. (1991), 'Culture publique, intégration et pluralisme', *Relations*, 574 (October), 239–41.

Hepburn, E. (2001), '"Citizens of the Region": Party Conceptions of Regional Citizenship and Immigrant Integration', *European Journal of Political Research*, 50, 504–29.

Iacovino, R. (2014), 'Canadian Federalism and the Governance of Immigration', in E. Hepburn and R. Zapata-Barrero (eds), *The Politics of Immigration in Multilevel States: Governance and Political Parties*, Basingstoke: Palgrave Macmillan, pp. 86–107.

Isajiw, W. (1981), 'Social Evolution and the Values of Multiculturalism', paper presented at the Ninth Biennial Conference of the Canadian Ethnic Studies Association, Edmonton, Alberta, 14–17 October 1981.

Joppke, C. (1996), 'Multiculturalism and Immigration: A Comparison of the United States, Germany and Great Britain', *Theory and Society*, 25, 449–500.

Kallen, E. (1982), 'Multiculturalism: Ideology, Policy and Reality', *Journal of Canadian Studies*, 17 (1), 51–63.

Kymlicka, W. (1995), *Multicultural Citizenship: A Liberal Theory of Minority Rights*, Oxford: Oxford University Press.

Kymlicka, W. (1997), 'Ethnicity in the USA', in M. Guibernau and J. Rex (eds), *The Ethnicity Reader: Nationalism, Multiculturalism and Migration*, Cambridge: Polity Press, pp. 229–47.

Kymlicka, W. (1998), *Finding Our Way: Rethinking Ethnocultural Relations in Canada*, Toronto: Oxford University Press.

Parekh, B. (2000), *Rethinking Multiculturalism: Cultural Diversity and Political Theory*, Basingstoke: Macmillan.

Perreault, R. (1999), 'Notes pour une allocution de Monsieur Robert Perreault sur la réforme des services d'intégration et de francisation', Quebec City: Ministère de Relations avec les citoyens et de l'Immigration.

Raz, J. (1986), *The Morality of Freedom*, Oxford: Clarendon.

Rocher, F., G. Rocher and M. Labelle (1995), 'Pluriethnicité, citoyenneté et intégration: de la souveraineté pour lever les obstacles et les ambiguités', *Cahiers de recherche sociologique*, 25, 213–45.

Rocher, F., M. Labelle, A.-M. Field and J.-C. Icart (2007), *Le Concept d'interculturalisme en contexte québécois: généalogie d'un néologisme*, rapport présenté à la Commission de consultation sur les pratiques d'accommodement reliées aux différences culturelles.

Sandel, M. (1982), *Liberalism and the Limits of Justice*, Cambridge: Cambridge University Press.

Semprini, A. (1997), *Le Multiculturalisme*, Paris: Presses universitaires de France.

Taylor, C. (1994), 'The Politics of Recognition', in A. Gutmann (ed.), *Multiculturalism and 'The Politics of Recognition'*, Princeton: Princeton

University Press, pp. 25–73.

Taylor, C. (2012), 'Interculturalism or Multiculturalism?', *Philosophy and Social Criticism*, 38 (4–5), 413–23.

Weinfeld, M. (1981), 'Myth and Reality in the Canadian Mosaic: "Affective Ethnicity"', *Canadian Ethnic Studies*, 13, 80–100.

Young, I. M. (2000), *Inclusion and Democracy*, Oxford: Oxford University Press.

The Case for Interculturalism, Plural Identities and Cohesion

Ted Cantle

Multicultural societies will inevitably become more multicultural as the world becomes more interdependent and as financial, commercial, cultural and other links increasingly entwine. But multicultural policies are not fit for purpose and have slowed down and inhibited the acceptance of difference. Interculturalism is based upon an entirely different conceptual and policy framework and offers a new and progressive approach to how we learn to live with diversity. Though many multicultural theorists have attempted to resist any change of approach – including those developed since 2001 under the banner of 'community cohesion' – there are now signs that this is beginning to change. Indeed, claims that the new principles of interculturalism were 'foundational' to multiculturalism all along (Meer and Modood 2012: 182) reflect this hasty revisionism. Such claims, however, are not supported by any evidence and many of the key tenets of interculturalism were ignored or rejected by multiculturalists.

This chapter therefore examines the similarities and differences between multiculturalism and interculturalism with particular reference to the impact of globalisation, especially changing patterns of interaction and communications, and ideas about collective and personal identity. It reflects briefly on the origins of multiculturalism, largely from a European perspective, with its preoccupation with 'race' and accompanying socio-economic analysis. This chapter suggests that while the focus on inequalities was justified, multiculturalism completely failed to adapt to super-diversity and the multifaceted aspects of difference and 'otherness', including those based on disability, age, sexual orientation and gender. Further, multiculturalism remained firmly rooted in intra-national differences, between minority and majority populations, and can be contrasted with interculturalism, which recognises that 'difference' now crosses national boundaries and also reflects the heterogeneity of national, ethnic and faith groups.

A fundamental aspect of this debate is therefore the way in which personal and collective identities are instrumentalised, in particu-lar the 'illusion of a unique identity' (Sen 2006: 175) in which conflict and violence are sustained today: the world is increasingly divided between religions (or 'cultures' or 'civilisations'), which ignore the relevance of other ways in which people see themselves, through class, gender, profession, language, literature, science, music, morals or politics. Sen thus challenges what he sees as 'the appalling effects of the miniaturisation of people' (2006: 175) in which the development of plural identities is generally presented as a threat to notions of community and cultural solidarity. But plural identities do not necessarily entail the weakening of tradi-tional forms, and can easily sit alongside each other. Indeed, the development of more plural identities – a process which is inherent in globalisation and diversity – should be viewed much more posi-tively, as it greatly increases the possibilities for peace, tolerance and cohesion, by building relationships across many divides.

But this is far from accepted and far-right and popular nationalist parties have grown across Europe, demonstrating that the 'threat' theory has some considerable popular resonance. These parties have based the threat on a supposed loss of cultural and national integrity and the very sovereignty of the nation. The response to this challenge has, however, been ambivalent in mainstream politi-cal arenas. On the one hand, there has been a reluctance to give any credence to suggestions of a loss of national powers or to sugges-tions that migration has diluted national identity through greater diversity; on the other hand, they have nevertheless tried to claw back some of their lost political support by suggesting a return of national powers and greater limits on immigration. This simply serves to reinforce the threat theory.

A new response is now necessary. First, there is a need to rec-ognise the new reality – that the powers of the state have been substantially eroded, along with a simple national identity. But the opportunity that this presents now also needs to be exploited, by enabling people to come to terms with diversity through intercultural education and experience. At the same time, the 'threat' needs to be countered with the development of more plural democratic arrangements and more multilevel and direct participation in the political system. In addition, the effects of globalisation – and immigration in particular – on those 'left behind', in both economic and political terms, have to be recognised. This will entail a more realistic assessment of the impact of migration on physical infrastructure and community services and revision of ideas about how economic growth is determined and managed. In short, the very fundamentals of our political systems need to change.

National identity also has to be set within a wider context of more plural identities in which people now see themselves in different ways and at different times and in different contexts. For example, mixed-race relationships, once subject to legal restrictions and social taboos, are now the fastest growing of all ethnic categories across Europe. Similarly, gay relationships are now celebrated more than challenged, and disabilities and health issues are openly discussed and publicly recognised. 'You can't put me in a box' (Fanshawe and Sriskandarajah 2010) is now a common plea, but still largely disregarded by multicultural orthodoxy and policy.

The legacy of multiculturalism

It is not intended here to give a full account of the history of multiculturalism, especially as the 'difference' brought by migration has been evident to some extent at least for a millennium. However, the mobility of people has become ever more entwined with globalisation and economic growth as the ease of travel and communications has improved. In Europe, the post-war increase in migration drew upon former colonies, building upon established cultural links, especially language. The migration was nevertheless characterised by 'visible' minorities who were often seen as a threat to the cultural integrity and values of the host nations, even though migration had helped post-war economies to grow by providing a source of (often cheaper) labour. This contradiction heralded an age of anti-discrimination legislation, positive action programmes and some integration measures to try to ensure that tensions and conflicts were minimised. The multicultural model in Britain was noted for its emphasis on tolerance, equal rights and the avoidance of assimilation. This enjoyed considerable, though by no means universal, support, but its 'success' was challenged by the finding in 2001 that communities had separate or 'parallel lives' based on ethnicity, with the report on the riots in English northern towns (Cantle 2001). Subsequent concerns about extremism in Muslim communities following 9/11 and the bombings in other cities added fuel (though more heat than light) to concerns about the multiculturalist model.

The multicultural policies followed by the UK and most European governments have become ever more exposed and, it is argued, are no longer appropriate to mediate the new era of globalisation and super-diversity. Despite some past successes, especially in terms of tackling discrimination and promoting equal opportunities, they have become far too blunt a tool to do this effectively. Multicultural policies have also failed to recognise that 'difference' is no longer simply defined by 'race' and that identity has become multifaceted and dynamic, developing support for a more intercultural model. They now enjoy neither governmental nor popular support, leading to a political paralysis in which the issues are only debated in a defensive mode, with little attempt to recognise that cultures are more fluid than ever before and the interconnectedness of the world demands a new and progressive approach which builds interaction between and within cultures. There has also been little attempt to develop the cultural navigational skills which help people to accept and endorse the change process, nor to remove the structural and institutional barriers that cause separation and lead to inequality. The opportunity to learn about each other through educational, experiential and routine intercultural contact is seldom supported on anything like a pervasive basis, with communities encouraged to view their identities as special and fixed.

Multicultural policies have also been slow to recognise how the fluidity of population change impacts on national solidarity and governance. In 2010 there were 214 million international migrants; if they continue to grow in number at the same pace, there will be over 400 million by 2050 (IOM 2010). The extent of population movement is such that all Western economies are now characterised by 'super' or 'hyper' diversity, with cities such as London, Stockholm, Toronto, New York and Amsterdam housing over 300 language groups. At the same time, 'horizontal' human movement has taken place and is increasing across countries in other regions, such as South America and southern Africa, with newer forms of multiculturalism emerging. Consequently, multiculturalism is now much more complex and community relations are multifaceted, no longer simply revolving around visible majority/minority distinctions underpinned by their distinct socio-economic positions. In so far as national identity has been considered, it has been from the limited perspective of how minority cultures are 'accommodated' within a national framework, rather than the impact on the majority community and how all identities are being remade. The political response has inevitably been to cling to the idea of clear national boundaries supported by strong national identities, and any suggestions of the loss of sovereignty or political plurality are quickly contested. Rather than reflecting the process of globalisation, the political class also feel threatened by the interconnectivity of the modern world. They believe that it is a threat to their own (national) power base and are not prepared to acknowledge, let alone argue for, a more collaborative approach between nations, or devolution within them (as the Scottish referendum debate has exposed).

The post-war ideal of a more integrated international community, in which ideas and cultures may bridge national boundaries to create a world in which we are more at ease with each other, is seldom now advanced as a desirable political objective, despite the evident interdependency of economic and political decision-making. Similarly, while people are themselves increasingly crossing borders, intermarrying, building new virtual networks and creating real and tangible personal relationships at all levels, this is seldom recognised, let alone championed. 'Identity politics', whether on the basis of narrow national, ethnic, faith or regional bases, often holds back transition rather than supporting and inspiring a new and interconnected world.

The population increase in the UK over the past ten years or so has been at the fastest rate since records began. The 2001 census reported the population as 58.789 million, which compares to 63.182 million found in the 2011 census – an increase of more than 7 per cent. Estimates vary as to what proportion of this growth is due to migration, but recent reviews by the left-leaning *Guardian* newspaper and the right-leaning organisation Migration Watch both attribute more than half of the total growth to migration. However, there is little by way of a positive narrative for the rising levels of immigration and its impacts, and it has become a very significant political issue in which it is seen to pose a 'threat' to the homogeneity and distinctiveness of national and regional identities. Whilst this may be based on real fears about competition over jobs and services, rising welfare costs and overcrowding, it may also be underpinned by 'racist' or xenophobic ignorance. But it is notable that far-right and popular nationalist parties in many countries are increasingly exploiting fear of the erosion of a simple national identity to build substantial support. This has grown across most of Europe, including France, Denmark, the Netherlands, Austria, Belgium, Germany, Greece and Italy. The recent European Parliament elections, in May 2014, illustrate the unprecedented growth – with France's support for the Front National at over 20 per cent and the UK's for the UK Independence Party (UKIP) at 26 per cent – and the failure of multiculturalism to respond to these concerns.

Community cohesion programmes had, however, in England at least, assuaged some of the concerns about growing diversity, largely on the basis of the new framework in which a sense of belonging and positive relationships between different groups would be promoted. Certainly, the annual Place Survey (DCLG 2009) of residents' attitudes was able to demonstrate, up until 2009 (it was subsequently discontinued by the new coalition government), that local authorities had had some success in improving perceptions of whether 'people from similar backgrounds got on well together', both in most of the local communities and on an aggregate basis. This mirrored the way in which community cohesion had largely been conceived – as a localised programme, which responded to local needs and was largely developed and implemented through local statutory and non-statutory agencies. The early definition reflected this approach:

A cohesive community is one where:
- There is common vision and a sense of belonging for all communities;
- The diversity of people's different backgrounds and circumstances are appreciated and positively valued;
- Those from different backgrounds have similar life opportunities; and
- Strong and positive relationships are being developed between people from different backgrounds in the workplace, in schools and within neighbourhoods. (LGA 2002: 6)

The success of these local narratives and programmes, however, have to be set against growing concerns about the extent and nature of immigration and anxieties about extremism which have been played out in the national press and media. These concerns have been well documented, featuring in the top five public concerns since 2005, with immigration often cited as the most important, even at times displacing concerns about the economy (Duffy and Frere-Smith 2014). (Interestingly, though, the concerns about immigration are generally lower in more diverse areas and greater in areas with a lower proportion of migrants (Kaufmann and Harris 2014: 33), supporting ideas about 'contact theory', which is central to both community cohesion and interculturalism.)

Whilst, at a local level, community cohesion had been embraced enthusiastically and soon developed a wide range of guidance and good practice (see Cantle 2008: 171–238), little was done at the national level to create a more positive view of diversity and change, nor to respond to the continuing concerns about the level of immigration and its perceived impact on cultural solidarity and integrity. Further, the nature of 'difference' became increasingly defined by international events and influences, through the supposed threat emanating from Muslim communities, both at home and abroad. The UK's counter-terrorism strategy (commonly known as 'Prevent') was rolled out at the national level, with little ownership by local authorities and their partners; indeed, they were often critical of the strategy and, together with a number of voluntary organisations, were reluctant to co-operate with the government on this issue. The Prevent strategy created a number of problems and contradicted many of the principles of community cohesion, in that it targeted and homogenised Muslims, creating a 'suspect community', through an undifferentiated approach in which widespread surveillance was introduced. However, more generally, the threat of terrorism became associated with the Muslim communities, and they became the focus of much of the developing public angst about multiculturalism. Local authorities found it difficult to maintain trust between their local Muslim communities and statutory agencies, and the key differences that they were trying to resolve were increasingly defined by government policy (including foreign policy) and by reference to wider notions of 'British values', over which they had no control. (For an excellent discussion of the problematic interaction of Prevent and community cohesion, see Thomas 2014.)

139

The positive approach of community cohesion at local level was not mirrored by a change in the national discourse of multiculturalism and, as explained above, the political narrative about both immigration and extremism served to weaken its appeal still further. The discourse of 'multiculturalism' had also failed to provide a reassuring public response across Europe, even to the extent that the Eminent Persons Report by the Council of Europe declined to even use the term, noting that it no longer had any real credibility (COE 2011: 5). Certainly, there are now few politicians who advocate on behalf of multiculturalism, with its 'failure' remarked upon at the highest level (Cantle 2012: 53–4), and with little attempt to develop and articulate an alternative vision of how we might live together in a shared society. Community cohesion has provided both a narrative and a programme for understanding and coping with difference at a local level, but multicultural theory and practice has failed to adapt to the new social and political reality and provide a supportive discourse at a national and international level. It is suggested that the concept of interculturalism can undertake such a role, forming a new meta-narrative, and transform our understanding of 'difference' and our policy and practice for 'living together'.

Multiculturalism and interculturalism: Key differences

There have, of course, been many different conceptions of multiculturalism and interculturalism and some similarities and overlaps at different points, though recent academic and policy debates are contributing to much clearer dividing lines. The Canadian/ Quebec Province use of interculturalism has been the most difficult to situate within such clear-cut divisions, as this approach (expounded, for example, by Bouchard 2011) mirrors much of the reified, static and defensive form of identity management found in European forms of multiculturalism, whereas the Canadian government form of 'multiculturalism' is a little closer to the European idea of interculturalism. This conation apart, the key difference between multiculturalism and interculturalism generally revolves around the way in which personal and collective identities are conceptualised and instrumentalised.

Plural identities enable people to bridge divides and to see both themselves and others in multifaceted ways. Plural identities therefore confound the 'miniaturisation' of people and their identities (Sen 2006: 175) which has been so apparent under multicultural theology. The prospects for cohesion and peace are enhanced by the breaking down of traditional and hardened boundaries, but this depends upon the development and facilitation of interaction and contact, which has rarely been part of any multicultural programme – indeed, it has often been seen as a threat – despite the clear evidence from recent studies that contact helps to reduce the apparent fear of 'others' and promote intergroup harmony (Hewstone et al. 2006), both directly and in a more contextual sense (Christ, Hewstone et al. 2014). These recent studies are based upon 'contact theory' which dates from the 1950s (Allport 1954) but contributions from social psychology (and anthropology) are absent from almost all of the work of multicultural theorists over the last half-century. Sociologists, in particular, have been subject to criticism for neglecting the value of 'cultural encounters' (Delanty 2011: 642), confirming that no notion of permeable community boundaries, and the beneficial impact of contact, interaction and exchange, was ever 'foundational' to multiculturalism.

In fact, a central tenet of multicultural theory was the idea that 'thick' or community boundaries helped to protect minorities against assimilation and that heritage should be preserved in the face of the overwhelming hegemony of the majority. Indeed, whilst minority communities were to be somehow preserved, the majority community was expected to adapt and change to accommodate a wider variety of social and cultural practices.

The desire to maintain cultural differentiation was actually laudable, but this approach failed to recognise that both minority and majority communities were in a constant state of flux, and that they were not simply adapting to each other but were exposed to external – and often far more profound – pressures. These included the de-industrialisation of Western economies, the growth of diaspora influence, the emergence of global corporations and brands, and the rapid development of transnational communications including social media. Again, transnational influences were not even considered as part of multicultural theory, let alone seen as 'foundational', and remained firmly rooted in the intra-national debate about majority and minority relationships.

Powell and Sze (2004) recognise that whilst identity is part of a dynamic process, it has been conceived as static and as ascribed under multicultural theory:

> multiculturalism is a policy based on the notion of personal autonomy. Interculturalism, in contrast, recognizes that in a society of mixed ethnicities, cultures act in multiple directions . . . Multiculturalism tends to preserve a cultural heritage, while interculturalism acknowledges and enables cultures to have currency, to be exchanged, to circulate, to be modified and evolve. (Powell and Sze 2004: 1)

The recent acceptance of multiculturalism's 'groupist' approach to identity (Meer and Modood 2012) is to be welcomed, but the majority of academic and policy literature on multiculturalism is founded on the protection of 'essentialised', ascribed and static identity boundaries, in which these 'pure' forms are privileged.

In this sense, multicultural theory also unfortunately embodied an element of racial purity. It was based upon certain bounded categories ('Black', 'Asian', 'White', 'Muslim', 'Jew', 'Irish' and so on), embedded in legislation and supported by policies in which leaders represented these entire and apparently homogeneous communities, funded exclusive centres and enabled services to be carried out by people who were of the same identity as the recipients of that service. This meant that certain communities were also privileged above others, who were too small to feature on the purist radar or who were more fluid and differentiated. In fact, it was not until the 1991 UK census that mixed race even featured as a category. Any sense that people could be 'mixed' in terms of heritage, or could be differentiated within boundaries, seemed to be absent from both conceptualisation and policy and practice. In the 1990s, academic texts did begin to refer to hybrid identities, often combining a national and an ethnic or religious category, but this simply extended the number of categories, resulting in what Sen called 'plural monoculturalism' (2006: 156), rather than challenging the whole notion of the artificial boundaries created, or creating any real acceptance of fluid and dynamic boundaries. The disaggregation of generic categories like 'Black' or 'Asian' was also proposed, but, as noted by one of the few academic texts to question identity boundaries, this was 'confined within an either/or model of identity which fails to recognise that social identity can be multi-faceted' (Solomos and Back 1996: 135). Multiculturalists seemed to have entirely missed the fact that during this period the UK was home to hundreds of ethnic, faith and language groups which were heterogeneous in themselves and knew no clear boundaries; and that the era of super-diversity had arrived. Perhaps, more importantly, their emphasis on the value of diversity, rather than cultural encounter and exchange, meant that any idea of a relational concept of culture was denied.

The principal differences and similarities between interculturalism and multiculturalism are set out in the table below. It is appreciated that there are a number of conceptions of multiculturalism (and a much smaller number of conceptions of interculturalism; see Zapata-Barrero 2013) and this therefore represents a generalisation of these differences and similarities. However, it should be noted that, with one or two notable exceptions, there has been a very established multicultural orthodoxy in the UK at least, and the table overleaf is thought to be a fair representation of these views.

Interculturalism and multiculturalism do share some characteristics. Both support the tackling of disadvantage and inequalities, though multiculturalists have tended to approach this through silo programmes within separate communities, such as care support to Jewish elders, IT skills programmes for Muslim women, and school targets for Black Caribbean or White working-class children – again reinforcing ideas about distinct and separate identities.

The early model of multiculturalism in the UK did apparently recognise the need to 'promote good relations' between groups, and this idea was in fact embedded in early race-relations legislation from the 1960s. However, it was never developed into any real or pervasive practice and lacked 'commitment, leadership and resources' (Cantle 2008: 40), with the focus of the legislation from 1976 focusing more on anti-discrimination and equality programmes (Cantle 2008: 43). At the same time, any attempt to develop an open public debate to help people come to terms with migration and diversity was trumped by the fear that the 'oxygen of publicity' would raise tensions. This made it more difficult to challenge negative views and created a culture of 'political correctness' in which the 'race debate' was off limits. Indeed, such debates have become increasingly circumscribed by legislation over the years, the same approach being extended to the 'terror debate' with the Home Secretary announcing a new ban on extremist

Multiculturalism and interculturalism: similarities and differences

Multiculturalism	Interculturalism
Tends to assume that ethnic, faith and other differences are ascribed and static – and protected as a 'birthright'. Also tends to regard identity groups as homogeneous.	Based on a dynamic concept of difference that welcomes evolution over time, with group identity to be challenged. Regards each group as fluid, with group identity seen as heterogeneous.
Minority differences are defended in face of what are seen as assimilationist tendencies. But any protection of majority identity (or national identity) has been opposed as exclusionary.	Interculturalists see both minority and majority identities as constantly being remade, partly because of their interrelation, but also due to external and global influences.
Personal identity is presented as self-defined and consolidated through reinforcement with people of the same background; emphasis on knowing self first through heritage and roots.	Personal identity is understood only in relation to others. Self is discovered by exploration and openness, not by building a protective shell to withstand possibility of exchange.
Difference is seen in 'groupist' terms with the idea of 'pure' identities tacitly supported through acceptance of categories like 'Black', 'White', 'Jewish', 'Sikh' and 'Irish'. These are treated as homogeneous groups in legal and policy terms (e.g. funding and representation). Cosmopolitan identities regarded with suspicion, or opposed.	Interculturalism recognises plural identities, with increasing numbers of mixed race and intermarriage, alongside growing numbers of dual- and multinational identities, with interventions that cross categories. Heterogeneous hybrid and cosmopolitan identities regarded as the new 'normal'.
'Difference' revolves around long-standing majority/minority divisions within each nation with a focus on 'accommodations' between them.	'Difference' goes beyond national references influenced by international events and exchange, for example, through diaspora and transnational social media communications.
'Difference' is defined in binary terms, usually in relation to 'race' or ethnicity (and faith as an ethnic group).	'Difference' is multifaceted, embracing gender, disability, sexual orientation and age, as well as that of nationality and faith.
Many proponents of multiculturalism believe that difference is determined by socio-economic factors (and that they can only be made less salient through	Interculturalists recognise socio-economic factors as important determinants of prejudices and stereotypes, but not as the sole determinant, and also emphasise

(continued)

Multiculturalism	Interculturalism
equality programmes) reflecting historical patterns of oppression and exploitation.	education/interaction programmes as a means of disconfirming stereotypes and preconceptions.
Multiculturalism has been passive, fearing that promotion of any sense of commonality or belonging would tend towards assimilation and loss of group identities.	Interculturalism is proactive: developing common values and belonging at a societal level; collective identity is multifaceted.
Multiculturalism has restricted debate about diversity to deny the 'oxygen of publicity' to extremists and fears the raising of tensions. Denying free speech has led to accusations of 'political correctness'.	Interculturalism encourages more open debate and 'dangerous conversations' to enable people to come to terms with change; supports looser legal framework. Also, less fearful of championing the creativity and innovation from diversity.

speakers in universities in 2014 – as though the lure of extremists is so strong that it cannot be resisted through rational argument. Multiculturalists could perhaps have justified their restrictions in the early post-war period, but have tended to argue for more, rather than less, over the years and seem not to have noticed that far-right parties are no longer able to attract support on the basis of crude biological racism (Goodwin 2011: 8).

It is also striking that there were few campaigns to promote a sense of commonality and belonging, until this developed under the community cohesion agenda in 2001 (see Cantle 2008: 178–86).

Multicultural theory has also been surprisingly silo-based, with few of the established theorists drawing upon social psychology and anthropology. For the most part, such theories have been limited to a sociological and structural analysis which draws heavily upon a Marxist position in which attitudes and values are determined almost entirely by socio-economic position. As Powell and Sze have therefore noted:

Understanding how cultures move around in a society, introduce social changes, and facilitate cultural integration requires an interdisciplinary approach: one that includes the obviously primary concerns of human rights, citizenship, work, education, health and housing, one that also

145

develops inclusive policies and supports the development of creative expression. (2004: 1)

A positive future for plurality

In terms of the current debate about national identity, it might be assumed that the sole beneficiaries are those on the far right and in popular nationalist parties who have galvanised the 'left behind'. But while this might be apparent in political terms, many people are eschewing identity politics and taking advantage of the more open borders and transnational communications. The fastest-growing ethnic group across Europe is that of mixed race, faith and nationality, with an enormous complexity in intercultural relations which defies political populism. Further, contrary to the popular narrative, people are developing more plural and cosmopolitan identities. Castells (2006: 57) draws upon the research of Professor Norris of Harvard University, who has analysed the World Values Survey to show that regional and local identities are trumping national loyalties. Professor Norris calculated that for the world as a whole, 13 per cent of respondents primarily considered themselves as 'citizens of the world', 38 per cent put their nation-state first, and the remainder (that is, the majority) put local or regional identities first.

A 2008 world public opinion survey (WOP 2008) of people in twenty-one nations around the world found that nearly 30 per cent of people now see themselves as a 'citizen of the world' (10 per cent) as much, or more than, as a citizen of their nation (20 per cent). Further, the more people know people from different regions of the world, the more they see themselves as a global citizen – rising to 47 per cent among those who know people from five or more regions. As might be expected, the larger number of respondents from around the world (66 per cent) said that they think of themselves primarily as citizens of their country, but this varied considerably by country. In the poll, the nations with the highest numbers saying they primarily think of themselves as 'citizens of the world' were Italy (21 per cent) and Germany (19 per cent). Very substantial numbers said they see themselves as either a citizen of the world or equally as a citizen of the world and of their country. These include France (51 per cent), China (50 per cent), Italy (48 per cent), India (46 per cent) and Mexico (44 per cent). The lowest levels are found in Azerbaijan (9 per cent), Kenya (12 per cent), Jordan (15 per cent) and South Korea (16 per cent). Younger people tend to be even more globally oriented than older people. Among those aged 60 years and older, 24 per cent see themselves as global citizens. This rises to 34 per cent among those aged 18–29. Global identity also increases with education. Among those with less than a high school education, 28 per cent think of themselves as global citizens. This rises to 39 per cent among those with education. These are, by any standards, remarkable results, and they demonstrate the enormous shift in patterns of self-identity.

Similarly, a more recent opinion poll carried out by Ipsos MORI, 'UK becoming "more local and global"' (Ipsos MOPI 2013), illustrates the extent of the change in the UK:

• Almost a quarter (24 per cent) say they feel a greater sense of connection to people in other countries around the world than they did ten years ago. For those aged 15–34, the figure is 31 per cent.
• More than four in ten (44 per cent) say that their leisure activities are important to their identity, with a similar proportion saying their values or outlook matter (38 per cent) and slightly fewer saying their personal views and opinions are important (34 per cent).
• Traditional factors of age (22 per cent), nationality (20 per cent), gender (13 per cent), class (7 per cent) and ethnicity (6 per cent) were viewed as less important to people's identity.
• Only 20 per cent said their nationality was among the top three or four things they would tell a stranger was important about them. Only 10 per cent said religion, while 7 per cent picked social class.

Despite having little by way of encouragement, a surprising number of people are thinking of themselves in more complex terms, and it is particularly striking that none of the new key aspects of identity are those that are generally ascribed at birth.

In the face of this broader diversity and changing patterns of identity, governmental responses have been ambivalent. For the most part, they have attempted to deny the change and reinforce their view of national identity through such measures as the

teaching of national history and promoting national citizenship
and identity, most recently through the idea of 'British values'. By
steadfastly retaining a pretence of the integrity of national borders
and governance, and by attempting to deny the interdependence
brought by globalisation, they reinforce a fear of 'others'. They
then also appear to lag behind the current reality of multifaceted
identities within their communities. Already there is clear evidence
of a decline in traditional democratic traditions across Europe,
with election turnouts and political party membership in decline.
The growth of new political movements, from the *indignados* in
Spain to that led by the comedian Beppe Grillo in Italy, and the
current lack of trust in and disconnection from mainstream parties
suggest that these movements could grow further still. Indeed, the
elections for members of the European Parliament across Europe
in 2014 saw many new parties (of the left and right) gain ground.

People are now often able to draw upon heritage, faith, language, diaspora and new national identities to create hybrid or
multiple identities. It is also the case that the variation within
ethnic groups is as great as those differences between them, and
there is a great danger in homogenising any particular identity. All
types of hyphenated identity – for example 'British-Asian', 'French-
Muslim' or 'Swedish-African' – also run the risk of simply replacing the limited notion of a single identity with an equally static
hybrid identity, becoming bounded and ascribed: what Sen (2006:
156) describes as 'plural monoculturalism'. Identity is a process
and not a fixed category, although it is often regarded as the latter.

A UK government report – interestingly, by the Government
Office for Science, rather than the Home Office or Communities
Department – recognised the dramatic change in people's identities (though it remains to be seen whether this has any impact on
multicultural policy):

Identity in the UK is changing. Over the next 10 years, people's identities are likely to be significantly affected by several important drivers of
change, in particular the rapid pace of developments in technology. The
emergence of hyper-connectivity (where people can now be constantly
connected online), the spread of social media, and the increase in online
personal information, are key factors which will interact to influence
identities. These developments need to be set within a wider context
of demographic change: the shift of the large post-war generation into

retirement, and the coming into adulthood of young people who have been immersed since birth in a digital environment. The increasing diversity of the UK's population means that dual ethnic and national identities will continue to become more common, while the gradual trend towards a more secular society appears likely to continue over the next decade. A key message for policy makers is that identities can be a positive resource for social change, building social capital, and promoting wellbeing, but they can also have a role in social unrest and antisocial behaviour. (Government Office for Science 2013: 1)

None of this should suggest that national identity could or should be downplayed. In fact, there is a great danger in suggesting that the one area of identity that some lower socio-economic groups feel able to cling to in a time of uncertainty should be wiped away. The reality is, however, that city, regional, national and cosmo-politan identities now need to sit alongside each other; they are not opposed – something that multiculturalism has never acknowl-edged. Interculturalism recognises that people can have more than one identity at the same time and that these are not necessarily in opposition to each other; rather, they simply represent different aspects of human relations.

Plurality of power and the state

The strength of national identity depends to some extent on the powers and responsibilities of the nation-state and to what extent they create a sense of solidarity. If the powers and responsibili-ties become diffuse and diluted as a result of both more localised and more transnational agencies, this may have an impact on feelings on solidarity, distinctiveness and allegiance. Though the nation-state is no longer in a simple alignment with distinct politi-cal communities, this is not to say that national identity is about to fade away, but feelings of solidarity may become more plural, in response to the political plurality, and sit alongside national, regional and other forms. For some, however, there has been a retreat into hardened national identities as people 'hunker down' and attempt to cling to what they believe are their own separate and distinct certainties.

Globalisation has brought many new international agen-cies and structures into being and fundamentally altered power relationships, with national politicians now appearing to be controlled by them rather than leading them. These new agencies have responded to a range of common issues, from international finance and crime to environmental concerns such as climate change, the proliferation of nuclear weapons and many more. The European Union perhaps stands out most in this regard. At the same time, non-governmental organisations are also developing and taking on new roles, again at the expense of nation-states. Held (1989: 196) charts the rise of these organisations and calculates that whereas there were 176 such organisations in 1905, there were 4,615 in 1984. Agg (2006: 2) suggests that the figure had reached nearly 45,000 by the end of the 1990s. This, together with the rapid growth of global business and brands, has created a popular sense of powerlessness and alienation. Castells (2010: 419) supports the view that the state has been bypassed by networks of wealth, power and information and has lost much of its sovereignty. Not everyone agrees with his view, but even defenders of state power such as Ignatieff (2014: 39), who would very much like to see the current role of the national sovereignty restored, are forced to recognise that 'we live in a world where power seems elsewhere. We feel that power lies somewhere in "the global market" and that we are its play-things.' Governments have even failed to recognise that there is now no barrier between domestic and foreign policies (Hill 2013).

The problem for the 'statists' is that they assume the boundaries and powers of the state have been fixed and become immutable (in much the same way as multicultural theory had regarded ethnic and faith boundaries). In fact, they have been made and remade many times over, with a clear trend towards smaller states. In 1950 there were just fifty nations, compared to over 200 today. There are indications that this number will increase further, with the growth of more ardent separatist movements and areas where people no longer feel able to share the same land or government. Around twenty nations have been created in recent years, which stem partly from the break-up of previously constructed federations in the Balkans and Eastern Europe or divisions being turned into official separation, for example in the recently divided Sudan. More divisions may be on the way, as states such as Belgium are becoming virtually ungovernable as single entities; there are around twenty secessionist movements in Europe alone, with Scotland (in which a pro-independencc referendum was narrowly defeated in 2014) and Catalonia being the most notable.

A more radical view of the fragmentation of states is provided by Barber (2013: 4), who believes that nation-states will be replaced by cities as the main instrument of the polity and suggests that this is not only inevitable but also desirable, because cities are a more functional democratic unit and more capable of responding to cross-border challenges than are states. States will resist change, however, as they 'are quintessentially indisposed to cooperation . . . too inclined to rivalry and mutual exclusion'. New ideas of solidarity and political agency are also moving in other directions and forming 'horizontally', particularly through social media – transcending traditional power structures and constantly redefining who 'we' are.

The power balance within states has also profoundly changed. Ford and Goodwin (2014) describe the 'left behind' not only in economic terms, but also in terms of their political influence – or lack of it. These mainly older, working-class voters, with few qualifications, were once central to the political and social debate; trade unions wielded real power, and no party could secure election without winning significant support from them. But this group is now rapidly declining, and in the meantime there has been a dramatic expansion of university education and professional white-collar employment, with middle-class graduates and professionals now at the centre of society and politics. The working class have become 'voiceless'.

It is remarkable that the multicultural theology, founded on race and ethnic divisions, has viewed national identity through the same lens. States tend to present their history and heritage as one of uniqueness, whereas in reality the British values (or those of any other Western economy) are virtually identical and have become universal in essence and largely based around the Universal Declaration of Human Rights. In the UK, it is notable that neither the previous Labour government nor the more recent Conservative-led coalition government was able to produce a statement of 'British values', despite both promising to do so. Citizenship has also become regarded as ascribed and static, unchanging and unchangeable, and the boundaries are fiercely guarded and defended, even where many individuals and families cross the boundaries. Few states are willing to grant dual citizenship and very reluctant to recognise plurality, or sanction hybrid forms.

A progressive way forward

The way in which we think about ourselves and others needs to reflect the modern-day reality of globalisation and super-diversity. Intercultural education and learning will need to become pervasive and to recognise the challenge that we must face to overcome a history of division. This will not be an easy process, as Lau Chek Wai suggests:

> it is important to view intercultural exchanges as periods of revolutions. Like in periods of scientific revolutions, intercultural exchanges involve a change of worldview, a change of meaning and a change of the repertoire of questions. Intercultural exchanges cannot be properly conceived as an accumulation of past cultural experiences. The hybrids must be regarded as new entities. (2004: 121)

In terms of national identity and power, the political class must begin to accept the reality of political change, rather than simply trying to claw back ground lost to the far right and popular nationalist parties by hoping that a little less migration, the tackling of alleged abuse of benefit rules and the improvement of integration will suffice. This is unlikely to convince the 'left behind' and simply confirms their perception that this is the problem. It fails to tackle the economic and political realities of an increase in population and also fails to address the changing reality of politics and power.

Clearly, the economic realities of the 'left behind' do have to be tackled. This means, first, recognising – in a more realistic way – the increased pressure upon the physical and social infrastructure that results from an increase in population. But it also means presenting a vision of a future world in which power has to be exercised more collaboratively, across boundaries, and at many different levels to tackle global issues – and, by championing more plural identities (simply supporting the existing trends), improving the chances for peace, security and prosperity.

It is not possible, as several commentators seem to believe, to simply turn back the clock. Ignatieff (2014: 37), for example, states that the survival of democratic politics depends on reviving sovereignty and 'regaining the sense that we're masters in our own house' – perhaps not unlike the views of UKIP and the other nationalist parties who are desperate to repatriate powers taken by the EU. Goodhart is also an advocate of a 'return to sovereignty', and positions this in binary terms as a choice between 'two liberalisms' of 'solidarity on the one hand (meaning a high trust/high sharing society) and an increasing diversity of values and ways of life on the other'. But he creates a false choice between 'a more individualistic and diverse society ... more dynamic and competitive [which] is likely to manifest lower levels of sharing and a weaker sense of belonging ... [with] common norms and mutual regard damaged by too much diversity' and the 'communitarian notion of club membership' in which 'people will always favour their own families and communities' (Goodhart 2014: 20). He also seems to posit the choice between simple national identity and culture and a universal or global culture. He fails to consider cosmopolitanism, which offers 'a reflexive condition in which the perspective of others is incorporated into one's own identity, interests or orientation in the world' (Delanty 2011: 634) – in other words, adding to, rather than threatening, national perspectives.

Similarly, the powers of states will become more diffuse, some powers exercised directly, others in combination with state and non-state actors, with some power devolved. Even Ignatieff (2014: 38) recognises that 'sovereigns need to combine ... we need sovereign co-operation more than ever, because no single power ... is in control of globalisation anymore'. A more profound change, accepting the need for more plural forms of democratic engagement, will enable people to participate in politics at different levels and in different forms – including the 'voiceless' part of majority populations. We therefore need to remake democratic institutions to reflect the reality of modern-day populations, in order to reinvigorate democracy and better respond to resource pressures at a local level. This may be through the thousands of 'city-states' as envisaged by Barber (2013) or through single-issue politics, at both the international and local levels. But it may also take the form of more 'horizontal' forms of direct citizenship engagement through social media. This has already begun to transcend established power structures and national and other boundaries. In fact, these could democratise international agencies which have clung to the ideal of representative democracy even though it has become increasingly remote. As part of 'reinventing the state' suggested by Micklethwait and Wooldridge (2014), power can now be pushed downwards much more easily if new technology is embraced. It is unfortunately notable that the only significant use of an international plebiscite is that of the Eurovision Song Contest!

There has also been little by way of any systematic attempt to develop a more global outlook through intercultural education, which might enable people to become more at ease with all aspects of diversity and globalisation. Many of our present programmes of education and socialisation doggedly attempt to promote a primordial sense of national, faith, ethnic and gender identity. Cannadine (2013) has recently illustrated how the state provides a historical account which depends upon an exaggerated 'them and us' perspective. He also sets out at length the way in which national identities have been created and reinforced through a Manichean concept of a 'divided past', ignoring the elements of collaboration and exchange between nations. The development of a plural democracy must now go hand in hand with a plural identity. The pretence of a homogeneous national or cultural identity has always been open to challenge, but the pace of change is increasing, with the very powers and nature of states and their democratic frameworks in flux. A static concept of democracy is as untenable as a static concept of national identity.

More generally, plural identities need to be promoted and developed, and by building understanding across divides, the prospects for tolerance, understanding, cohesion and peace are greatly enhanced. The support for simple homogeneous identities through categorisation, funding and representation must be curtailed and reflected with more heterogeneous and multifaceted forms. This will mean an acceptance that much of our existing, simplistic and 'groupist' forms of identity will have to change, along with the way in which they are instrumentalised through public policy:

> In an age of super diversity where people do not identify around single identities and feel conflicted allegiance (if any allegiance at all) to predefined groups, activism around particular 'strands' seems irrelevant to many people and may not even be that effective in addressing the true causes of inequality. Even the very categorisations that we rely on (for example, 'black', 'gay', 'Asian' or 'disabled') no longer seem to be able to tell us much about who people are, what lives they lead, who they identify with, or what services they need from government and society. And the tick box approach seems to be missing out on growing numbers of people who fall outside or across standard classifi-

cations. Yet society seems to treat ethnic identities as if they are clearly bounded, static and meaningful, and public bodies insist on a tick box classification. (Fanshawe and Sriskandarajah 2010: 11)

For many people who live in diverse areas there will be 'everyday' and banal encounters which enable their stereotypes and pre-conceptions to be directly challenged and the fear of 'others' to be reduced (Christ, Hewstone et al. 2014). But many countries around the world, including in the West, have highly segregated residential and other environments in which the possibilities for cultural exchange are limited. In the longer term segregation has to be challenged (including the economic determinants), but its worst effects – ignorance, intolerance and enmity – can be mitigated by relatively simple and low-cost programmes to encourage people to see the human face of the 'other'. Such exchanges, however, also begin to change not only our personal identities, but also our collective and community identities – and this represents a challenge to our political arrangements.

References

Agg, C. (2006), *Trends in Government Support for Non-Governmental Organizations: Is the 'Golden Age' of the NGO Behind Us?*, Civil Society and Social Movements Programme, Paper 23, Geneva: United Nations Research Institute for Social Development.

Allport, G. W. (1954), *The Nature of Prejudice*, Cambridge, MA: Addison Wesley.

Barber, B. (2013), *If Mayors Ruled the World*, New Haven: Yale University Press.

Bouchard, G. (2011), 'What Is Interculturalism?', *McGill Law Journal/Revue de Droit de McGill*, 56 (2), 435–68.

Cannadine, D. (2013), *The Undivided Past: History Beyond Our Difference*, London: Allen Lane.

Cantle, T. (2001), *Community Cohesion: A Report of the Independent Review Team* (The 'Cantle Report'), London: Home Office.

Cantle, T. (2008), *Community Cohesion: A New Framework for Race and Diversity*, Basingstoke: Palgrave Macmillan.

Cantle, T. (2012), *Interculturalism: For the Era of Cohesion and Diversity*, Basingstoke: Palgrave Macmillan.

Castells, M. (2006), 'Globalisation and Identity: A Comparative Perspective', in *Transfer: Journal of Contemporary Culture*, 1 (November), 56–66.

Castells, M. (2010), *The Power of Identity: The Information Age, Economy, Society and Culture*, Chichester: Wiley-Blackwell.

Christ, O., M. Hewstone et al. (2014), 'Contextual Effect of Positive Intergroup Contact on Outgroup Prejudice', *Proceedings of the National Academy of*

Sciences, 111 (11), <http://www.pnas.org/content/111/11/3996> (last accessed 10 June 2015).

Council of Europe (COE) (2011), *Report of the Group of Eminent Persons: Living Together – Combining Diversity and Freedom in 21st-Century Europe*, available at <http://www.coe.int/t/dg4/highereducation/2011/kyiv%20website/report%20on%20diversity.pdf> (last accessed 10 June 2015).

Delanty, G. (2011), 'Cultural Diversity, Democracy and the Prospects of Cosmopolitanism: A Theory of Cultural Encounters', *The British Journal of Sociology*, 62, 633–56.

Department for Communities and Local Government (DCLG) (2009), *Place Survey 2008, England*, London: DCLG.

Duffy, B., and T. Frere-Smith (2014), *Perceptions and Reality: Public Attitudes Towards Immigration*, London: Ipsos MORI.

Fanshawe, S., and D. Sriskandarajah (2010), *You Can't Put Me in a Box: Super Diversity and the End of Identity Politics*, London: Institute for Public Policy Research.

Ford, F., and M. Goodwin (2014), *Revolt on the Right: Explaining Support for the Radical Right in Britain*, London: Routledge.

Goodhart, D. (2014), 'A Post-Liberal Future', *Demos Quarterly*, available at <http://quarterly.demos.co.uk/article/issue-1/a-postliberal-future/> (last accessed 10 June 2015).

Goodwin, M. (2011), *New British Fascism: The Rise of the British National Party*, London: Routledge.

Government Office for Science (2013), *Foresight Future Identities: Final Project Report*, London: Government Office for Science.

Held, D. (1989), 'The Decline of the Nation State', in S. Hall and M. Jacques (eds), *New Times*, London: Lawrence & Wishart.

Hewstone, M., S. Paolini, E. Cairns, A. Voci and J. Harwood (2006), 'Intergroup Contact and the Promotion of Intergroup Harmony', in R. J. Brown and D. Capozza (eds), *Social Identities: Motivational, Emotional, Cultural Influences*, Hove: Psychology Press.

Hill, C. (2013), *The National Interest in Question: Foreign Policy in Multicultural Societies*, Oxford: Oxford University Press.

Hirst, P., and G. Thompson (1999), *Globalization in Question: The International Economy and the Possibilities of Governance*, 2nd edn, Cambridge: Polity Press.

Ignatieff, M. (2014), 'Sovereignty and the Crisis of Democratic Politics', *Demos Quarterly*, available at <http://quarterly.demos.co.uk/article/issue-1/sovereignty-and-the-crisis-of-democratic-politics-2/> (last accessed 10 June 2015).

International Organisation for Migration (IOM) (2010), *World Migration Report 2010*, Geneva: IOM.

Ipsos MORI (2013), 'UK Becoming "More Local and Global"', available at <http://www.ipsos-mori.com/researchpublications/researcharchive/3365/UK-becoming-more-local-and-global.aspx> (last accessed 10 June 2015).

Kaufmann, E., and G. Harris (2014), *Mapping the White Response to Ethnic Change*, London: Demos.

Lau Chek Wai, E. (2004), 'The Ownership of Cultural Hybrids: Creativity, Culture and Performance', in D. Powell and F. Sze (eds), *Interculturalism: Exploring Critical Issues*, Oxford: Inter-Disciplinary Press, pp. 121–5.

Local Government Association et al. (LGA) (2002), *Guidance on Community Cohesion*, London: LGA.

Meer, N., and T. Modood (2012), 'How Does Interculturalism Contrast with Multiculturalism?', *Journal of Intercultural Studies*, 33 (2), 175–96.

Micklethwait, J., and A. Wooldridge (2014), *The Fourth Revolution: The Global Race to Reinvent the State*, London: Allen Lane.

Powell, D., and F. Sze (2004), *Interculturalism: Exploring Critical Issues*, Oxford: Inter-Disciplinary Press.

Sen, A. (2006), *Identity and Violence: The Illusion of Destiny*, New York: W. W. Norton.

Solomos, J., and L. Back (1996), *Racism and Society*, Basingstoke: Macmillan Press.

Thomas, P. (2014), 'Divorced but Still Co-habiting? Britain's Prevent/Community Cohesion Policy Tension', *British Politics*, 9, 472–93.

World Opinion Poll (WOP) (2008), available at <http://worldpublicopinion. org/pipa/articles/views_on_countriesregions_bt/608.php?lb=brglm&pnt=608 &nid=&id> (last accessed 10 June 2015).

Zapata-Barrero, R. (2013), *The Three Strands of Intercultural Policies: A Comprehensive View*, GRITIM-UPF Working Paper Series, 17, Barcelona: UPF.

7

Defending Diversity in an Era of Populism: Multiculturalism and Interculturalism Compared

Will Kymlicka

Introduction

In both academic and public debates, one of the current fashions is to defend a (new, innovative, realistic) interculturalism against a (tired, discredited, naive) multiculturalism. In an influential recent article, Meer and Modood argue that there is little intellectual substance underlying this trend.[1] The two approaches are often said to rest on different underlying assumptions about the nature of individual and collective identities, the sources of social cohesion, the practices of democratic citizenship and the norms of justice. In reality, however, these contrasts typically rest on a misrepresentation, even caricature, of multiculturalist theories and approaches. Nor is the trend based on a systematic empirical comparison of the actual policy outcomes associated with the two approaches, since defenders of interculturalism rarely make clear how their policy recommendations differ from those defended by multiculturalists. As a result, Meer and Modood argue, the 'good interculturalism vs bad multiculturalism' literature is essentially rhetorical rather than analytical.

Meer and Modood's conclusions have not gone unchallenged, and various commentators continue to insist that some versions of interculturalism really do represent an important intellectual alternative to some versions of multiculturalism.[2] While I remain

---

[1] See Meer and Modood 2012, reprinted in this volume.
[2] See, for example, the responses in *Journal of Intercultural Studies* (vol. 33, 2012), and the essays collected in Barrett 2013.

convinced of Meer and Modood's conclusions, in this chapter I want to set aside that debate and approach the issue from a different perspective.[3] There may or may not be compelling intellectual or academic reasons to distinguish interculturalist from multiculturalist approaches, but it seems clear to me that drawing a sharp contrast between them can also serve certain political purposes. In the current political climate, the trope of replacing a tired old multiculturalism with a new innovative interculturalism can serve certain rhetorical functions, and we need to be aware of this.

My goal in this chapter, therefore, is to consider the interculturalism/multiculturalism contrast as a form of political rhetoric, and to ask what is the purpose of this rhetoric? Who are the proponents of this rhetoric, and who are the intended audiences? Which political actors, and which political projects, are being enabled by this new rhetoric, and who/what is being marginalised? In places, Meer and Modood imply that if the contrast between interculturalism and multiculturalism is primarily rhetorical rather than substantive or analytical, it is therefore of less interest, and perhaps even a distraction. I want to suggest, on the contrary, that the politics of rhetoric in this field is itself very interesting and revealing.

Interculturalism as political myth

Consider, in this regard, the influential 2008 White Paper on Intercultural Dialogue from the Committee of Ministers of the Council of Europe (COE 2008). It argues that interculturalism should be the preferred model for Europe because multiculturalism has failed:

> In what became the western part of a divided post-war Europe, the experience of immigration was associated with a new concept of social order known as multiculturalism. This advocated political recognition of what was perceived as the distinct ethos of minority communities on a par with the 'host' majority. While this was ostensibly a radical departure from assimilationism, in fact multiculturalism frequently shared the same, schematic conception of society set in opposition of

---

[3] This chapter is a revised and expanded version of my 'Comment on Meer and Modood', *Journal of Interculturalism Studies*, 33 (2012), 211–16.

majority and minority, differing only in endorsing separation of the minority from the majority rather than assimilation to it ... Whilst driven by benign intentions, multiculturalism is now seen by many as having fostered communal segregation and mutual incomprehension, as well as having contributed to the undermining of the rights of individuals – and, in particular, women – within minority communities, perceived as if these were single collective actors. The cultural diversity of contemporary societies has to be acknowledged as an empirical fact. However, a recurrent theme of the consultation was that multiculturalism was a policy with which respondents no longer felt at ease.

The intercultural approach, it argues, avoids these failed extremes of assimilation and multiculturalism, by both acknowledging diversity and insisting on universal values:

Unlike assimilation, [the intercultural approach] recognises that public authorities must be impartial, rather than accepting a majority ethos only, if communalist tensions are to be avoided. Unlike multiculturalism, however, it vindicates a common core which leaves no room for moral relativism.

All of this repeats the tropes that Meer and Modood identify in the literature. And, as they would predict, it does so without a shred of evidence. The White Paper gives no examples of multiculturalist policies in post-war Europe that were premised on moral relativism, and it does not cite any evidence that the problems of social segregation or gender inequality are worse in European countries that embraced multiculturalism than in those countries that rejected multiculturalism. This is not surprising since, as I have argued elsewhere, there is no evidence for this claim.[4] And, as Meer and Modood would predict, the White Paper's defence of interculturalism stays at such a level of generality that it is impossible to tell which real-world multiculturalist policies it would reject.

---

[4] To state the obvious, countries which have embraced multiculturalism are not ethnic utopias, and they confront many challenges relating to the inclusion of immigrants, including social isolation, economic inequality, poor educational outcomes, prejudice and stereotyping. The question is whether these problems are any worse in countries that have adopted multiculturalism policies, as compared to those countries that have rejected multiculturalism in favour of some alternative approach. And the answer here, I believe, is no. For a review of the evidence, see Kymlicka 2010, 2012. See also Kesler and Bloemraad 2010; Wright and Bloemraad 2012.

In all of these respects, the White Paper nicely illustrates the Meer and Modood analysis.[5] But I mention the White Paper not primarily to support the Meer/Modood analysis, but rather to suggest its limits. In light of the White Paper, we need to step back and ask deeper questions about the political context within which these debates take place, and about how progressive intellectuals can constructively intervene in them.

To understand the problem, it's worth pausing to consider how remarkable the 2008 White Paper is. The White Paper was approved by the Council of Ministers representing all the member states of the Council of Europe, and the Paper itself is derived from consultations with policy-makers in the member states. The result is an official statement by a pan-European organisation stating that it is the consensus of member states that multiculturalism has failed. And note that this was in 2008. When three conservative politicians – Cameron, Merkel and Sarkozy – made such claims in early 2011, this was considered newsworthy. But the claim that multiculturalism has failed had already been endorsed in 2008 by all member states, whether governed by left-wing or right-wing parties, whether traditionally pro-multicultural (like Britain or the Netherlands) or anti-multicultural (like France or Greece). There was a clear political consensus that we need a post-multicultural alternative, to be called 'interculturalism'.

Moreover, this is not just a European phenomenon. When UNESCO prepared its 2008 World Report on Cultural Diversity, it too started from the premise that there was a consensus on the need for a post-multiculturalist alternative at the global level, which it too framed in the language of interculturalism (UNESCO 2008). Both the Council of Europe and UNESCO have histori-cally been seen as standard-bearers for multiculturalism, yet as of 2008 both had declared the need to shift from multiculturalism to interculturalism.

---

[5] Not all defenders of interculturalism engage in these anti-multiculturalist tropes. Many interculturalists view themselves as allies of multiculturalists (and vice versa), differing only in choice of terminology or in level of analysis. My focus here, like Meer and Modood's, is only with that branch of the interculturalist literature that offers itself as categorically different from multiculturalism, and as a remedy for its failures. Even more specifically, I'm interested in how this trope is invoked at the level of political rhetoric, and so my focus is on public discourse and policy docu-ments rather than on academic theories.

How should we respond to such documents? One response, consistent with the Meer/Modood analysis, is to ask whether the White Paper or the World Report provides any good arguments or evidence for the claim that interculturalism is superior to multiculturalism. For example, when the White Paper claims that post-war Western Europe embraced relativist and segregationist multiculturalism, we certainly want to know if that is a fair characterisation or not. And here I agree with Meer and Modood that it is not a fair characterisation: indeed, it strains all credibility.[6]

But this just pushes the puzzle back a level: why would policy-makers from across Europe endorse this caricature? One possibility is that this is a sincere error, due perhaps to misinformation or inadequate research, and that if we bring this error to light, the member states of the Council of Europe and UNESCO might reconsider their rhetoric of abandoning a failed multiculturalism for a new interculturalism.

It's not clear if Meer and Modood believe something like this is possible, but in my view it is implausible. I suspect that the authors of the White Paper and UNESCO World Report – and the policy-makers they consulted – are already aware that they are presenting a caricature. Or perhaps more accurately, I suspect they are not particularly concerned one way or the other about whether their characterisation is fair. The interculturalism-as-remedy-for-failed-multiculturalism trope is not offered as an objective social science account of our situation, but rather, I believe, is intended to serve as a new narrative or, if you like, a new myth. As I read these reports,[7] the authors have concluded that it is politically useful to construct a new narrative in which interculturalism emerges in Europe from the failed extremes of assimilation and multiculturalism. Such a narrative, they believe, can

[6] For my own critique of these mischaracterisations, see Kymlicka 2007, chapters 2 to 4.

[7] In the interests of full disclosure, I should note that I was invited to write a background paper for the UNESCO report, and in that paper I argued (not unlike Meer and Modood) that there were no good arguments or social science evidence for claiming that multiculturalism has failed or that an intercultural alternative would be superior. (It has been published as 'The Rise and Fall of Multiculturalism? New Debates on Inclusion and Accommodation in Diverse Societies', *International Social Science Journal*, 199 (2010), 97–112.) I now think that my paper, while more or less sound on its own terms, was largely irrelevant to the political task that the UNESCO World Report team had taken on.

better sustain public support for progressive agendas and inclusive politics. Like all such narratives or myths, it is intended to enable certain political projects while disabling others, and the Council of Europe and UNESCO authors believe that this new narrative can enable inclusive politics while disabling xenophobic politics.

Viewed this way – as an enabling political myth – I think that the interculturalist rhetoric is interesting and important. It is an attempt to tell a story that can revive the flagging political commitment to diversity. Across Europe, and around the world, we see popular discontent with diversity, but this new narrative tells people that their discontent is not with diversity as such, but with a misguided and naive 'multiculturalism'. Multiculturalism is offered up as a handy scapegoat for popular discontent, in the hope that this will undercut support for populist, anti-immigrant or anti-Roma, xenophobic parties. The narrative says 'don't take your frustrations out on minorities; your objection is not to diversity, which is a good thing, but to the extreme multiculturalist ideology that we have now safely put behind us'.[8]

Viewed as a social science diagnosis of popular discontent, this blaming of multiculturalism is implausible. The evidence suggests that popular discontent with immigrants is in fact higher in countries that didn't embrace multiculturalism, and there's no evidence that adopting multiculturalism policies causes or exacerbates anti-immigrant or anti-minority attitudes. The authors of these reports sometimes reveal their awareness that their narrative is stretching the facts.[9] But viewed as a political myth, it may be useful.

---

[8] For critics, the term 'extreme multiculturalist ideology' is a pleonasm – as Grillo notes, for critics, 'multiculturalism is always already "unbridled"' (2007: 987).

[9] We can see this, for example, in the report on interculturalism produced by the Consultation Committee on Accommodation Practices Relating to Cultural Differences, created in 2007 by the government of Quebec, and co-chaired by the philosopher Charles Taylor and the sociologist Gerard Bouchard. In its main narrative, the Bouchard-Taylor report engages in the familiar anti-multiculturalist tropes identified by Meer and Modood (that it is fragmenting, relativist, and so on), and argues instead for interculturalism as a 'counter' to multiculturalism (e.g. pp. 120, 123, 205, 281). But in several places the report acknowledges in passing that these anti-multiculturalist tropes may not actually be true, and that the Committee does not have the empirical evidence to assess them (e.g. pp. 118, 192, 214). It's clear that the report hopes that readers will embrace their narrative of interculturalism as a counter to multiculturalism without inquiring too closely into the social science evidence for it. And, as with the White Paper and UNESCO reports, the Bouchard-

Something needs to be done to bolster the flagging commitment to diversity in Europe, and drawing a rhetorical contrast between a new interculturalism and an old multiculturalism may be politically effective, at least in some contexts. And precisely because the contrast is rhetorical rather than real, policy-makers can retain much or all of what they adopted as multiculturalism and simply relabel it as interculturalism (or as 'diversity policies', 'pluralism polices' or 'community cohesion policies').

And this, arguably, is what we see. There have been two systematic attempts to empirically measure the adoption of multiculturalism policies across Europe, and both indicate that the rhetorical retreat from the word 'multiculturalism' is not matched by any comparable retreat from actual multiculturalism policies, which are often simply relabelled. The appendix at the end of the chapter provides the scores from the Multiculturalism Policy Index that Keith Banting and I developed, which measures the diffusion of multiculturalism policies across 21 democracies. The results indicate a modest but steady strengthening from 1980 to 2000 to 2010.[10] Similar results were arrived at independently by Ruud Koopmans in the 'cultural rights' battery of his 'Indicators of Citizenship Rights Index' (Koopmans et al. 2012).[11] These results are what we would expect if the political champions of interculturalism are engaged primarily in the rhetorical rebranding of multiculturalism, rather than any substantive intellectual rethinking of it.

Viewed this way, the rhetorical trope of replacing a discredited multiculturalism with a new interculturalism can be seen as a rather shrewd strategy by progressive policy makers. It may have helped defend pro-diversity policies in the face of rising populist and anti-immigrant political forces. In order to preserve the commitment to diversity, perhaps we need to drop the poisoned term of 'multiculturalism', and to engage in a conscious act of political mythmaking in which interculturalism emerges providentially to rescue us from the twin failed extremes of assimilationism and

Taylor narrative may well be an effective piece of political drama to defend diversity within Quebec.

[10] See the appendix to this chapter, and the more detailed explication in Banting and Kymlicka 2013.

[11] See also the various articles in Vertovec and Wessendorf 2010 which show that the rhetorical retreat from the word 'multiculturalism' is not matched by any comparable retreat from actual multiculturalism policies.

multiculturalism. I think we need to take that possibility seriously, and ask what work this myth can do, for whom, and in which contexts, and how this compares with alternative strategies for addressing popular discontents.

My aim in this chapter is not to come up with a definitive judgement about how well this myth is working. The answer to that question surely varies across different countries, and perhaps even across different domains of policy within a country, in ways that would require extensive empirical analysis to track. My aim here is more modest: I hope to identify some of the potential benefits and risks involved in the rhetorical reframing of diversity, and to suggest some reasons why this new rhetoric might not be as benign as some of its defenders have assumed.

The risks of rhetorics

As noted earlier, the crux of this new rhetoric is not just that 'interculturalism is good' but also that 'multiculturalism is bad'. It is the conjunction of these two claims that defines the new intellectual fashion. Viewed in the abstract, there is nothing intrinsic to the words 'interculturalism' and 'multiculturalism' that makes one preferable to another, and there is no reason in principle why all the experiments in 'multiculturalism' which emerged in the West starting in the late 1960s could not equally have been called experiments in interculturalism, or perhaps have been called both interchangeably. And so there is nothing intrinsically right or wrong about deciding, from this point forward, to label diversity policies as interculturalism policies. Indeed, in those countries where the 'm word' has been poisoned, abandoned even by its former champions, it may be inevitable. In these contexts, it is quixotic at best to try to redeem the word, and it makes sense for progressive policy-makers to prefer another label such as 'interculturalism' for their policy recommendations.[12]

But what is distinctive to the new fashion is not simply the label of 'interculturalism', but also the narrative of 'failed multiculturalism'.

---

[12] 'Multiculturalism' has not yet become a poisoned term in every country – I think it is still a viable term in Canada and Australia, for example – and in such countries, I would argue that the fight for diversity can and should still be fought in the name of multiculturalism. And this means tackling head-on the myths and the misrepresentations, in just the way that Meer and Modood do in their paper.

We need interculturalism precisely to rescue us from the failures of multiculturalism. This is the central plot line. The casting of multiculturalism as the scapegoat is vital to the rhetorical strategy, which, as I noted earlier, responds to popular discontent by saying 'don't take your frustrations out on minorities; your objection is not to diversity, which is a good thing, but to the extreme multiculturalist ideology that we have now safely put behind us'.

I suggested earlier that we can see this as a shrewd political strategy, but it is also a dangerous one. Consider again the claim in the Council of Europe's 2008 report that by defending the 'common core' of universal values, interculturalism can rescue us from the 'moral relativism' inflicted by multiculturalism. This is an extraordinary claim, implying that for twenty years mainstream political elites across Europe were indifferent to fundamental principles of human rights and liberal democratic principles, and indeed adopted policies that conflicted with these principles. I noted earlier that the report provides no evidence for this claim, which is demonstrably false. But my concern here is with the rhetorical effects. Is this rhetoric likely to undercut support for populist and nativist parties, as the report's authors hope, or is it more likely to legitimise those parties and their worldviews? After all, the claim that multiculturalism policies rested on moral relativism has been a staple of populist parties for years, and is indeed a central lynchpin in the populist worldview. According to populists, mainstream political elites – and their allied elites in the media and corporate world – cannot be trusted to protect the core values of the society. These elites have been passive and indifferent in the face of threats to our civilisation and way of life, cowed by shibboleths of political correctness. The claim that multiculturalism rests on moral relativism is tied in the populist mind to paranoia about the liberal elites who promoted multiculturalism.

The 2008 Council of Europe report is, in effect, endorsing and legitimising key components of this populist worldview. The report says that the populists were right all along to view multiculturalism as based on moral relativism, and were right to believe that liberal elites failed to defend the 'common core'. Of course, the report goes on to ask readers to trust that these same elites can now implement an improved form of interculturalism, and asks readers to reject populist movements and parties. But why would any reader draw this conclusion? Why isn't the natural conclusion that citizens are right to distrust mainstream politicians, bureaucrats and other elites, and should look instead to populists to defend the 'common core'?

Interculturalists may think that they are defending diversity, but their crude anti-multiculturalist rhetoric may play into the hands of xenophobes who reject both multiculturalism and interculturalism. Since much of the anti-multiculturalist discourse in Europe is a thinly veiled form of racism and xenophobia, for the Council of Europe and UNESCO to also play the anti-multiculturalist card risks licensing and legitimating anti-diversity views. And indeed the rhetorical repudiation of multiculturalism by organisations like the COE and UNESCO seems to have done little if anything to actually stem the tide of xenophobia, or the rise of anti-immigrant political parties.[13] On the contrary, these forces now feel vindicated in their diagnosis, crowing 'we told you so', and insisting that only they can be trusted to tell the unvarnished truth, unlike the politically correct liberal elites who now concede multiculturalism's failure but who are still pushing interculturalism.

This is one example of a larger point – namely, that the risks of new narratives or rhetorics depend on how they interact with other narratives and rhetorics in the political domain. The 'interculturalism-as-remedy-for-failed-multiculturalism' narrative cohabits in public space with the 'populist-parties-as-remedy-for-failed-elites' narrative, and the interaction of the two can be toxic, at least if explicit efforts aren't made to prevent this. In my view, the 2008 Council of Europe report, far from preventing these toxic effects, practically invites them.

In order to prevent these perverse unintended effects, we need to think in a more systematic way about the larger rhetorical field, and how narratives of interculturalism or multiculturalism interact with other narratives in the field. I cannot provide this sort of systematic analysis here, but I will briefly suggest some of the main issues that such an analysis would need to consider.

---

[13] Ambrose and Mudde (2015) argue that firm state commitment to multiculturalism in Canada helps explain the absence of far-right parties.

167

Mapping the rhetorical field

The rhetorical field of contemporary Western societies is dense and complicated, and singling out individual elements from that field always involves a simplification. But I would argue that narratives of interculturalism/multiculturalism need to be understood, first and foremost, as existing in intimate relations with narratives of liberal democratic nationhood. It is the interaction of these narratives, I suggest, that most directly determines the prospects for pro-diversity policies.

So let me begin with how I see this interaction in the case of multiculturalism, and then consider whether interculturalism can offer a more constructive approach. Narratives of multiculturalism emerged at a particular time and space and, like all new narratives, were intended at least in part to solve some problem that seemed pressing. So what was the problem to which multiculturalism was offered as a possible solution?

The most plausible answer lies in the unusual way that contemporary liberal democratic politics is structured around ideas of nationhood. The contemporary world order is defined as an order of nation-states, each of which is the vehicle by which a distinctive nation or people exercises self-determination. Liberal democracy entered the world in conjunction with the rise of nation-states, and for a variety of reasons this link has proven to be durable. Liberal democracy and nationhood have 'elective affinities', as Margaret Canovan (1996) puts it, in part because nationhood helps to provide a stable basis for territorial boundaries and social solidarities that liberal democratic principles by themselves cannot provide.

However, we also know that this link between nationhood and liberal democracy creates systemic risks for all those who are not seen as belonging to the nation, including indigenous peoples, sub-state national groups and immigrants. Since they are not seen as members of the nation or people in whose name the state governs, and may indeed be seen as potentially disloyal fifth columns, they cannot be trusted to govern themselves or to share in the governing of the larger society. And this exclusion is typically then buttressed and justified by ideologies of racial inferiority or cultural backwardness. In short, while liberal democracy has benefited in important ways from its link with nationhood, minorities have often paid a high price. They have been faced with social stigmatisation and racialisation, at best offered a stark choice of assimilation or exclusion, and at worst subject to expulsion or genocide.

Multiculturalism emerged as one answer – or rather part of one answer – to this dilemma. Multiculturalism aims to mitigate the costs to minorities – particularly immigrant minorities – of the elective affinity between liberal democracy and nationhood.[14] If liberal democracy had not entered the world tied to ideas of nationhood, it is quite possible that we would not need multiculturalism, at least not in the form we know in the West. But in our historical situation, some remedy was required for the unjust and exclusionary consequences of the privileging of nationhood and its associated ideologies.

This genealogy helps to explain many of the dilemmas that confront both multiculturalism and interculturalism as narratives. On the one hand, the *justification* for multiculturalism rests at least in part on highlighting how nationhood has been exclusionary and unjust, and this in turn requires highlighting how a self-identified dominant nation has stigmatised various minorities. This justification presupposes that a certain kind of majority/minority cognitive schema is operative in society: multiculturalism is a response to the chronic problem that members of the majority nation in liberal democratic nation-states exclude and stigmatise minorities who are seen as non-nationals.

But of course the *goal* of multiculturalism is to overcome this chronic tendency, and to create a form of political community without exclusion or stigmatisation. And how can we achieve this? According to critics, multiculturalism's solution is to include and recognise minorities outside of the nation, as separate groups who live outside and alongside the nation, in 'parallel societies'. And this solution is then criticised as simply reproducing the very majority/minority schema that created the problem in the first place. We can see this interpretation of multiculturalism in the Council of Europe report, which refers to

> a new concept of social order known as multiculturalism. This advocated political recognition of what was perceived as the distinct ethos

---

[14] The remedy required for indigenous peoples takes a different form from that for immigrant groups, and in most countries these different remedies appear under different labels. 'Multiculturalism' is the label typically used in reference to immigrant groups, while other terms are used for indigenous peoples.

of minority communities on a par with the 'host' majority. While this was ostensibly a radical departure from assimilationism, in fact multiculturalism frequently shared the same, schematic conception of society set in opposition of majority and minority, differing only in endorsing separation of the minority from the majority rather than assimilation to it. (2008: 3.3, §53)

Similarly, when Sarkozy, Merkel and Cameron proclaimed that multiculturalism was a 'failure', they all defined it in precisely these terms – as the encouragement of separate societies parallel to the majority national society (Cameron 2011).

Was this ever really the goal of multiculturalism? No. This is another example of the crude caricatures of multiculturalism that Meer and Modood point out. There may be isolated cases where multiculturalism took this form of parallel societies. I think this is particularly true of countries such as Germany and the Netherlands where multiculturalism initially emerged in the context of guest-worker programmes, intended to encourage and enable temporary migrants to return home. In this 'returnist multiculturalism', the goal wasn't to make immigrants feel welcome and at home in their new country, but on the contrary to reiterate that their real home was in the country of origin to which they should return.[15] Surveys at the time showed that many guest-workers in the 1960s and 1970s did indeed plan to return home, and did not intend to put down roots. And while those expectations of return were gradually abandoned, the initial models of returnist multiculturalism were not systematically rethought to serve immigrants who were now acknowledged to be permanent residents and future citizens.

But this model of parallel societies was never the operative model of multiculturalism in most countries, where immigrants were from the start understood to be settling permanently. In these countries, multiculturalism was always seen as a way of staking a claim to belonging and to membership in the larger society, and as a mode of contributing to it. It was a way of staking a claim to citizenship in a multicultural nation-state – in effect, a claim to multicultural nationhood.

[15] As Karen Schönwälder notes in the case of Germany, mother-tongue education, where it does occur, was not introduced 'as a minority right but in order to enable guest worker children to reintegrate in their countries of origin' (2010: 160).

Some commentators have claimed that the very idea of multi-cultural nationhood is incoherent, but I think we now have over-whelming evidence that it is indeed possible to develop conceptions of national identity in which multiculturalism is a defining feature of the nation. Much has been written about this in the Canadian and Australian cases, but also in Britain, including in Scotland.[16]

Viewed this way, the Council of Europe's critique of multi-culturalism rests on conflating the diagnosis and the remedy. Multiculturalists do tend to perceive a majority/minority schema in operation in society, underpinned by ideologies and practices of nationhood, but this is their diagnosis of the problem, not their solution. Their remedy is precisely to create a new form of mul-ticultural nationhood that avoids this schema, by creating forms of multicultural citizenship that enable participation, belonging and contribution. That this is a possible aim of multiculturalism is never considered in the Council of Europe's report.

Still, to be fair, one might worry that multiculturalism's diagno-sis and remedy stand in some tension with each other. If multicul-turalism's diagnosis highlights the pervasiveness of the majority/minority schema, does that not, perhaps unintentionally, 'set in opposition' majority and minority, as the Council of Europe report claims, and thereby make it more difficult to achieve the remedy of multicultural nationhood?

This perhaps explains why defenders of interculturalism tend to downplay the impact of majoritarian nationalism on minorities, and to instead formulate the issue as primarily one of interpersonal contact within meso and micro settings. For many interculturalists, the task is to encourage more constructive forms of interaction across ethnic and religious lines, primarily at the local level and in civil society, as an effective means of reducing prejudice, and thereby reducing the appeal of populist nativism, and reaping the benefits of cultural diversity (see, for example, Zapata-Barrero 2011). And all of this can be achieved without even entering into heated and emotional debates about nationhood – debates that all too often get captured by right-wing nativists and populists. We can win arguments for intercultural neighbourhoods without having to win arguments for multicultural nationhood, and perhaps the prospects for the former are better if we don't even raise the latter.

---

[16] See Kernerman 2005, Uberoi 2008, Levey 2008, and Hussain and Miller 2006.

This contrast between an interculturalist focus on local-level interactions and a multiculturalist focus on state policy can of course be overdrawn. As Meer and Modood note, multiculturalism has always operated at both levels, and interculturalists rarely, if ever, explicitly disavow the need to reform state conceptions and practices of nationhood. Still, there is at least a rhetorical difference in the relative emphasis and priority attached to these two levels, and this raises an interesting strategic judgement. Is it better, rhetorically, to highlight or to obscure the relationship between multiculturalism and nationhood?

I have elsewhere argued that to achieve justice, we need both intercultural citizens, who are able to interact constructively with their co-citizens across ethnic and religious lines, and multicultural nation-states, which conceptualise nationhood (and hence national sovereignty, national identity, national interest and so on) in multicultural terms (Kymlicka 2003). Neither level is sufficient on its own. I won't repeat that argument, and in any event the issue here is not whether both are required in the long term, but about rhetorical emphasis. Is it better to emphasise bottom-up, local, civil-society-based projects of intercultural interaction, as interculturalists imply, and save state-centred projects of redefining multicultural nationhood for later? Or will local projects of intercultural interaction always be fragile in the absence of an explicit state commitment to redefining nationhood?

I am not aware of any systematic studies that would enable us to draw confident conclusions about the merits of these different strategies. So let me simply raise two worries about the interculturalist strategy. The first is that interculturalism offers a rather tepid and apolitical diagnosis of the problem facing minorities. Rather than diagnosing the problem in terms of the deep structures of liberal democratic nationhood, as they are institutionalised in the nation-state and sedimented in state-sponsored national identities, interculturalists tend to diagnose the problem as one of individual capacities and dispositions to interact across ethnic and religious lines. It may well be true that we would all be better off, individually and collectively, if we were more able and willing to engage in intercultural dialogue, but it's difficult to see why this is an issue of justice or collective obligation. Multiculturalism, by contrast, highlights the problem in the state-sponsored privileging of nationhood, and in the exclusions this has entailed, which makes clear why it is a matter of justice and collective responsibility.

And this raises the second concern, which is that interculturalism not only renders invisible the privileging of nationhood, but effectively consigns control over nationhood to conservative and populist forces. Many interculturalists seem to believe that arguing over nationhood is doomed to fail, as if nationhood is a field that is inherently tilted against the forces of diversity. They therefore seek a field of possible intervention, such as neighbourhoods and cities, where progress can be made without triggering anxieties about nationhood.

I fully understand this desire to avoid triggering anxieties about nationhood. Studies have repeatedly shown that when national identities are 'primed', people's attitudes to minorities and diversity grow harsher.[17] But the net result is not just to defer debates about redefining nationhood, but to leave the entire field of nationhood to the forces of populism. And this is indeed what seems to be happening across much of Europe. The progressive defenders of diversity are fighting for intercultural neighbourhoods and intercultural cities, while conservatives are defining the agenda around national security, national citizenship, national solidarity and national identity – all in ways that systematically marginalise and stigmatise minorities.[18]

I'm sceptical that we can make enduring progress on diversity unless or until we explicitly tackle ideas of nationhood and show how multiculturalism (or interculturalism) can be a constitutive feature of nationhood. Nationhood is too powerful a force to be ignored, and too dangerous a force to be left in the hands of populists. Figuring out how to redefine nationhood in a multicultural direction is a huge task, and requires careful conceptual analysis

[17] For example, studies have compared two randomly selected groups who are asked their attitudes towards immigrants. One group is asked, 'Do you think immigrants are responsible for increased crime?' The other group is asked the same question, but with national identity primed – for example, they are asked, 'You are Dutch: do you think immigrants are responsible for increased crime?' These are called 'mere mention' studies, and they show that the mere mention of national identity typically triggers greater antipathy to immigrants (although, interestingly, this effect is not found in Canada, see Breton 2013). Given these studies, it is understandable to seek a forum for discussing diversity that does not bring nationhood to the front of the mind.

[18] Consider the rise of 'welfare chauvinism' – excluding immigrants from the protection of the national welfare state. It is difficult to see how this can be countered by interculturalist tropes.

and public policy analysis, as well as symbolic and rhetorical changes.[19] But I see no alternative if we wish to make durable reforms that support diversity and pluralism.

Conclusion

Faced with growing public disenchantment, new strategies are required to revive the flagging political project of diversity in Europe and elsewhere. One such strategy is to build a new political narrative in which interculturalism emerges from the failed extremes of assimilation and multiculturalism. In their work, Meer and Modood have challenged this narrative as historically inaccurate and conceptually shoddy. In this chapter, I have tried to shift the focus, and to evaluate this narrative as a rhetorical strategy rather than a social scientific analysis. Can this new narrative work to energise pro-diversity forces and to undercut support for populism? I have not offered a definitive answer, but have suggested that the progressive potential of the interculturalist narrative will depend heavily on how it interacts with narratives about populism and nationhood. And to date, I fear, the interculturalist narrative has too often left untouched exclusionary narratives of nationhood, and unintentionally legitimised populist narratives about the untrustworthy nature of mainstream elites on issues of diversity. The search for new narratives of diversity will have to continue.

---

[19] One important task here is to evaluate the recent explosion of 'civic integration' policies (Goodman 2010), to see which (if any) are compatible with ideas of multicultural nationhood. While many commentators have assumed that civic integration policies and multiculturalism policies are inherently at odds, this assumption rules out of court precisely what we should be looking for: namely, innovative ways of linking multiculturalism and nationhood. For some preliminary reflections on how to incorporate multiculturalist thinking into civic integration policies (and vice versa), see Kymlicka 2012, and for the contrasts between enabling and prohibitive forms of civic integration, see Goodman 2010, Adamo 2008, Peucker 2008 and Paquet 2012.

Appendix: Multiculturalism Policy Index for 21 OECD Countries, 1980, 2000, 2010

	1980	2000	2010
Australia	5	8	8
Austria	0	1	1.5
Belgium	1	3	5.5
Canada	5	7.5	7.5
Denmark	0	0.5	0
Finland	0	1.5	6
France	1	2	2
Germany	0	2	2.5
Greece	0.5	0.5	2.5
Ireland	1	1.5	3
Italy	0	1.5	1
Japan	0	0	0
Netherlands	2.5	5.5	2
New Zealand	2.5	5	5.5
Norway	0	0	3.5
Portugal	1	2	3.5
Spain	0	1	3.5
Sweden	3	5	7
Switzerland	0	1	1
United Kingdom	2.5	5.5	5.5
United States	3	3	3
Average Europe	0.7	2.1	3.1
Average All	1.29	2.71	3.48

Note: Countries could receive a total score of 8, one for each of the following eight policies: (a) constitutional, legislative or parliamentary affirmation of multiculturalism at the central and/or regional and municipal levels and the existence of a government ministry, secretariat or advisory board to implement this policy in consultation with ethnic communities; (b) the adoption of multiculturalism in the school curriculum; (c) the inclusion of ethnic representation/sensitivity in the mandate of public media or media licensing; (d) exemptions from dress codes; (e) allowing of dual citizenship; (f) the funding of ethnic group organisations or activities; (g) the funding of bilingual education or mother-tongue instruction; and (h) affirmative action for disadvantaged immigrant groups. Source: Multiculturalism Policy Index, <http://www.queensu.ca/mcp> (last accessed 10 June 2015).

References

Adamo, S. (2008), 'Northern Exposure: The New Danish Model of Citizenship Test', *International Journal on Multicultural Societies*, 10 (1), 10–28.

Ambrose, E., and C. Mudde (2015), 'Canadian Multiculturalism and the Absence of the Far Right', *Nationalism and Ethnic Politics*, 21, 213–36.

Banting, K., and W. Kymlicka (2006), *Multiculturalism and the Welfare State: Recognition and Redistribution in Contemporary Democracies*, Oxford: Oxford University Press.

Banting, K., and W. Kymlicka (2013), 'Is There Really a Retreat from Multiculturalism Policies? New Evidence from the Multiculturalism Policy Index', *Comparative European Politics*, 11 (5), 577–98.

Barrett, M. (ed.) (2013), *Interculturalism and Multiculturalism: Similarities and Differences*, Strasbourg: Council of Europe.

Breton, C. (2013), 'Priming National Identity and its Impact on Attitudes Towards Immigration and Multiculturalism', Toronto: Environics Institute, available at http://www.environicsinstitute.org/news-events/news-events/new-study-shows-national-identity-in-english-canada-compatible-with-inclusive-view-of-immi gration (last accessed 15 January 2016).

Cameron, D. (2011), 'Speech at the Munich Security Conference', 5 February 2011, available at <https://www.gov.uk/government/speeches/pms-speech-at-munich-security-conference> (last accessed 11 June 2015).

Canovan, M. (1996), *Nationhood and Political Theory*, Cheltenham: Edward Elgar.

Council of Europe (COE), Committee of Ministers (2008), *Living Together as Equals in Dignity: White Paper on Intercultural Dialogue*, Strasbourg: Council of Europe.

Goodman, S. (2010), 'Integration Requirements for Integration's Sake? Identifying, Categorizing and Comparing Civic Integration Policies', *Journal of Ethnic and Migration Studies*, 36 (5), 753–72.

Grillo, R. (2007), 'An Excess of Alterity? Debating Difference in a Multicultural Society', *Ethnic and Racial Studies*, 30 (6), 978–98.

Hussain, A., and W. Miller (2006), *Multicultural Nationalism: Islamophobia, Anglophobia, and Devolution*, Oxford: Oxford University Press.

Kernerman, G. (2005), *Multicultural Nationalism: Civilizing Difference, Constituting Community*, Vancouver: UBC Press.

Kesler, C., and I. Bloemraad (2010), 'Does Immigration Erode Social Capital? The Conditional Effects of Immigration-Generated Diversity on Trust, Membership, and Participation across 19 Countries, 1981–2000', *Canadian Journal of Political Science*, 43 (2), 319–47.

Koopmans, R., I. Michalowski and S. Waibel (2012), 'Citizenship Rights for Immigrants: National Political Processes and Cross-National Convergence in Western Europe, 1980–2008', *American Journal of Sociology*, 117 (4), 1,202–45.

Kymlicka, W. (2003), 'Multicultural States and Intercultural Citizens', *Theory and Research in Education*, 1 (2), 147–69.

Kymlicka, W. (2007), *Multicultural Odysseys*, Oxford: Oxford University Press.

Kymlicka, W. (2010), 'Testing the Liberal Multiculturalist Hypothesis: Normative Theories and Social Science Evidence', *Canadian Journal of Political Science*, 43 (2), 257–71.

Kymlicka, W. (2012), 'Multiculturalism: Success, Failure, and the Future', in

Migration Policy Institute (ed.), *Rethinking National Identity in the Age of Migration*, Berlin: Verlag Bertelsmann Stiftung, pp. 33–78.

Levey, G. B. (2008), *Political Theory and Australian Multiculturalism*, New York: Berghahn Books.

Meer, N., and T. Modood (2012), 'How Does Interculturalism Contrast with Multiculturalism?', *Journal of Intercultural Studies*, 33 (2), 175–96.

Modood, T. (2007), *Multiculturalism: A Civic Idea*, Cambridge: Polity Press.

Paquet, M. (2012), 'Beyond Appearances: Citizenship Tests in Canada and the UK', *Journal of International Migration and Integration*, 13 (2), 243–60.

Peucker, M. (2008), 'Similar Procedures, Divergent Functions: Citizenship Tests in the United States, Canada, Netherlands and United Kingdom', *International Journal on Multicultural Societies*, 10 (2), 240–61.

Schönwälder, K. (2010), 'Germany: Integration Policy and Pluralism in a Self-Conscious Country of Immigration', in S. Vertovec and S. Wessendorf (eds), *The Multiculturalism Backlash: European Discourses, Policies and Practices*, London: Routledge, pp. 152–69.

Tavan, G. (2012), 'No Going Back? Australian Multiculturalism as a Path-Dependent Process', *Australian Journal of Political Science*, 47 (4), 547–61.

Uberoi, V. (2008), 'Do Policies of Multiculturalism Change National Identities?', *Political Quarterly*, 79, 404–17.

UNESCO (2008), *Investing in Cultural Diversity and Intercultural Dialogue: World Report on Cultural Diversity*, Paris: UNESCO.

Vertovec, S., and S. Wessendorf (eds) (2010), *The Multiculturalism Backlash: European Discourses, Policies and Practices*, London: Routledge.

Wright, M., and I. Bloemraad (2012), 'Is There a Trade-off between Multiculturalism and Socio-Political Integration? Policy Regimes and Immigrant Incorporation in Comparative Perspective', *Perspectives on Politics*, 10 (1), 77–95.

Zapata-Barrero, R. (2011), 'Anti-Immigration Populism: Can Local Intercultural Policies Close the Space?', Discussion Paper, London: Policy Network, <http://www.policy-network.net/uploads/media/160/7726.pdf > (last accessed 23 June 2015).

8

Models of Diversity in the Americas: Avenues for Dialogue and Cross-Pollination

Ana Solano-Campos

In the last decades, scholars in Canada and Europe have engaged in widespread debates about the distinctive features of multicultural-ism and interculturalism. At the same time, discussions about these distinctions have also been ongoing in Latin America,[1] but these are not as widely documented in the anglophone and francophone literature. In this chapter, I argue that looking at intercultural and multicultural orientations to diversity outside of North American and European contexts can both enrich and problematise con-versations about multiculturalism and interculturalism. First, I provide an overview of scholarly debates about multiculturalism and interculturalism in the Americas, with occasional references to the European context. Next, I explore Latin American discus-sions on intercultural and multicultural orientations to diversity, drawing connections and comparisons to the debates in Europe and Canada. Finally, I interrogate normative trends that largely prescribe and dichotomise models of diversity in all three settings – advocating for a contextual approach that locates diversity par-adigms along a diversity spectrum and identifying current and potential avenues for dialogue and cross-pollination.

---

[1] Although Latin American countries share a history of colonial rule and indige-nous legacies, they have developed along different *temporalidades* (temporalities) (Ansaldi 2001; Hopenhayn 2002), where a common history is expressed in quite distinctive ways or *singularidades* (singularities). It is not within the scope of this chapter to provide a comprehensive account of how intercultural and multicultural approaches to diversity have developed in all of the countries in the Latin American context, but to provide a broad overview of intercultural and multicultural scholarly thought across the region.

The multicultural-intercultural dichotomy

Contemporary debates about diversity in European and North American countries take place in the context of a discursive shift from multiculturalism to interculturalism. Banting and Kymlicka explain,

> In much of the western world, and particularly in Europe, there is a widespread perception that multiculturalism has 'failed' and that governments who once embraced a multicultural approach to diversity are turning away, adopting a strong emphasis on civic integration. (2012: 3)

Although there is a documented 'retreat from the use of the term "multiculturalism" in political discourse' in Europe and Canada (Barrett 2013: 22; Kymlicka 2012), research from the Multiculturalism Policy Index – which monitored the evolution of multiculturalism in twenty-one Western democracies – indicates that 'the larger picture in Europe is one of stability and expansion of multicultural policies in the first decade of the 21st century' (Banting and Kymlicka 2012: 18).

In Latin America, where intercultural orientations to diversity have dominated, there has been a shift toward multiculturalist rhetoric *and* policies. However, across the continent, normative approaches that prescribe and dichotomise interculturalism and multiculturalism have led these debates: scholars have positioned multicultural and intercultural orientations to diversity in opposition to – and competition with – each other. In the following sections I contextualise the nature and evolution of these debates.

MULTICULTURALISM IN THE AMERICAS

In the United States and Canada, scholars have both interrogated and advocated the merits of multiculturalism to best address the needs of immigrant and ethno-cultural groups in each country. Multiculturalism is often presented as 'a particular kind of policy approach that may be used for the management of culturally diverse societies' (Barrett 2013: 16). Scholars have identified and proposed various theories of multiculturalism – among them cultural studies (Hall and du Gay 2003), post-colonial (Bhabha 2002), liberal (Kymlicka 2006; Levy 2003), and communitarian (Taylor 1993) – each communicating different perspectives on the status of collective versus individual rights of ethno-cultural and immigrant groups (Arriarán Cuéllar and Hernández Alvídrez 2010). Scholars have also highlighted that multiculturalism is highly influenced by the particular context in which it is implemented. For Meer and Modood, 'the idea of multiculturalism might be said to have a "chameleonic" quality' (2012: 179). Similarly, Barrett argues that multiculturalism varies 'across countries' and also 'within countries over time' (2013: 19).

United States multiculturalism is often linked to the civil rights movement and to the struggle of African-Americans for equality in the 1960s and 1970s (Banks 1994; Sleeter 1996; Gay 2010). It is also associated with a 'modern' strand of education – multicultural education – that attends to issues of oppression, resistance, social justice and cultural democracy in school policy and curriculum (Meer and Modood 2012). In reference to the United States context, May and Sleeter (2010) argue that a new form of multiculturalism, 'critical multiculturalism', 'has emerged over the last decade as a direct challenge to liberal or benevolent forms of multicultural education'. They contend that 'by integrating and advancing various critical theoretical threads such as anti-racist education, critical race theory, and critical pedagogy, critical multiculturalism has offered a fuller analysis of oppression and institutionalization of unequal power relations in education'.

In Canada, the emergence of multiculturalism has been linked to various historical events, among them the arrival of older immigrants of non-British origin during the twentieth century who 'dethroned' the traditional Canadian 'anglo-normative understanding' (Taylor 2012: 417); the influx of immigrants from developing countries during the 1960s and 1970s (Joshee 2004); and 'the rise of a nationalist and secessionist movement in French-speaking Quebec' (Meer and Modood 2012: 180). Unlike in the United States, multiculturalism in the Canadian context is understood as a public policy (Castles 2004: 25). Canada was one of the first countries in the Americas to enforce multiculturalism at the legislative level, with the creation of the Official Languages Act in 1969, the Policy of Multiculturalism in 1971, and the Multiculturalism Act in 1988. For Taylor, 'multiculturalism became a marker of the new Canadian political identity, and Canadians . . . [spread] the word internationally about their own success and its status as paradigm and model for everyone' (2012: 417). Over time, Canadian multiculturalism has stressed different aspects of diversity, evolving from a focus on plurality and citizenship in the 1950s and 1960s, an emphasis on identity, social justice and education in the 1970s and 1980s, and from the 1990s onwards highlighting social cohesion and peace education (Joshee 2004).

During the late 1960s, in the midst of increased immigration flows, the Canadian province of Quebec – where over 70 per cent of people are descendants from francophone settlers – demanded the rights to preserve their French culture and language. As Ghosh recounts, some Quebecers perceived multiculturalist policies as 'an imposition by English Canada' (2011: 7) and tried to retain their sovereignty by introducing French language legislation and a policy of interculturalism in 1977. Ghosh explains that

> While Canadian multiculturalism is built on the assumption of not pointing to a dominant culture, interculturalism in Quebec is based on the understanding of the predominance of francophone culture: to build and integrate other cultural communities into a common public culture based on the French language, while respecting diversity. (2011: 7)

Taylor argues that interculturalism, with its emphasis on integration rather than on the recognition of difference, was most appropriate for the Quebec context because Quebecers have to 'ensure that the integration [of immigrants] takes place in French rather than English' (2012: 417).

In reference to the Canadian context, scholars have put forth hard and soft claims for interculturalism's distinctiveness (Levey 2012), with the former encompassing definitions of the two paradigms as fundamentally different (Bouchard 2011) and the latter viewing the distinctiveness between the two paradigms as a matter of emphasis (Taylor 2012). For example, Taylor argues that both multiculturalism and interculturalism are 'subspecies' from a common trunk and that their main difference 'concerns rather the story that we tell about where we are coming from and where we are going' (2012: 413).

Other scholars, such as Maxwell, Waddington, McDonough, Cormier and Schwimmer (2012), highlight the similarities while at the same time positively comparing interculturalism to multiculturalism. Maxwell et al. argue that interculturalism addresses multiculturalism's limitations. For example, they contend that interculturalism and multiculturalism are 'conceptual cousins' (2012: 431) because both promote integration, increase intercultural awareness, embrace cultural diversity as a characteristic and asset, reject assimilationist and racist tendencies, and encourage political participation of ethnic groups. Yet, using the metaphors of 'the mosaic' and 'the story' to refer to multiculturalism and interculturalism respectively, they claim that whereas multiculturalism 'capitalizes on the promotion and valorization of cultural diversity as a political end in itself', interculturalism 'regards the integration of new citizens as part of a dynamic, open-ended process of transforming a common societal culture through dialogue, mutual understanding, and intercultural contact' (2012: 432). For Maxwell et al. Canadian interculturalism 'focuses on identifying and implementing means by which to encourage cultural and religious groups to enter into a national dialogue' (2012: 432). They state that interculturalism has three important elements that differentiate it from multiculturalism: an emphasis on dialogue to build a common culture, an establishment of sociological asymmetry in which newcomers and citizens take on different roles for integration and acceptance of each other, and the creation of a moral, legal, civic contract for immigrants.

On the other hand, Meer and Modood contend that interculturalism is not an 'updated version' (2012: 177) of multiculturalism and critique positive comparisons of interculturalism to multiculturalism, particularly in regard to what they identified as the four main claims in those comparisons: (1) interculturalism's emphasis on dialogue; (2) its focus on the group rather than the individual; (3) its commitment to social cohesion; and (4) its critique of illiberal cultural practices. Meer and Moddod maintain that these characteristics, which are often attributed to interculturalism, are also present in multiculturalism, and that, in fact, 'multiculturalism presently surpasses interculturalism as a political orientation' (2012: 192). The nature of this discussion becomes more complex when we ask, as does Dussel, 'what happens when these multiculturalism discourses, predominantly performed by North American and other Anglo-Saxon scholars, are restaged in different national settings, which have their own ways of dealing with difference within the nation-states?' (2001: 96).

The Latin American debates

Across Latin America, *interculturalidad* has arguably been the predominant diversity paradigm. Latin American academic debates have questioned the merits of multiculturalism in contrast to those of *interculturalidad*. Scholars have focused on whether multiculturalism fits Latin America's history of colonialism and racial hybridity (Maldonado Ledezma 2011; Tubino 2002; Walsh 2001; Williamson 2004) – which *interculturalidad* presumably does – and examined multiculturalism's perceived neoliberal underpinnings (Hale 2006; Warren 2013). Whereas in Europe and anglophone/francophone America there has been a rhetorical departure from multiculturalism, in many Latin American countries multiculturalist discourses are on the rise (Arriarán Cuéllar and Hernández Alvídrez 2010; Wieviorka 2014).

Latin American scholars define *interculturalidad* as a prescriptive rather than a descriptive term, a political democratic project with various social dimensions (Mendoza 2011; Dietz 2009, 2012; López 1997). A common theme in most definitions of *interculturalidad* is its focus on creating 'dialogic equitable relations among members of different cultural universes' (Godenzzi Alegre 1996: 15). Yet, there is not one simple or agreed-upon definition of *interculturalidad* among scholars, particularly because *interculturalidad* in the Latin American context is conceived as a eutopia or work in progress (Godenzzi Alegre 1996; Walsh 2001; Gómez and Hernández 2010).

THE REIGN OF *INTERCULTURALIDAD*

One of the main arguments in favour of *interculturalidad* is that it encapsulates the cultural clash and racial miscegenation that ensued upon the conquest and colonisation of the region. Comprising several geographical, ethnic, linguistic and epistemological clusters, Latin America was already a diverse setting before the arrival of the Europeans. Mesoamerican and Andean peoples, the former inhabitants of the region that spread from Mexico to Costa Rica (Carrasco and Sessions 1998) and the latter residents of today's Colombia, Ecuador, Peru, Bolivia, Argentina and Chile (McEwan 2006), were not monolithic groups. Historians Carrasco and Sessions explain, 'Mesoamerica was a diverse space and time

... There were several hundred ethnic groups among the natives of Mesoamerica who spoke many different languages' (1998: 25). This statement can be expanded to the Andean world as well.

The cultural and linguistic diversity also extended to indigenous epistemologies. Aikman (1996) makes clear that in the past as well as today, 'there is no single coherent body of indigenous knowledge. Indigenous peoples do not comprise one homogenous epistemological and ontological alternative to the Western educational paradigm encountered in schools. On the contrary, they present a diverse panorama of philosophies and world views' ('Indigenous Conceptions of Education and Intercultural Education' section, paragraph 7). With the conquest, the diversity of the region grew in new, complex ways, incorporating Eurocentric hierarchies and power dynamics that were enforced by the Spanish, Portuguese, French, Dutch and British colonisers.

In addition to reflecting the indigenous and colonial legacy of the region, *interculturalidad* aligns with the political discourses of *mestizaje*, transculturation, and *indigenismo*, discourses that perpetuate ideas of racial hybridity. Now a contested concept, *mestizaje*, the idea of racial mixing or miscegenation (Wade 2005), was championed by political leaders such as José Martí (1891) and José Vasconcelos (1925) as a narrative of racial unity and co-operation, becoming a marker of national identity for many people in Latin American countries. Immortalised in art and literature, the narrative of *mestizaje* led political, economic and social conventions across the region. It was a narrative that Miller (2004: 15) posits 'could be enlisted in the development of a regional identity that both recognized internal differences and unified Latin America in its distinction from Europe and the United States'. Related to the concept of *mestizaje* is the political ideology of *indigenismo*, 'an effort by Europeans or their American-born descendants (criollos) to represent an indigenous "other"' (Marentes 2013).

Later on, Ortiz introduced the concept of 'transculturation' as a multidirectional process of cultural transfer, in opposition to the unidirectional idea of 'acculturation'. Transculturation, he described, was 'the complex process of adjustment and re-creation – cultural, literary, linguistic, and personal – that allow for new, vital, and viable configurations to arise out of the clash of cultures and the violence of colonial and neocolonial appropriations' (1940: 2). The concept of 'transculturation' was initially used in reference to Cuban society. It was later expanded by Rama (1982) to the Latin American reality, and has been further developed and debated by other scholars (Trigo 1996; García Canclini 2004).

Interculturalidad is also said to problematise political discourses about the indigenous subaltern. *Interculturalidad*'s origins are found at the centre of movements of agency and resistance surrounding – and emerging in – indigenous communities, particularly in Mexico and the Andean region (Aikman 1996; Hamel 2008; López 2009; Gómez and Hernández 2010).

Since the 1970s, indigenous movements in Latin American countries – predominantly those countries with larger indigenous populations, like Mexico, Ecuador, Bolivia, Guatemala, Venezuela and Peru – established the cornerstone for educational policies and practices that promoted the linguistic and cultural identities of indigenous groups. At the core of indigenous movements lies a statement about the role of language identity and linguistic practices – in addition to political participation and territorial rights – as crucial expressions of citizenship. Such is the case of Peru, Bolivia, Paraguay and Colombia, where indigenous languages have gained legitimate and, in some cases, co-official or official status along with Spanish.

The dialogic and linguistic dimension of *interculturalidad* is strongly present in education policy and practice – initially via *Educación Indígena Bilingüe* (Indigenous Bilingual Education), then through *Educación Bilingüe Bicultural* (Bicultural Bilingual Education), and later on through *Educación Intercultural Bilingüe* (Intercultural Bilingual Education) (López 2009). Hornberger states that 'the earliest use of the term "intercultural" in Latin America may have been in Venezuela's 1979 bilingual intercultural education policy' and 'in a [1980] meeting of indigenists in Mexico' (2000: 178) – around the same time that increasing attention from organisations like the United Nations granted greater regional and international recognition to interculturalism. However, Aman argues that 'when adopted by the government, *interculturalidad* came merely to signify bilingual education, and the decolonial dimension, which was profoundly emphasized by the indigenous movements in their articulations of the concept, was effectively erased' (2014: 13).

In the 1990s a regional and political movement that scholar Patricio Ortiz (2009: 93) refers to as the 'Indigenous Emergence' continued to encourage 'indigenous people across the Americas to begin deconstructing Western paradigms and (re)constructing Indigenous ones'. Since then, several scholars have extensively studied the way in which individual Latin American nation-states have incorporated *interculturalidad* in their educational policies and practices (Zimmerman 1997; Moya 1997, 1998; Hamel 2008; López 1997, 2009; López and Küper 1999; López and Giménez 2001; Cunningham 2001; Herdoíza-Estévez and Lenk 2010; López and Sapón 2011; Maldonado Ruiz 2011).

Latin American scholars, particularly supporters of *interculturalidad*, have frequently critiqued North American and European discourses of multiculturalism (Tubino 2002; Maldonado Ledezma 2011). Discourses of *interculturalidad* have been often intertwined with dominant European intercultural discourses, specifically because of the influence of organisations like UNESCO. However, the differences between Canadian, European and Latin American intercultural paradigms have rarely been debated (Aman 2014).

Conceptually, *interculturalidad* shares many characteristics with Canadian and European interculturalism: an emphasis on dialogue, relationship-building, conflict resolution, universal values and democracy. This is, in part, because 'gran parte de la filosofía de nuestro continente se ha desarrollado y se desarrolla aun en estrecho dialogo con la filosofía europea' ('a great part of our continent's philosophy has been developed and continues to develop in close dialogue with European philosophy') (Fornet-Betancourt 2004: 28; my translation). In addition, there has been constant influence from international organisations in the Latin American region that promote intercultural agendas.

However, *interculturalidad* is different from Quebecan interculturalism and European interculturality in two important ways. First, Latin American *interculturalidad* emerged as a response not to post-immigrant social formations but to colonial and post-colonial dynamics. Second, although *interculturalidad* might traditionally be associated with modernity, it can also 'be theorized as an act of resistance to the vestiges of colonialism, with the purpose of delinking from the rhetoric of modernity and the logic of coloniality' (Aman 2014: 8). For Aman, unlike *interculturalidad*, European interculturality 'continues to be written in the imperial languages, as UNESCO reiterates the imperative to embrace their concept of universally shared values' (2014: 23).

INTERCULTURALISING MULTICULTURALISM

Many Latin American scholars seem to align with European and North American trends to positively compare interculturalism to multiculturalism. However, their impetus is not new and does not necessarily come from European discourses about failed multiculturalism. Instead, rejection of the multiculturalist rhetoric can be considered an anti-neocolonial or anti-neoliberal narrative.

Some Latin American scholars see multiculturalism as lacking an integrative element to breach differences among various cultural groups (López 1997; Cunningham 2001; Walsh 2001; Tubino 2001, 2002; García Canclini 2004). For instance, they contrast multiculturalism with *interculturalidad* as focusing on recognition rather than dialogue, as encouraging affirmative action rather than transformative action, as creating parallel societies rather than integrated societies, as promoting tolerance but not *convivencia*. In fact, Tubino has spoken of the need to 'interculturalize multiculturalism' (2002: 63). These scholars seem to actively distance themselves from the discourse of multiculturalism because it is often perceived as an imposition from the North America canon. For example, Maldonado Ledezma warns that 'to apply [multicultural] postulates to other multicultural contexts implies significant challenges and theoretical deficiencies that arise from borrowing approaches originated in contexts foreign to our realities; thus, their uncritical application becomes inadequate' (2011: 60; my translation).

Maldonado Ledezma adds that *interculturalidad* is 'a proposal that seeks to overcome the obvious differences of a theoretical standpoint – multiculturalism – created in Western social contexts different to ours, with extremely different histories, and particular challenges that need to be addressed, that are profoundly divergent from indigenous concerns in Latin America' (2011: 63; my translation). In addition, Walsh sustains that *interculturalidad* reflects the Latin American experience of *mestizaje* as 'part of the reality and of the cultural resistance' in the region (2001: 6), something that multiculturalist theories do not include. Williamson points out that even if 'multiculturalism is understood as a framework that allows for a better study of reality, it cannot be used [in Latin America] as a political statement' (2004: 18).

However, Viaña, Tapia and Walsh have pointed out that

interculturalidad 'fue asumiendo un sentido socioestatal de buro-cratización' ('has taken on a bureaucratising socio-statal sense'), making it 'parte del aparato de control y de la política educativa estatal' ('part of the control apparatus and of the state educational policy') (2010: 81; my translation). Critics of *interculturalidad* argue that it 'lacks a political project or vision' (Arriarán Cuéllar and Hernández Alvídrez 2010: 100; my translation), which multi-culturalism is presumed to possess. Not only that, Arriarán Cuéllar and Hernández Alvídrez claim that 'contrary to what is com-monly stated, we are witnessing a transition from the intercultural paradigm to multiculturalism' (2010: 87; my translation).

The Multicultural Turn in Latin America

Although multiculturalism is commonly thought of as a Western European and North American political discourse (Dussel 2001; Wieviorka 2014), the last two decades have brought about an increased interest in and influence of multiculturalism in Latin America (Arriarán Cuéllar and Hernández Alvídrez 2010; Wieviorka 2014). Wade studied the multicultural policies that have taken place in Latin America in the last twenty years and looked at various arguments to explain this shift. He found that – since the early 1990s – international organisations like the World Bank and the United Nations have shown an 'increased interest in the social inclusion of marginalised groups in general and of indigenous and afro-Latin populations in particular' (2006: 69; my translation). This has prompted intra-national and international pressure (Van Cott 2000) to align with democratic and human rights principles policed by those organisations (Wade 2006). Other arguments that might explain the shift towards multiculturalist policies are state interests to 'use difference as a new form of government' (Wade 2006: 69, as in Gros 1997; my translation) – in contrast to seemingly problematic development programmes – and, to a lesser degree, 'the political mobilization of indigenous and black social movements' across the region (Wade 2006: 70).

Overall, scholars perceive multiculturalist policies in Latin America either as challenging the assimilationist rhetoric of *mes-tizaje* (Hopenhayn 2002; Wade 2013) or as perpetuating seem-ingly undesirable neoliberal discourses (Hale 2006; Warren 2013). Whereas the political and social discourses of *mestizaje* and transculturation embedded in *interculturalidad* are at the core of the national identity of Latin American masses, some scholars argue that these discourses have perpetuated the invisibilisation and denial of the indigenous and African 'other' (Hopenhayn 2002) and – in countries like Brazil – the myth of a racial democracy (Freyre 2003). For Hopenhayn, the rhetoric of *mestizaje*

> has been the assimilation (and acculturation) of indigenous and afro-Latin groups into the culture of the conquerors and colonizers—and later on, of republicans and modernists. Mestizaje can be understood as mediation, but also as subordination and renunciation; as a historical representation of the encounter, and as a dominant strategy in the absorption of the dominated . . . Mestizaje has served as a symbolic lever to institute a national 'ethos' as the ideology of the nation-state. (2002: III, paras 1–4; my translation)

In a way, *interculturalidad* has not been successful in addressing racial and religious exclusion, something that multiculturalism is presumed to do in the form of anti-racism and affirmative action policies. In that regard, it can be argued that *interculturalidad* in the Latin American context has to some extent been colour blind and colour mute – a by-product of the complexity of racial hybridity and colonial structures and of the challenges that come with trying to identify racial boundaries and label racial identities within that context.

Thus, scholars studying Latin American multiculturalism describe it as 'challenging ideologies of mestizaje or mestiçagem as the core identity of the nation' (Wade 2013: 212) and argue that 'the adoption of multicultural discourses entails recognition of the damaging effects of the assimilationist policies that accompanied mestizaje discourses' (Richards 2010: 65). For Arriarán Cuéllar and Hernández Alvídrez,

> The limitations of interculturalidad become increasingly evident as the insufficiency of the neoliberal democratic state comes to the surface, a state only willing to recognise all members of its society under the condition that they remain static in their inequality. (2010: 100; my translation)

Arriarán Cuéllar and Hernández Alvídrez explain that Latin American – and more specifically Mexican – multiculturalism has

189

kept its distance from Eurocentric foci in order to stay grounded in the reality of Latin American countries. They point out,

> Mexican multicultural thought in recent years is composed of four trends that are different from multiculturalism in the United States, Canada, and Europe: 1) the liberal multiculturalism of Fernando Salmerón (1993) and Leon Olive (1995); 2) Luis Villoro's (1998) communitarian multiculturalism; 3) the analogic pluralist multiculturalism of Mauricio Beuchot (1999); and 4) the baroque multiculturalism of Samuel Arriarán (2009). (Arriarán Cuéllar and Hernández Alvídrez 2010: 88–9; my translation)

However, Latin America's 'new' (Horton 2006) multiculturalism has been widely critiqued, often described negatively in the scholarly literature as state-led and state-sponsored – what Wade et al. (2014: 1) call 'official' multiculturalism – and it is perceived as a top-down policy tool for state-remaking influenced by international organisations and globalising forces. In a study on the Mapache nation in Chile and Argentina, Warren (2013: 243) explains that 'the state is engaged in what some have called "neo-liberal multiculturalism": visibly supporting indigenous activities that fit with state visions of the nation while criminalising others by applying anti-terrorist laws to indigenous activism'. In Bolivia and Guatemala, scholars talk about the idea of *indio permitido* ('authorised indian') (Hale 2006; McNeish 2008), a phrase originally borrowed by Hale from sociologist Silvia Rivera Cusicanqui which refers to 'how governments are using cultural rights to divide and domesticate indigenous movements' (2006: 17).

In Brazil, policies of affirmative action and university quotas established by the government to facilitate access of Afro-Brazilians to higher education programmes have been highly critiqued by scholars and met with logistical challenges that reveal the complexity of racial self-identification. As Loveman (2014: xii) states, 'Latin American national myths long celebrated the idea that distinctive peoples were formed through the mixture of races and thus a dissolution of racial differences.' Official ethno-racial classification was a common practice in post-colonial Latin America, but it was abandoned during the mid-twentieth century harvesting an official colourblindness. The practice has recently re-emerged following 'shifts in international criteria for how to be a modern nation and promote national progress' (Loveman 2014: 209). Genomic research (Wade 2013) is part of this social trend. However, the Brazilian experience is a testament to the difficulties of addressing the gaps seemingly left by *interculturalidad* with multicultural policies.

Although multiculturalism in Latin America is currently associated with prescriptive, neoliberal and state-led management of difference, grassroots multicultural movements like *Quilombismo* also exist. *Quilombos* were originally military communities in Africa; however, during the seventeenth century, the word 'quilombo' became associated with the community of Palmares in Brazil, a community of runaway enslaved people. Artist and scholar Abdias do Nascimento has studied extensively the history of *quilombos* and their significance in challenging dominant constructions of race in Latin America. He notes that *quilombos*, which were common in Suriname, Mexico, Venezuela, Cuba, Colombia, Jamaica and the United States, allowed African enslaved people 'to recover their liberty and human dignity through escape from captivity, organizing viable free societies in Brazilian territory' (1990: 182). He explains that 'Quilombismo, an anti-imperialist struggle, identifies itself with Pan-Africanism and sustains a radical solidarity with all peoples of the world who struggle against exploitation, oppression, and poverty, as well as with all inequalities motivated by race, colour, religion, or ideology' (1990: 185).

Contextualising models of diversity

The debate on the distinctions and merits of multiculturalism and interculturalism is ongoing and evolving. In the United States scholars have interrogated various iterations of multiculturalism. In the Canadian context, scholars have debated the characteristics of each model (Bouchard 2011; Levey 2012), some positively comparing interculturalism to multiculturalism (Taylor 2012; Maxwell et al. 2012) and some advocating to various degrees a multiculturalist approach (Meer and Modood 2012; Kymlicka 2012; Wieviorka 2012). In Latin America, discussions about multiculturalism and *interculturalidad* are taking place amidst increasing multicultural rhetoric and policies. However, in all settings, most scholars seem to perpetuate normative and dichotomous understandings of these diversity models. Definite statements about the superiority of one model over the other or about their incompatibility defeat the purpose that those models of diversity aim to address.

'Multiculturalism [and, I argue, interculturalism] is read differently in different contexts, according to particular histories and traditions' (Dussel 2001: 96). For Barrett, 'multiculturalism has taken so many different forms across countries and over time that it is vital to know which form of multiculturalism is being used in the comparison with interculturalism before the accuracy of any conclusions about the relationship between the two can be assessed' (2013: 21). The same is true of intercultural orientations to diversity.

Likewise, Mendoza argues that *interculturalidad*, interculturalism and multiculturalism each have 'distinctive connotations and meanings for its participating actors . . . Their differences have to do with the emphasis they place on relationships and dialogue, and with the prescriptive or descriptive/analytical character of the realities in which they are embedded' (2011: 314; my translation). 'In that sense,' she continues, 'the proposals for transformation and/or improvement of relationships, for attending to and recognising difference and diversity depend on those realities' (2011: 316; my translation). I agree with Mendoza that conversations about models of diversity in the Americas need to take place within 'the realities in which they are embedded' (2011: 316), as social processes responding to particular social realities.

Levey (2012) points out that the political claims for the distinctiveness between multiculturalism and interculturalism are a response to the semantic limitations that both terms have to describe and prescribe ways to address diversity in modern societies. A potential avenue to expand semantic reach would include exploring a multicultural-intercultural continuum, or diversity spectrum, rather than a multicultural/intercultural dichotomy. Bouchard's work can be useful in contextualising the diversity spectrum of different countries. He presents three levels of analysis, each nesting the next: paradigms, models and societal structure (2011: 443). He notes that a nation can adhere to one or more paradigms and 'that a paradigm can accommodate more than one model—and sometimes very different models' (2011: 444).

Other avenues would involve investigating the circulation of ideas about diversity through continental cross-pollinations and 'multicultural policy web[s]' (Joshee and Johnson 2007: 5). Joshee and Johnson have already pointed out the existence of an 'ongoing dialogue about diversity policies in Canada and the United States' (2007: 6) which has involved teaching, professional development and scholarship. For them,

> [C]onsidering policy in the context of a web of interrelated, ongoing policies (Oquist 2000) provides a powerful metaphor for thinking about and mapping multicultural education policies ... [T]his web has rings that represent the different levels at which policy is formally located, and cross-cutting threads that, while connected, are not necessarily harmonious. The points at which the threads cross the rings represent discrete policy texts, each of which is the result of historical struggles. Significantly, the web draws our attention to the open spaces between the threads. In these spaces individuals have some freedom to act in ways that support, extend, or undermine stated policy objectives and to introduce new ideas that may influence the policy discourse. The web metaphor acknowledges that the policy process is complex and involves actors from both within and outside the state. (2007: 6)

Less well-known are the webs of cross-pollination between Anglo-American or francophone countries and Spanish or Portuguese America. However, this does not mean they are non-existent, rather that they are mainly not easily accessible (McLaren 1998).

Concluding remarks

In this chapter, I have highlighted how debates about multiculturalism and interculturalism have developed differently in Latin America than in Canada and Europe. I pointed out that Latin American *interculturalidad* presents important differences from interculturalism and multiculturalism in North America and Europe. Specifically, *interculturalidad* emerged as a response not to post-immigrant social formations but to colonial and post-colonial dynamics, for which multiculturalism is perceived as inadequate. However – although contested – multicultural discourses in Latin America are rising, both as tools for the remaking of the state and as alternatives to the perceived assimilationist rhetoric of *mestizaje*.

After an examination of contemporary debates on the distinctions between multiculturalism and interculturalism in Europe and the Americas, I interrogated current tendencies to perpetuate normative and dichotomous understandings of diversity models rather than contextual and complementary perspectives. Instead, I proposed increasing current engagement in cross-continental and multilingual collaborations and examining the intersections of national trajectories, global processes and circulation of ideas from a comparative perspective. As conversations expand to include areas of the world like Latin America, Africa and Asia, scholars should keep in mind that the study of multiculturalism and inter-culturalism should not be carried out in English only (Macedo and Bartolomé 1999; Wieviorka 2014), nor should it be conducted in academic, disciplinary or geo-political bubbles (Conell 2007).

References

Aikman, S. (1996), 'The Globalisation of Intercultural Education and an Indigenous Venezuelan Response', *Compare*, 26 (2), 153–65.

Aman, R. (2014), 'Why Interculturalidad Is Not Interculturality: Colonial Remains and Paradoxes in Translation between Indigenous Social Movements and Supranational Bodies', *Cultural Studies*, 1–24, <http://dx.doi.org/10.1080/09502386.2014.899379> (last accessed 11 June 2015).

Ansaldi, W. (2001), 'La temporalidad mixta de América Latina, una expresión del Multiculturalismo', in H. Silveira (ed.), *Identidades comunitarias y democracy*, Madrid: Editorial Trotta, pp. 167–83, <http://www.catedras.fsoc.uba.ar/udishal/art/temporalidad.pdf> (last accessed 12 June 2015).

Arocena, F. (2006), 'Multiculturalismo, mestizaje y nacionalidad. Un studio comparado sobre Brasil, Bolivia, y Perú', *Barbarói*, 25 (2), 30–50, <http://online.unisc.br/seer/index.php/barbaroi/article/view/727/587> (last accessed 12 June 2015).

Arocha, J. (ed.) (2004), *Utopía para los excluidos: El multiculturalismo en África y América Latina*, Bogota: Universidad Nacional de Colombia, <http://www.bdigital.unal.edu.co/1561/> (last accessed 12 June 2015).

Arriarán Cuéllar, S. (2009), *Hermenéutica, multiculturalismo y educación*, Mexico City: Colegio de Posgraduados.

Arriarán Cuéllar, S., and E. Hernández Alvídrez (2010), 'El paradigma del multiculturalismo frente a la crisis de la educación intercultural', *Cuicuilco*, 48, 87–105.

Banks, J. (1994), *Multiethnic Education: Theory and Practice*, 3rd edn, Boston, MA: Allyn and Bacon.

Banks, J. (ed.) (2009), *The Routledge International Companion to Multicultural Education*, New York: Routledge.

Banting, K., and W. Kymlicka (2012), 'Is There Really a Backlash Against Multiculturalism Policies? New Evidence from the Multiculturalism Policy Index', GRITIM-UPF Working Paper Series, 14, <http://repositori.upf.edu/bitstream/handle/10230/17066/GRITIM%2814%29.pdf?sequence=1> (last accessed 19 June 2015).

Barrett, M. (ed.) (2013), *Interculturalism and Multiculturalism: Similarities and Differences*, Strasbourg: Council of Europe.

Becker, M. (1995), '*Indigenismo* and Indian Movements in Twentieth-Century Ecuador', *XIX Latin American Studies Association Congress*, <http://lanic.utexas.edu/project/lasa95/becker.html> (last accessed 12 June 2015).

Bernal, A. (2003), 'La educación entre la multiculturalidad y la interculturalidad', *Estudios sobre educación*, 4, 85–101.

Beuchot, M. (1999), 'Filosofía y barroco', in S. Arriarán Cuéllar and M. Beuchot (eds), *Filosofía, neobarroco y multiculturalismo*, Mexico City: Editorial Itaca.

Bhabha, H. (2002), *El lugar de la cultura*, Buenos Aires: Manantial.

Bouchard, G. (2011), 'What Is Interculturalism?', *McGill Law Journal*, 54, 435–68.

Carrasco, D., and S. Sessions (1998), *Daily Life of the Aztecs: People of the Sun and Earth*, Westport, CT: Greenwood Press.

Castles, S. (2004), 'Migration, Citizenship, and Education', in J. Banks (ed.), *Diversity and Citizenship Education: Global Perspectives*, San Francisco: Jossey-Bass, pp. 17–48.

Chasteen, J. C. (2001), *Born in Blood and Fire: A Concise History of Latin America*, New York: W. W. Norton & Company.

Conell, R. (2007), *Southern Theory: The Global Dynamics of Knowledge in Social Science*, Cambridge: Polity Press.

Cunningham, M. (2001), *Educación intercultural bilingüe en los contextos multiculturales: Proceedings from the Primera feria hemisférica de educación indígena*, Guatemala City: PAEBI-USAID, <http://www.beps.net/publications/parteiii.pdf> (last accessed 19 June 2015).

Diaz-Polanco, H. (2005), *Elogio de la diversidad: Globalizacion, multiculturalismo y etnofagia*, Mexico City: Siglo XXI Editores.

Dietz, G. (2009), *Multiculturalism, Interculturality and Diversity in Education: An Anthropological Approach*, Münster and New York: Waxmann.

Dietz, G. (2012), *Multiculturalismo, interculturalidad, y diversidad en educación: una aproximación antropológica*, Mexico City: Fondo de Cultura Económica.

Dussel, E. (2004), *Transmodernity and Interculturality: An Interpretation from the Perspective of Philosophy of Liberation*, Mexico City: UAM, <http://enriquedussel.com/txt/Transmodernity%20and%20Interculturality.pdf> (last accessed 12 June 2015).

Dussel, I. (2001), 'What Can Multiculturalism Tell Us about Difference? The Reception of Multicultural Discourses in France and Argentina', in C. Grant and J. Lei (eds), *Global Constructions of Multicultural Education: Theories and Realities*, Mahwah, NJ: Lawrence Erlbaum, pp. 93–114.

Eisenstadt, T., M. Danielson, M. Bailón Corres and C. Sorroza Polo (eds) (2013), *Latin America's Multicultural Movements: The Struggle between Communitarianism, Autonomy, and Human Rights*, Oxford: Oxford University Press.

Escobar, A. (1997), 'Cultural Politics and Biological Diversity: State, Capital and Social Movements in the Pacific Coast of Colombia', in R. G. Fox and O. Starn, *Between Resistance and Revolution: Cultural Politics and Social Protest*, New Brunswick, NJ: Rutgers University Press, pp. 40–64.

Fornet-Betancourt, R. (2004), *Filosofar para nuestro tiempo en clave intercultural*, Aachen:Wissenschaftsverlag Mainz.

Freyre, G. (2003), *Casa-Grande e Senzala: Formação de família brasileira sob o regime da economia patriarcal*, 48th edn, São Paulo: Global Editora, <http://www.usp.br/cje/anexos/pierre/freire_gilberto_casa_grande_senzala.pdf> (last accessed 12 June 2015).

García Canclini, N. (2004), *Diferentes, desiguales, y desconectados. Mapas de la interculturalidad*, Barcelona: Editorial Gedisa.

Gay, G. (2010), *Culturally Responsive Teaching: Theory, Research, and Practice*, New York: Teachers College Press.

Ghosh, R. (2011), 'The Liberating Potential of Multiculturalism in Canada', *Canadian Issues*, Spring, 3–8.

Giménez Romero, C. (2000), 'Guía sobre interculturalidad', in *Colección Cuadernos Q'anil 1*, Guatemala City: Editorial Serviprensa.

Godenzzi Alegre, J. (1996), 'Introducción. Construyendo la convivencia y el entendimiento: educación e interculturalidad en América Latina', in J. Gondenzzi Alegre (ed.), *Educación e Interculturalidad en los Andes y la Amazonia*, Cuzco: Centro de Estudios Regionales Andinos 'Bartolomé de las Casas', pp. 23–82.

Gómez, J. T., and J. G. Hernández (2010), 'Relaciones interculturales, interculturalidad y multiculturalismo: teorías, conceptos, actores y referencias', *Revista Cuicuilco*, 17 (48), 11–34.

González Oviedo, M. (2009), 'Pluralidad, derechos humanos y educación intercultural', in M. González Oviedo (ed.), *Educación e interculturalidad: lo nuestro, lo propio, lo de todos*, San José: Ministerio de Educación Pública.

Gros, C. (1997), 'Indigenismo y etnicidad: el desafio neoliberal', in M. V. Uribe and E. Restrepo (eds), *Antropologia en la modernidad: Identidades, etnicidades y movimientos sociales en Colombia*, Bogota: Instituto Colombiano de Antropologia.

Gutierrez Martinez, D. (ed.) (2006), *Multiculturalismo: Desafios y Perspectivas*, Mexico City: Siglo XXI Editores.

Hale, C. (2006), 'Rethinking Indigenous Politics in the Era of the "Indio Permitido"', in *Dispatches from Latin America: On the Frontlines against Neoliberalism*, Cambridge, MA: South End Press, pp. 16–37, <http://www.utexas.edu/law/centers/humanrights/events/adjudicating/papers/hale.pdf> (last accessed 12 June 2015).

Hall, S., and P. du Gay (2003), *Cuestiones de identidad cultural*, Buenos Aires: Amorrortu.

Hamel, R. E. (2008), 'Plurilingual Latin America: Indigenous Languages, Immigrant Languages, Forcign Languages – Towards an Integrated Policy of Language and Education', in C. Hélot and A. De Mejía (eds), *Forging Multilingual Spaces: Integrated Perspectives on Majority and Minority Bilingual Education*, New York: Multilingual Matters, pp. 58–108.

Herdoíza-Estévez, M., and S. Lenk (2010), 'Intercultural Dialogue: Discourse and Realities of Indigenous and Mestizos in Ecuador and Guatemala', *Interamerican Journal of Education for Democracy*, 3 (2), 196–223.

Hopenhayn, M. (2002), 'El reto de las identidades y la multiculturalidad', *Pensar Iberoamerica*, <http://www.oei.es/pensariberoamerica/ric00a01.htm> (last accessed 12 June 2015).

Hopenhayn, M. (2009), 'La educación intercultural: entre la igualdad y la diferencia', *Pensamiento Iberoamericano*, 4, 49–72.

Hornberger, N. H. (2000), 'Bilingual Education Policy and Practice in the Andes: Ideological Paradox and Intercultural Possibility', *Anthropology & Education Quarterly*, 31 (2), 173–201, <http://isites.harvard.edu/fs/docs/icb.topic653581.files/Bilingual%20Formal%20Education/Hornberger%20Article.pdf> (last accessed 19 June 2015).

Horton, L. (2006), 'Contesting State Multiculturalisms: Indigenous Land Struggles in Eastern Panama 1', *Journal of Latin American Studies*, 38 (4), 829.

Joshee, R. (2004), 'Citizenship and Multicultural Education in Canada: From Assimilation to Social Cohesion', in J. Banks (ed.), *Diversity and Citizenship Education: Global Perspectives*, San Francisco: Jossey-Bass, pp. 127–56.

Joshee, R., and L. Johnson (2007), *Multicultural Education Policies in Canada and the United States*, Vancouver: University of British Columbia Press.

Kymlicka, W. (2006), *Ciudadania multicultural. Una teoria liberal de los derechos de las minorias*, Barcelona: Paido's.

Kymlicka, W. (2012), 'Comment on Meer and Modood', *Journal of Intercultural Studies*, 33 (2), 211–16.

Lazo Briones, P. (2008), *Etica, hermeneutica y multiculturalismo*, Mexico City: Publicaciones Universidad Iberoamericana.

Levey, G. B. (2012), 'Interculturalism vs. Multiculturalism: A Distinction without a Difference?', *Journal of Intercultural Studies*, 33 (2), 217–24.

Levy, T. (2003), *El multiculturalismo del miedo*, Madrid: Tecnos.

López, L. E. (1997), 'La diversidad étnica, cultural y lingüística latinoamericana y los recursos humanos que la educación requiere', *Revista Iberoamericana*, 13, 47–98.

López, L. E. (2009), *Reaching the Unreached: Indigenous Intercultural Bilingual Education in Latin America*, paper commissioned for the EFA Global Monitoring Report 2010, *Reaching the Marginalized*, Paris: UNESCO, <http://unesdoc.unesco.org/images/0018/001866/186620e.pdf> (last accessed 24 June 2015).

López, L. E., and C. Giménez (2001), 'Educación intercultural', *Cuadernos pedagógicos no. 5*, Guatemala City: Ministerio de Educación.

López, L. E., and W. Küper (1999), 'La educacion intercultural bilingue en Latin America: balance y perspectivas', *Revista Iberoamericana de educación*, 20, 17–85.

López, L. E., and F. Sapón (eds) (2011), *Recreando la EIB en América Latina: trabajos presentados en el IX congreso Latinoamericano de educación intercultural bilingüe*, Guatemala City: Ministerio de Educación.

Loveman, M. (2014), *National Colors: Reclassification and the State in Latin America*, Oxford: Oxford University Press.

Macedo, D., and L. Bartolomé (1999), *Dancing with Bigotry: Beyond the Politics of Tolerance*, New York: Palgrave Macmillan.

McEwan, G. (2006), *The Incas: New Perspectives*, Santa Barbara: ABC-CLIO.

McLaren, P. (ed.) (1998), *Multiculturalismo revolucionario*, Mexico City: Siglo XXI Editores.

McNeish, J. (2008), 'Beyond the Permitted Indian? Bolivia and Guatemala in an Era of Neoliberal Developmentalism', *Latin American and Caribbean Ethnic Studies*, 3 (1), 33–59, <http://www.cmi.no/publications/file/2847-beyond-the-permitted-indian.pdf> (last accessed 24 June 2015).

Maldonado Ledezma, I. (2010), 'De la multiculturalidad a la interculturalidad: la reforma del estado y los pueblos indígenas en México', *Andamios*, 7 (14), 287–319.

Maldonado Ledezma, I. (2011), 'Estados-nación, identidades subalternas e interculturalismo en América Latina', *Revista Lider*, 18, 53–67.

Maldonado Ruiz, L. (2011), 'Refundación de los Estados y sistemas de educación en América Latina', in L. E. López and F. Sapón (eds), *Recreando la EIB en América Latina: trabajos presentados en el IX congreso Latinoamericano de educación intercultural bilingüe*, Guatemala City: Ministerio de Educación, pp.

19–32, <http://www.rniu.buap.mx/infoRNIU/feb12/2/lib_ciesas_recreando_tomoi.pdf> (last accessed 24 June 2015).

Marentes, L. (2013), 'Latino *Indigenismo* in a Comparative Perspective', *Oxford Bibliographies Online: Latino Studies*, <http://www.oxfordbibliographies.com/view/document/obo-9780199913701/obo-9780199913701-0040.xml> (last accessed 12 June 2015).

Marti, J. (1891), 'Nuestra América', *El Partido Liberal*, Mexico City.

Martínez, C. (2007), '¿Es el multiculturalismo estatal un factor de profundización de la democracia en América Latina?: una reflexión desde la etnografía sobre los casos de México y Ecuador', in V. Bretón, F. García, A. Jove and M. J. Vilalta (eds), *Ciudadanía y exclusión: Ecuador y España frente al espejo*, Madrid: Catarata, pp. 182–202.

Maxwell, B., D. I. Waddington, K. McDonough, A.-A. Cormier and M. Schwimmer (2012), 'Interculturalism, Multiculturalism, and the State Funding and Regulation of Conservative Religious Schools', *Educational Theory*, 62 (4), 427–47.

May, S., and C. Sleeter (eds) (2010), *Critical Multiculturalism: Theory and Praxis*, New York: Routledge.

Meer, N., and T. Modood (2012), 'How Does Interculturalism Contrast with Multiculturalism?', *Journal of Intercultural Studies*, 33 (2), 175–96.

Mendoza, R. (2011), 'Políticas educativas para la interculturalización de la educación superior en México: participación y ejercicio de derechos', in L. E. López and F. Sapón (eds), *Recreando la EIB en América Latina: trabajos presentados en el IX congreso Latinoamericano de educación intercultural bilingüe*, Guatemala City: Ministerio de Educación, pp. 311–36.

Miller, M. G. (2004), *Rise and Fall of the Cosmic Race: The Cult of* Mestizaje *in Latin America*, Texas: University of Texas Press.

Moya, R. (1997), 'Interculturalidad y reforma educativa en Guatemala', *Revista Iberoamericana de educación*, 13, 129–55.

Moya, R. (1998), 'Reformas educativas e interculturalidad en América Latina', *Revista Iberoamericana de educación*, 17, 105–87.

Nascimento, A. d. (1990), 'Quilombismo: The African Road to Socialism', in M. K. Asante and K. W. Asante (eds), *African Culture: The Rhythms of Unity*, Trenton, NJ: Africa World Press.

Naseem, A. M. (2011), 'Conceptual Perspectives on Multiculturalism and Multicultural Education – A Survey of the Field', *Canadian Issues*, Spring, 9–14.

Olivé, L., and L. Villoro (eds) (1995), *Filosofía moral, educación e historia*, Mexico City: UNAM.

Ortiz, F. (1940), *Contrapunteo cubano del tabaco y el azúcar*, Caracas: Ayacucho.

Ortiz, P. (2009), 'Indigenous Knowledge and Language: Decolonizing Culturally Relevant Pedagogy in a Mapuche Intercultural Bilingual Education Program in Chile', *Canadian Journal of Indigenous Education*, 32 (1), 93–114.

Rama, A. (1982), *Transculturacion narrativa en America Latina*, Mexico City: Siglo XXI Editores.

Richards, P. (2010), 'Of Indians and Terrorists: How the State and Local Elites Construct the Mapuche in Neoliberal Multicultural Chile', *Journal of Latin American Studies*, 42 (1), 59–90.

Salazar Tetzagüic, M. (2009), *Multiculturalidad e interculturalidad en el ámbito educativo: Experiencias de países latinoamericanos*, San José: Instituto Interamericano de Derechos Humanos.

Salmerón, F., and E. Garzón Valdéz (eds) (1993), *Epistemología y cultura*, Mexico City: UNAM.

Sansone, L. (2007), 'Apresentação: que multiculturalismo se quer para o Brasil?', *Ciência e Cultura*, 59 (2), 24–8, <http://cienciaecultura.bvs.br/scielo.php?pid=S0009-67252007000200013&script=sci_arttext> (last accessed 12 June 2015).

Sleeter, C. E. (1996), *Multicultural Education as Social Activism*, Albany, NY: State University of New York Press.

Spitta, S. (1995), *Between Two Waters: Narratives of Transculturation in Latin America*, Houston: Rice University Press.

Taylor, C. (1993), *El multiculturalismo y 'la political del reconocimiento'*, Mexico City: FCE.

Taylor, C. (2012), 'Interculturalism or Multiculturalism?', *Philosophy and Social Criticism*, 38 (4–5), 413–23.

Torres, C. A. (2007), *Democracia, educación y multiculturalismo*, Mexico City: Siglo XXI Editores.

Trigo, A. (1996), 'On Transculturation: Toward a Political Economy of Culture in the Periphery', *Studies in Latin American Popular Culture*, 15, 99.

Tubino, F. (2001), 'Interculturalizando el multiculturalismo', in Y. Onghena, *Interculturael*; available at <http://www.cidob.org/en/media2/publicacions/monografias/interculturael/08_tubino_cast> (last accessed 24 June 2015).

Tubino, F. (2002), 'Entre el multiculturalismo y la interculturalidad: más allá de la discriminación positiva', in F. Tubino (ed.), *Interculturalidad y política: desafíos y posibilidades*, Lima: Red para el desarrollo de las ciencias sociales en el Perú, pp. 51–76.

Tubino, F. (2005), 'La praxis de la interculturalidad en los estados nacionales latinoamericanos', *Cuadernos interculturales*, 3 (5), 83–96.

Us Soc, P. (2009), *La práctica de la interculturalidad en el aula*, San José: Coordinación Educativa y Cultural Centroamericana.

Van Cott, D. (2000), *The Friendly Liquidation of the Past: The Politics of Diversity in Latin America*, Pittsburgh: University of Pittsburgh Press.

Vasconcelos, J. (1925), *La Raza Cósmica*, Madrid: Agencia Mundial de Librería, <http://www.filosofia.org/aut/001/razacos.htm> (last accessed 12 June 2015).

Viaña, J., L. Tapia and C. Walsh (2010), *Construyendo Interculturalidad Crítica*, La Paz: Instituto Internacional de Integración del Convenio Andrés Bello.

Villoro, L. (1998), *Estado plural, pluralidad de culturas*, Mexico City: Paidós-UNAM, <http://escuelapnud.org/biblioteca/pmb/opac_css/doc_num.php?expl num_id=551> (last accessed 24 June 2015).

Wade, P. (2005), 'Rethinking *Mestizaje*: Ideology and Lived Experience', *Journal of Latin American Studies*, 37 (2), 239–57.

Wade, P. (2006), 'Etnicidad, multiculturalismo y políticas sociales en Latinoamérica: Poblaciones Afrolatinas e indígenas', *Tabula Rasa*, 4, 59–81.

Wade, P. (2013), 'Blackness, Indigeneity, Multiculturalism and Genomics in Brazil, Colombia and Mexico', *Journal of Latin American Studies*, 45 (2), 205–33.

Wade, P., C. López Beltrán, E. Restrepo and R. Ventura Santos (2014), *Mestizo Genomics: Race Mixture, Nation, and Science in Latin America*, Durham, NC: Duke University Press.

Walsh, C. (2001), *La interculturalidad en la educación*, Lima: DINEBI.

Warren, S. (2013), 'A Nation Divided: Building the Cross-Border Mapuche Nation in Chile and Argentina', *Journal of Latin American Studies*, 45 (2), 235–64.

Wieviorka, M. (2012), 'Multiculturalism: A Concept to be Redefined and Certainly Not Replaced by the Extremely Vague Term of Interculturalism', *Journal of Intercultural Studies*, 33 (2), 225–31.

Wieviorka, M. (2014), 'The End of Multiculturalism?', <http://wieviorka.hypoth eses.org/321> (last accessed 12 June 2015).

Williamson, G. (2004), '¿Educación multicultural, educación intercultural bilingüe, educación indígena o educación intercultural?', *Cuadernos Interculturales*, 2 (3), 16–24.

Zimmermann, K. (1997), 'Modos de interculturalidad en la educación bilingüe: reflexiones acerca del caso de Guatemala', *Revista Iberoamericana de educación*, 13, 113–27, <http://www.oei.es/oeivirt/rie13a05.htm> (last accessed 12 June 2015).

9

Diversity, Duality and Time

Geoffrey Brahm Levey

Introduction

The terms 'interculturalism' and 'multiculturalism' have occupied the same discursive space for a few decades now, especially in continental Europe and Quebec. Where they have engaged, it has typically been interculturalists seeking to nudge multiculturalism out of the way or into a specific corner. Nasar Meer and Tariq Modood (2012) helpfully brought this background tussle to a head by questioning the standard suggestions for interculturalism's distinctiveness and superiority over multiculturalism. At the same time, Gérard Bouchard (2011: 463), focusing on the Canadian case, argues that interculturalism and multiculturalism are 'rooted in opposite paradigms'. Where interculturalism turns on a 'duality' paradigm that endorses a foundational majority culture and 'ad hoc majority precedence', multiculturalism operates on a 'diversity' paradigm that does not recognise a majority culture and instead places all constituent groups and individuals on an equal footing. In subsequent work, Modood now agrees that how 'majority precedence' is treated marks a key difference between multiculturalism and interculturalism, at least on the Quebec model (see Chapter 11). While recognising the fact of such precedence, he argues that multiculturalism is mainly concerned with eliminating or offsetting it.

This is an important debate. In the symposium occasioned by Meer and Modood's original essay, I expressed my general scepticism about interculturalism being fundamentally different from multiculturalism (Levey 2012).[1] However, I share Bouchard's and

Modood's conviction that how one views the status of a 'foundational culture' and 'majority precedence' are pivotal issues. I am less interested or invested in the labels, as such, than I am in the underlying philosophical and practical issues at stake. The debate is, however, a useful vehicle for thinking about these issues. Although I agree that the foundational culture/majority precedence questions are pivotal regarding how one thinks about cultural diversity in liberal democracies, my contention is that these issues divide multiculturalists themselves rather than them from interculturalists. I will, however, suggest another possible point of differentiation between multiculturalism and one version of interculturalism – Quebec's – related to the acceptability of losing the established culture over time.

Situating the argument

It is important to delineate the ambit of my remarks in this chapter. The debate about multiculturalism and interculturalism is fraught not least because these rubrics and their respective self-identifying camps are so multifarious as to frustrate clear-cut demarcations between them. Geographical and historical variations abound. 'Multiculturalism' means different things in different places. In Canada, for example, multiculturalism is official state policy set out in the Canadian Multiculturalism Act (1988) and section 27 of the Canadian Charter of Rights and Freedoms (1982). Across the border in the United States, however, multiculturalism is not government policy at any level. Rather, there it arose as a protest movement from 'below' among African-Americans and other assorted identity groups who felt that the 'difference-blind' policies flowing from the 1964 Civil Rights Act were not working for them, and that henceforth their difference should be a matter of emphasis and pride. Accordingly, multiculturalism in the US has been strongly associated with affirmative action programmes and the question of whose cultures and 'narratives' should be taught in college curricula (Glazer 1998). Such country variations could be multiplied.

[1] I thank the Barcelona workshop participants for their helpful comments on aspects of this chapter, and Tariq Modood for subsequent conversations on these issues. I am also grateful to him and Ricard Zapata-Barrero for their editorial comments on the original version of this chapter, and to Will Kymlicka and Gérard Bouchard for their generous comments on the penultimate version.

The meaning of 'interculturalism' also varies contextually. A decade or so ago, interculturalism as used in continental Europe tended to focus on the relations among citizens and groups in civil society rather than on the state's relation to its cultural minorities, arguably the predominant concern of multiculturalism.[2] On this basis, interculturalism and multiculturalism could be regarded as perfectly compatible and even complementary strategies of integration. This localised meaning of interculturalism is still common in Europe (see Wood and Landry 2007; Pampanini, Adly and Napier 2010) and in Latin America (see Solano-Campos 2013; Tubino 2013), and has particular currency in the area of education (see Gundara 2012). However, this focus was never true of Québécois interculturalism, which always defined itself in opposition to federal Canada's multiculturalism. Quebec seeks to protect its French language and culture against the tide of anglophone Canada (and the US). As such, its policy of interculturalism is expressly concerned with the province's management of cultural minorities within the context of its own national-cultural commitments. Bouchard (2011: 444) describes this difference in terms of a focus on the 'societal or macrosocial level where the challenge is to define principles and general guidelines for integration', compared with the level of 'interculturality', and its focus on 'the micro-social scale of neighbourhoods, community relations, and the daily life of institutions (schools, hospitals, workplaces, etc.)'.

Two developments have complicated these regional contrasts. One is that some European bodies now advocate intercultural dialogue and interculturalism as fully fledged alternatives to multiculturalism, offering a more acceptable set of principles and arrangements for the state management of cultural diversity. The Council of Europe's (2008) White Paper on Intercultural Dialogue is one such example.[3] Similarly, in Britain, Ted Cantle (2012) has sought to recast interculturalism as a model of integration that has none of the foibles of multiculturalism and a clean slate of potential for addressing incessant globalisation and the 'super-diversity'

---

[2] A situation aptly captured by Will Kymlicka's (2003) title 'Multicultural States and Intercultural Citizens'.

[3] See, more recently, the Platform for Intercultural Europe, a civil society initiative that followed the European Commission's designation of 2008 as the European Year of Intercultural Dialogue: <http://www.intercultural-europe.org/site/> (last accessed 12 June 2015).

now confronting Western democracies. The Council of Europe's interest in interculturalism, in particular, followed general anxieties over multiculturalism in the wake of Muslim immigration and integration and a perception that 'multiculturalism' has become so controversial and tarnished that a fresh rubric is needed to represent an inclusive approach to cultural diversity.

The second development is that some researchers working on problems of integration at the micro-social level have begun to present interculturalism as an approach that tackles issues or aspects that they see as being overlooked by multiculturalism. For example, it is suggested that interculturalism values 'dialogue' or 'interaction' between groups and their members that is essential to successful social integration but which goes unheralded by multiculturalism policy or principles (see, for example, Wood et al. 2006; Zapata-Barrero 2015 and Chapter 3). In the *Journal of Intercultural Studies* symposium, I paid these arguments some credence by distinguishing between 'hard' and 'soft' claims underpinning the alleged contrast between interculturalism and multiculturalism (Levey 2012). 'Hard' claims for interculturalism's distinctiveness view it as fundamentally different from multiculturalism, as, for example, in Cantle's analysis and Bouchard's contention that the two brands operate according to different paradigms. In contrast, 'soft' claims see its distinctiveness more as a matter of emphasis. I suggested that some of the 'softer' claims differentiating interculturalism around dialogue and interaction have merit. However, I also accepted Meer and Modood's point, which follows from a 'soft' claim, that there is nothing in multiculturalism that precludes an emphasis on dialogical exchange or on the kinds of choice, cultural hybridity and cultural interactions trumpeted by interculturalists (see, for example, Parekh 2000; Modood 2013; Mookherjee 2011).

Against this background and complexity, the specific contrast I wish to pursue in the remainder of this chapter is the one drawn by Bouchard (2011) between multiculturalism and Québécois interculturalism. This returns us to the question of paradigms and attitudes to a foundational culture and 'ad hoc majority precedence'.

The duality paradigm and ad hoc majority precedence

Bouchard, a sociologist, was a joint author with the philosopher Charles Taylor of the high-profile report on 'reasonable accommodation' in Quebec commissioned by the provincial government (Bouchard and Taylor 2008). As noted, in his 2011 article Bouchard ventures the 'hard' claim that multiculturalism and interculturalism operate on fundamentally different paradigms. Where multiculturalism is said to operate on a 'diversity' paradigm, in which individuals and groups have equal status under the same laws and there is 'no recognition of a majority culture', interculturalism is said to operate on a 'duality' paradigm, where 'diversity is conceived and managed as a relationship between minorities and a cultural majority that could be described as *foundational*' (Bouchard 2011: 441–2; original italics).

An initial difficulty with this picture is Bouchard's own categories. In his general discussion, he distinguishes between *paradigms* as a first level of analysis and *models* as a second level of analysis. Paradigms include diversity, homogeneity, bi- or multi-polarity, duality and mixité, whereas models include multiculturalism, interculturalism, melting pot, hyphenation, republicanism, assimilationism, consociationalism and so on. Bouchard makes the sensible point that paradigms can accommodate more than one model, while states can adopt more than one paradigm. Yet he then goes on to argue that the models of interculturalism and multiculturalism operate on different paradigms. So what was presented as fluid and promiscuous is suddenly fixed and loyal: specific models belong to certain paradigms.[4]

Bouchard should have stuck with the promiscuous! Take interculturalism first. Bouchard defines the 'duality' paradigm (which he associates with interculturalism) in terms of a dominant cultural majority and then the rest. Yet the Council of Europe's White Paper on Intercultural Dialogue (2008: 18–20) and the Opatija Declaration on Intercultural Dialogue and Conflict Prevention (Council of Europe 2003) both frame the intercultural approach as rejecting or de-emphasising the majority/minority dichotomy. The principle of cultural diversity, states the Opatija Declaration,

---

[4] Bouchard (2011: 445) allows that the interculturalism model can also operate in the '(bi)pluri-polarity' paradigm.

cannot be applied exclusively in terms of 'majority' or 'minority', for this pattern singles out cultures and communities, and categorises and stigmatises them in a static position, to the point at which social behaviour and cultural stereotypes are assumed on the basis of groups' respective status. (Council of Europe 2003)

So different paradigms would seem to govern European and Québécois interculturalisms.

The multiculturalism side of the equation also resists singularity. There are several ways of distinguishing versions of multiculturalism. For example, some distinguish between 'soft' and 'hard' multiculturalisms, where the former refers simply to welcoming a culturally diverse society, and the latter refers to state interventions affirming this diversity. More common, perhaps, is the distinction between 'liberal' and 'radical' multiculturalisms, which typically turns on whether the accommodation of cultural difference is limited by respect for liberal values. Depending on the purpose, one might further differentiate 'liberal' (e.g. Kymlicka 1995), 'democratic' (e.g. Young 1990), 'political' (e.g. Modood 2007) and 'pluralist' (e.g. Crowder 2002) models of multiculturalism, each emphasising different fundamental values or ways of proceeding. In the present case the issue is the acknowledgement of and appropriate response to a foundational culture and ad hoc majority precedence. I think multiculturalists divide on this issue, so I believe another typology is called for to capture this contrast. Naming these positions, however, is hazardous, as it risks suggesting that exemplars have more in common than their position on the issue in question. Nevertheless, some identification is unavoidable, so I can only disclaim any such broader implication or inference. For convenience I will call one position 'parity multiculturalism' and the other, rather more conventionally, 'liberal nationalism'.

Parity multiculturalism is similar to Bouchard's 'diversity' paradigm in which no cultural group is entitled to a privileged position. The Council of Europe's White Paper on Intercultural Dialogue (2008: 18) caught the position exactly in stating that multiculturalism 'advocated political recognition of what was perceived as the distinct ethos of minority communities *on a par* with the "host" majority' (my emphasis). Not all in this camp go so far as to advocate literal parity between minorities and the dominant cultural majority; many, for example, grant some pragmatic privileging of the majority culture, such as that the lingua franca will privilege one (or more) cultural groups over others in the society. To this extent, the position might more accurately be dubbed 'quasi-parity' or 'even-handed' multiculturalism. Still, the position is grasped not according to where particular multiculturalists end up on policy questions; protagonists of opposing theoretical perspectives on cultural diversity often converge on substantive cases. Rather, it is the starting point or orientating assumptions that define the position. What is key for this group of multiculturalists, however we refer to them, is that the institutional privileging of a majority culture is inherently suspect and problematic. That is the baseline sensibility from which concessions might then be entertained. I would include in this camp Iris Marion Young (1990), Nancy Fraser (2002), Veit Bader (2007), many multiculturalists trained in sociology, anthropology and cultural studies (who tend to see an injustice in every disparity in power and status), and most radical multiculturalists.

On the other hand, there is an important group of multiculturalists who begin from the assumption that some significant institutional privileging of the foundational culture is not only inevitable but also legitimate. They typically go by the name of 'liberal nationalists', and their orientating assumptions resemble Bouchard's 'duality' paradigm and its picture of the majority culture and then the rest. Far from distrusting the idea of a foundational culture and majority precedence, liberal nationalists tend to think it is societally beneficial. A national identity grounded in the established institutions and culture, on this account, plays an important role in generating and sustaining social cohesion, a sense of belonging, and a commitment to the commonweal. These features are deemed to be legitimate interests of democratic states. What makes liberal nationalists multiculturalists is, however, their belief that such cultural privileging – typically, of a majority group – should be limited and matched by some redress for cultural minorities who are also members of the political community.[5] They also hold that the cultural contributions brought by immigrants and other minorities should extend the traditional national culture

---

[5] In ordinary language, 'liberal nationalism' often refers to the simple proposition that nations or the nation-state are the appropriate vehicle for realising a liberal political order. As Tamir (1993: 139) notes, on this basis, 'nowadays most liberals are liberal nationalists'. Obviously, liberal nationalists in this sense need not be multiculturalists.

and identity. However, where parity multiculturalists are impatient for this reform of 'the national' to occur, liberal nationalists are more likely to draw limits to the privileging of the majority culture, grant some minority cultural rights, and then allow the national culture to evolve over generations.

Liberal nationalists notably include Will Kymlicka (1995), Avishai Margalit and Joseph Raz (1990), Yael Tamir (1993), David Miller (1995), Margaret Canovan (1996), Chaim Gans (2003) and Tim Soutphommasane (2012). I have argued that Australian multicultural policy is almost a textbook example of liberal nationalism in action (Levey 2008, 2014).[6] Some liberal nationalists focus on indigenous, subnational and ethnic groups (e.g. Kymlicka), some take religious minorities as their main exemplar of minority cultural claims (e.g. Tamir, Margalit), while others treat religious, ethnic and racial minorities within the framework of liberal nationalist multiculturalism (e.g. Gans, Levey, Miller, Soutphommasane). Again, my earlier caveat bears repeating as there is also wide variation within this camp regarding the specific arguments made and their normative implications. Miller's liberal nationalism, for example, emphasises the importance of the established national-cum-public culture, whereas Kymlicka promotes a much 'thinner' national culture and emphasises the rights of cultural minorities.

Indeed, in places, Kymlicka has advocated minority accommodation to such an extent that his position resembles parity multiculturalism.[7] He writes:

> we need to ensure that the common institutions into which immigrants are pressured to integrate provide the same degree of respect, recognition and accommodation of the identities and practices of immigrants as they traditionally have of the identities and practices of the majority group. (Kymlicka 2001: 30)

For example, he has even suggested that public holidays should be more evenly distributed, with Christmas as perhaps the one Christian holiday and Easter and Thanksgiving replaced with Muslim and Jewish holidays (Kymlicka 1995: 223, n. 9). Still,

---

[6] Cf. Bouchard (2011: 441), who – mistakenly, in my view – cites Australia as an example of the 'diversity' paradigm at work.

[7] I thank Tariq Modood for challenging me on this point.

Kymlicka's point of departure is vintage liberal nationalism: his main point is that the terms of integration need to be properly monitored and debated as to their fairness once the idea of state neutrality is abandoned. His suggestion of redistributing public holidays appears in an endnote as a thought experiment and is not central to his argument or discussion. And the passage quoted above follows a caution that 'we need to recognize that integration does not occur overnight, but is a difficult and long-term process that operates inter-generationally' (Kymlicka 2001: 30). This long-term view contrasts with the haste of parity multiculturalists. If Kymlicka's theory of minority rights begins from liberal nationalist assumptions, there is no denying, however, that it is elaborated at the position's most egalitarian and, perhaps, Canadian-inspired edge.

An interesting aspect of liberal nationalists is that they tend to have spent time researching or teaching at Oxford (Canovan studied at Cambridge). Of course, not every writer on multiculturalism who has studied at Oxford is a liberal nationalist. Charles Taylor, who took two degrees at the University of Oxford and held its Chichele Professorship of Social and Political Theory, is no exception, however. Parity multiculturalists often cite Taylor's (1992) seminal essay 'The Politics of Recognition' in support of their case for equal respect of minorities. It is also true that the modern ideal of authenticity, which he champions for individuals and collectives, is claimed to generate widespread rights to political recognition (Levey 2015). However, both in his 1992 essay and more recently, Taylor's position resembles Bouchard's in being concerned with preserving the foundational francophone culture in Quebec.[8] Taylor (2012: 420) even suggests that Quebec's interculturalism model, with its openness to ad hoc majority precedence, may suit many European countries whose cultural majorities are also concerned with preserving their 'historic identities'. Most liberal nationalists would find interculturalism based on the 'duality' paradigm both familiar and generally agreeable; a parity multiculturalist would be likely to find it challenging.

Modood's work is an interesting case in this respect. One might expect him to find liberal nationalism congenial. After all, he

[8] Kymlicka (2001: 39, n. 1) includes Taylor as a liberal nationalist, also citing his 1992 essay.

accepts that national-cultural contexts differ and these will inform the kind of multiculturalism appropriate in each case. He acknowledges the influence of Michael Oakeshott on his 'sense of the importance of subjectivities, and of conserving them, of national traditions, and of antirationalism and anti-monism in political theory and social sciences more generally' (Modood quoted in Martínez 2013: 739). His self-styled political or 'multicultural citizenship' approach attaches particular importance to national identity as a vehicle for building cohesion among a society's constituent communities. He even invokes the language of a 'normative concept of Britishness' (Modood 2007: 151). This aspect distinguishes Modood from many multiculturalists, including most 'parity' multiculturalists, for whom ignoring or disparaging the idea of national identity is commonplace.[9] He defends at least one important institution of majority precedence beyond language, namely the established Church in England and its role in British lawmaking (Modood 1994, 2005, 2007, 2013). And he has consistently maintained that equality among groups should be realised not through state neutrality or by denying the cultural majority its established customs but rather by adding comparable entitlements for minorities. So where majority precedence prevails, Modood's multiculturalism is likely to be a less-wrenching experience for the majority than state neutrality or a crude even-handedness. Finally, Modood's political multiculturalism approach would seem to be open to some majority precedence in that a 'truly multiculturalist society' is said to amount to a 'variable geometry' in which recognition 'is taken to work differently for different groups' (Modood 2007: 83, 48).

Yet Modood does not apply his approach in this way. Instead, he focuses on the situation of minorities and tends to give short shrift to the standing of the established culture other than as background context. His discussion of national identity invariably emphasises how it needs to be 'multiculturalised', opened up and broadened to include cultural minorities. As he puts it, 'for multiculturalists a renewing of national identity has to be distinctly plural and hospitable to the minority identities', and has to involve 'rethinking the national story' (2013: 164). Such points are unexceptionable

---

[9] Modood was a Fellow at Nuffield College, Oxford, in the early 1990s, and then lived in Oxford for many years while commuting to work in cosmopolitan London.

for most multiculturalists who address national identity. It is the absence of attention to or concern with the other side of the equation, the established majority culture and any aspects of its possible precedence, which is telling. His defence of establishment is something of an exception in that he acknowledges the force of history and tradition and seeks a way to reconcile it with multifaithism. His solution is to construe establishment as signifying a public place for religion in general and as a bulwark against an overzealous secularism. However, the emphasis, again, is on what this means for religious minorities and, especially, Muslims in publicly expressing themselves. His 'variable geometry' of differing recognition is illustrated exclusively by reference to minority organisations. And, of course, adding minority entitlements is another way of attaining parity instead of subtracting majority privileging.

So, all told, it is not surprising that Modood takes issue with Bouchard's argument that ad hoc majority precedence has some legitimacy. He could not be more explicit in saying that, for him, multiculturalism is unconcerned with the interests of the established cultural majority: 'It is true that an emphasis on majoritarian anxieties is a radically different starting point from [multiculturalism]'. And again: 'The idea of majority precedence I believe is a significant difference from most accounts of [multiculturalism]' (Chapter 11).

There is, then, a real philosophical dispute among multiculturalists over the status of a foundational culture and majority precedence that matches that between interculturalist Bouchard and multiculturalist Modood. The respective parties to this dispute understand equality from different baselines and betray different inclinations, sympathies and, perhaps, interests regarding a foundational culture and a national cultural identity. Where Modood and parity multiculturalists resist attaching normative precedence to the empirical reality of majority cultural precedence, Bouchard, like liberal nationalists, does attach some normative precedence to this historical reality, believing it to have considerable legitimacy. Whether this philosophical difference translates into different policy positions in actual cases is, however, another matter. We should not be surprised to find some convergence at the practical level between Québécois interculturalism, liberal nationalist multiculturalism and parity multiculturalism, as all these models are committed to limiting majority precedence and building a more inclusive society. But nor should we be surprised if the tug of their philosophical assumptions leads protagonists of these respective models to decide cases somewhat differently.

Before looking at how cases are interpreted and decided by advocates of these vying approaches, I need to say something more about what 'ad hoc majority precedence' involves.

Assessing ad hoc majority precedence

Ad hoc majority precedence raises difficult questions. If all states endorse particular cultures to some extent, what is left of the distinction between the diversity and duality paradigms? Does it matter that some states, such as the United States, strive to be neutral regarding religious and cultural matters even if they're not in fact? That is, do they differ from states that conscientiously endorse particular cultures? If cultural commitments, at some deep level, are unavoidable, when or where do these commitments violate or compromise liberal democratic values? These are obviously complex and involved questions and I don't propose trying to answer them here. Rather, let me distinguish between three levels of majority precedence, whose differentiation is, I think, helpful in confronting these sorts of questions.

The first and deepest level of majority precedence is *civilisational*. This level includes the societal language(s) spoken and the calendar that governs the rhythm of the day and the organisation of the year; for example, whether the Gregorian calendar prevails, or one of the approximately thirty other calendars in use around the world today. The civilisational level also includes the governing ethical worldview, such as, in much of the West, a Judeo-Christian ethics coupled with progressive Enlightenment values. Prime Minister John Howard (2006) addressed this civilisational level in trying to capture the dominant Australian ethos:

> Most nations experience some level of cultural diversity while also having a dominant cultural pattern running through them. In Australia's case, that dominant pattern comprises Judeo-Christian ethics, the progressive spirit of the Enlightenment and the institutions and values of British political culture. Its democratic and egalitarian temper also bears the imprint of distinct Irish and nonconformist traditions.

A second level of majority precedence is *historical-institutional*. This level includes long-established institutions, formal and informal: liberal democratic rights and institutions of government, including church-state separation; the design of the national flag and other national emblems; public holidays; how the nation's history is taught in schools; the recitation of benedictions in Parliament or the legislature; and cultural norms, such as social space and queuing. The historical-institutional level will, in many cases, reflect or express the civilisational level. However, analytically the levels are distinct, both because they do not necessarily overlap (changing a public holiday or foregoing a queue scarcely touches on the civilisation) and because reforming a particular institution that does embody civilisational values does not necessarily undermine the civilisation's hold on the society.

The third level of majority precedence is the realm of *policy*, which covers contemporaneous laws and measures. Of course, new policies might be taken to reaffirm or reform historical institutions; however, I construe such policies as still addressing the 'historical-institutional' level. Rather, the ambit of 'policy' I am trying to capture here entails new initiatives that have little or no historical precedent. Examples include prohibitions against wearing religious signs or certain traditional garments, the scheduling of public ceremonies or events that effectively exclude some minorities, and crafting racial hatred laws based on what the majority thinks is unacceptable.

With this distinction between the three levels of majority precedence in hand, a few general observations may be made. Being pervasive and deep-seated, the civilisational level cannot really be considered ad hoc. In any case, it is clearly harder to overturn or reform the civilisational aspects of majority precedence than the other two levels. The policy level is the most accessible of the three levels to manage, and therefore also tends to furnish the cases of majority precedence that are hardest to defend. Still, the legitimacy of majority precedence is likely to depend on the specifics of each case, and no more so than at the historical-institutional level. We see these aspects reflected in Modood's and Bouchard's respective treatment of cases. The only 'civilisational' example they mention is language, and they both accept as legitimate the cultural privileging that accompanies the need for a lingua franca. Their focus is rather on what I am calling the 'historical-institutional' level.

Table 9.1 Gérard Bouchard on ad hoc precedence (from Bouchard 2011).

Legitimate Applications	Abusive Extensions
1. the institution of French as the common public language; 2. allocating a prominent place to the teaching of the francophone past in history courses, or, in other words, a national memory that is inclusive but gives predominance to the majority narrative; 3. the current priority position given to the presentation of Christian religions in the new course on ethics and religious culture; 4. the official burials of heads of state in Catholic churches; 5. keeping the cross on the Quebec flag (which has already been subject to challenges); 6. laying Christmas decorations in public squares or buildings; and 7. the sounding of bells in Catholic churches at various moments throughout the day.	1. keeping a cross on the wall of the National Assembly and in public courtrooms; 2. the recitation of prayers at municipal council meetings; 3. the funding of chaplain or Catholic pastoral care positions in public hospitals with state funds, to the exclusion of other religions; 4. the general prohibition against wearing religious signs for all employees in the public and semi-public sectors; 5. the reference to the supremacy of God in the preamble of the Canadian Charter of Rights and Freedoms; 6. including articles or clauses in a charter that establish a formal hierarchy between the cultural majority and minorities; and 7. the prohibition against wearing a burka in streets and public places (except for security or other compelling reasons).

Modood (2014: 312) declines to be drawn on the specifics of Bouchard's varied set of Quebec examples (summarised in Table 9.1). This is a pity, as engaging them would help to clarify what is at stake in this debate in practical terms. Instead, Modood discusses two 'institutional' cases: the teaching of historical narratives and minority religious instruction in schools.

Bouchard cites six examples of legitimate majority precedence besides language, all of which I would classify as 'historical-institutional'. He cites seven instances of illegitimate extensions of majority precedence, four being 'historical-institutional' and three being at the 'policy' level. Both Modood and Bouchard canvass the teaching of history and both stress the need for this to be inclusive of minority experiences, perspectives and contributions. However, Bouchard contends that prominence should still be given in the curriculum to the 'majority narrative', in Quebec the 'francophone past'. Modood (2014: 312) seems to accept the empirical likelihood of such prominence in making the case for inclusiveness: 'a national history will be for the most part what today's majority thinks of as its history'.

Both of them also address religion in schools. Bouchard refers to Quebec's mandatory ethics and religious culture course and makes the point that priority should be given to the 'presentation of Christian religions'. Modood (2014: 313) disposes of religious education (RE) – that is, learning about various traditions – with the comment that it is relatively uncontroversial in liberal democracies (the US excepted). He thinks the main issue regarding majority precedence concerns religious instruction (RI), in which school students have the opportunity to be taught their own faith and traditions. In Quebec, however, these issues were joined as parents lost the choice to enrol their children in Catholic, Protestant or non-religious moral instruction with the introduction of the ethics and religious culture course in 2008. There was much opposition in the province, including several court challenges, to the kind of generalised RE known in Britain (Carpay 2009). In any case, Modood's bracketing of RE is, I think, too quick, as he does not consider the question of *prioritising* the majority within an otherwise inclusive curriculum, which goes to the heart of the majority precedence issue.

Be that as it may, Modood contends that RI should be an option for students of all religious backgrounds, and that the majoritarian alternatives of only Christian students having this opportunity or religious instruction being abolished for everyone aren't consistent with multiculturalism. The United States is cited as an example of the latter, 'neutralist' approach, but we are entitled to wonder whether Modood's criticism also applies to Quebec's secular approach to religious education.

The significance of context is well seen from a few of Bouchard's 'historical-institutional' examples that outwardly appear to be comparable and yet are assessed differently. To wit, the cross on the Quebec flag is deemed legitimate, whereas a cross on the wall of the National Assembly and in public courtrooms is considered illegitimate. The Bouchard-Taylor report (2008) suggests the reasoning behind this disparate assessment. Public bodies of governance such as the National Assembly and the courtroom should be free of prominent displays of Catholic symbolism and 'intervention'. For the same reason, prayer recitation at municipal meetings (item 2) is considered illegitimate. In contrast, Bouchard's four 'societal' examples of Catholic and Christian privileging (items 3, 4, 6 and 7) are deemed legitimate presumably because 'certain practices or symbols may originate in the religion of the majority without . . . playing a regulatory role' (Bouchard and Taylor 2008: 152).

Less clear is why Bouchard thinks the reference to the supremacy of God in the preamble to the Canadian Charter of Rights and Freedoms (item 5) is an unacceptable extension of majority precedence. The Bouchard-Taylor report does not mention it. Instead, the report notes how the preamble to the Constitution Act, 1982 contains a reference to the supremacy of God, and dismisses this as insignificant precisely because 'the Charter guarantees the primacy of basic rights over the terms of the preamble' (Bouchard and Taylor 2008: 140, n. 9). Given God's invocation in the founding documents and legal tender of the United States, notwithstanding its high wall of separation between church and state, Bouchard's negative judgement, in this instance, seems a tad stretched.

Arguably, the clearest examples of illegitimate extensions of majority precedence are, as expected, the two 'policy' cases involving prohibitions against wearing religious signs and the burka in public places (items 4 and 7). A third 'policy' case is, however, especially interesting: 'including articles or clauses in a charter that establish a formal hierarchy between the cultural majority and minorities' (item 6). The Bouchard-Taylor report is similarly emphatic: 'it is a question here of *de facto* precedence that cannot be converted into the precedence of law, i.e. into a hierarchy' (Bouchard and Taylor 2008: 214). Now, one can appreciate this concern to leave cultural privileging ad hoc, informal, fluid and fungible. This way the advantages aren't 'locked in' and minorities aren't officially slighted. However, this ostensible commitment to ad hoc and de facto arrangements is also a bit odd in the present context for a number of reasons.

First, recall that Quebec's interculturalism model, as Bouchard outlines it, rests on a 'duality' paradigm based on the majority culture, which is legitimately privileged (within limits), and then the rest. Second, Bouchard (2011: 463) differentiates Quebec's interculturalism from federal Canadian multiculturalism precisely by noting that the latter does not recognise a majority culture in

Canada. Third, most of the items in Bouchard's list of legitimate majority precedence are presumably authorised in law or administrative regulations, which may leave them ad hoc but scarcely only de facto. Fourth, if the privileging of francophone culture in Quebec is considered legitimate, then there is surely something to be said for stating this situation up front and publicly justifying it.

Take the initial Australian multicultural policy, *National Agenda for a Multicultural Australia* (OMA 1989). This did what Canadian multiculturalism and Bouchard's interculturalism apparently decline to do, namely formally recognise the foundational culture and therewith majority precedence. The *National Agenda*, for example, acknowledges the importance of 'our British heritage' in helping 'to define us as Australian', and emphasises that multiculturalism 'does not entail a rejection of Australian values, customs and beliefs'. (It also expressly excludes from this recognition the relevance of ethno-cultural aspects such as skin colour, style of dress, mode of worship, or other languages spoken.) As it happens, the subsequent national multicultural policy statements, including the current one (DIAC 2011), have omitted these 'heritage' references to the national culture and instead emphasised multiculturalism itself as being central to Australian national identity, which is more in keeping with Bouchard's account of multiculturalism and his qualms about formalising hierarchies. The trouble is that the words of the policy documents are belied by how multicultural Australia continues to operate in practice. One example is the persisting custom of commencing sessions in both houses of federal parliament with the Lord's Prayer, and this despite multicultural lobbying to have these rituals better reflect Australia's diversity (Cahill et al. 2004).

So the risk is that leaving majority precedence de facto or ad hoc only accentuates the hollowness of the formal position against the lived reality. A perception of bad faith or hypocrisy can breed cynicism towards government and public institutions. It is better to call a spade a spade and explain why it is in the tool shed. The key, here, is that acknowledging the cultural heritage of the society, its language, symbols and public institutions can be instituted without creating a hierarchy among citizens or precluding a public conversation about what the collective culture and identity should look like. If executed sensitively, citizens will be furnished with the resources to be able to fit cases of ad hoc majority precedence that catch their attention into a public narrative that helps to make sense of them.

These various case examples serve to underscore a crucial point about both Québécois interculturalism and liberal nationalist multiculturalism. As both models accept a foundational culture and majority precedence whilst also being committed to the inclusion and rights of cultural minorities, drawing lines – and, in some cases, fine lines – between cases is standard operating procedure. Crucial to both models is that majority precedence be appropriately delimited.

How the future is meant to unfold

I have thus far focused on the convergences between liberal nationalist multiculturalism and Québécois interculturalism and their shared contrast with parity multiculturalism on the issues of a foundational culture and majority precedence. The question remains whether there is any significant difference between Québécois interculturalism and the liberal nationalist school of multiculturalism. I believe there may be, though my sense of it is necessarily impressionistic and ultimately speculative. I can best elucidate it through again comparing the Australian case.

Australia does not face a comparable challenge to Quebec's quest for national-cultural survival in anglophone North America. The respect for and privileging of Anglo-Australian institutions and culture have not been sustained, therefore, through existential threat, although historically White Australia saw itself as a far-flung outpost of the 'British race' fending off the 'yellow peril' from Asia. In contemporary Australia, there is now widespread acceptance that Australian national identity and culture will inevitably change with the changing composition of Australian society (where the overseas born are already approaching 30 per cent of the population). This proposition has been integral to Australian multiculturalism policy alongside respect for the established institutions and culture. As the most recent national multicultural policy states: 'Australia's multicultural composition is at the heart of our national identity and is intrinsic to our history and character' (DIAC 2011: 2).

Indeed, the decentring of Anglo-Australian institutions and culture is begrudgingly accepted even among those who are most wedded to them, namely cultural nationalists. 'The statistical evidence is that there will probably come a time when the celebrations of other faiths will loom larger in Australian life,' editorialised Brisbane's conservative *Sunday Mail* newspaper (in the Murdoch stable) a decade ago. 'In the meantime, Christians will continue joyously to observe their important celebrations in a manner that will reflect their historical dominance' (*Sunday Mail* 2005). Many of those who came to maturity in pre-multiculturalism Australia face the changed landscape with nostalgia but also realism. As the moral philosopher Raimond Gaita (b. 1946), himself a young immigrant, puts it with evident concern:

> Each generation of immigrants will change the tone and resonances of the Anglo-Celtic voice that invites them into the conversation about what it means to be Australian. That voice may change radically, but never, I hope, to a degree that makes it unrecognisable to, or in ways that would alienate, those whose sense of what it means to be Australian has been nourished by the Anglo-Celtic pioneers . . . [Still] genuine conversation must be open to the unforeseeable. (Gaita 2011: 201)

Are Québécois interculturalists similarly open to the diminution and loss of the majority francophone culture? Or is the 'unforeseeable' unthinkable? In their report, Bouchard and Taylor (2008: 121) speak of their belief 'that Canadian multiculturalism, inasmuch as it emphasizes diversity at the expense of continuity, is not properly adapted to Québec's situation'. In places, Bouchard (2011) sounds as if he means the conversation to be genuinely open-ended, with no limits on where it might lead, hence his insistence that majority precedence remain fluid and ad hoc. But the openness surely has limits, otherwise it would vitiate the whole point of the duality paradigm and its foot soldier, the interculturalism model. As Bouchard (2011: 438) explains, 'interculturalism concerns itself with the interests of the majority culture, whose desire to perpetuate and maintain itself is perfectly legitimate, as much as it does with the interests of minorities and immigrants'. And speaking of Quebec, he says: 'it is necessary to develop a form of pluralism that acknowledges that the francophone majority is itself a precarious minority that needs protection in order to ensure its survival and development' in North America and in a globalised world (Bouchard 2011: 441).

In the same vein, Taylor explains the difference between federal Canadian *multi*culturalism and Québécois *inter*culturalism in terms of their contrasting stories. 'The "multi" story', he says, 'decentres the traditional ethno-historical identity, and refuses to put any other in its place.' In contrast, the '"inter" story starts from the reigning historical identity but sees it evolving in a process in which all citizens, of whatever identity, have a voice, and no-one's input has a privileged status' (Taylor 2012: 418). While the latter reassurance applies to individuals and groups in Quebec, the reigning historical identity and the language and institutions that sustain it are not envisaged to evolve into oblivion. Québécois interculturalism is all about 'the over-all story of what we are trying to do, and of how things are meant to unfold' (Taylor 2012: 422).

If this analysis is correct, then openness to losing the majority culture over time marks an important difference between liberal nationalist multiculturalism and at least Québécois interculturalism. And since parity multiculturalism shares this openness with liberal nationalism only more so, we can conclude that there might well be here a fundamental difference between some interculturalisms and multiculturalism in general.

Bouchard is right, then, to identify the acceptance of a foundational culture and of ad hoc majority precedence as pivotal issues. They divide the duality and diversity paradigms. They also separate the interculturalism and multiculturalism models in so far as the former operates on a duality paradigm and the latter on a diversity paradigm. However, as I have sought to show, multiculturalism in theory and in practice actually divides on the status of a foundational culture and majority precedence. The liberal nationalist version operates on a duality paradigm whereas parity multiculturalism follows a diversity paradigm. In this sense, the two pioneers in institutionalising multiculturalism, Canada and Australia, took somewhat different turns. Courtesy of its peculiar bilingual circumstances and the challenge posed by Quebec, Canada officially pursued a multiculturalism that champions 'diversity' and does not recognise a majority culture.[10] In contrast, Australia overwhelmingly embraced 'duality' and a transparent form of liberal national-

---

[10] This still leaves official Canadian multiculturalism at some remove from parity multiculturalism, which is a philosophical position and not something that is enacted in the real world. I thank Will Kymlicka for this point.

ist multiculturalism that accords some significant precedence to the established culture. But multiculturalism writ large might plausibly be distinguished from Quebec's interculturalism if the question were adjusted. Instead of the acceptability of a foundational culture and (some) majority precedence, the question would be whether a foundational culture and ad hoc majority precedence are envisaged to last in perpetuity. Multiculturalists, including liberal nationalists, do not appear to be committed to such a proposition. For Québécois interculturalists, on the other hand, duality in perpetuity is the name of the cultural survival game.

Bouchard and Taylor stress how Canadian multiculturalism is ill suited as a model for Quebec due to the former's pursuit of 'diversity' instead of 'duality' and the acceptance of ad hoc majority precedence. However, even had Canada not opted for a multiculturalism that 'decentres the traditional ethno-historical identity' in favour of 'diversity' – which, according to some observers, actually is the situation beneath the official rhetoric[11] – a federal 'duality' model or liberal nationalist regime would hold little appeal for Québécois interculturalists. As a national policy, it would, of course, have the same deficit as Canada's official 'diversity' model of multiculturalism; bilingualism aside, the precedence accorded English Canada would leave francophone Canada simply a part of 'the rest', a minority like the others. As a model for managing Quebec's own internal cultural diversity, liberal nationalist multiculturalism lacks the very element of duality sought by Québécois interculturalists – a commitment to the survival of the established culture. It was precisely for this reason that Taylor (1992: 40, n. 16) found wanting Kymlicka's pioneering liberal nationalist theory of minority rights.

[11] For example, Will Kymlicka in an email to the author, 12 January 2015. The suggestion raises interesting questions about how we should think about the differences and similarities between the Canadian and Australian experiences with multiculturalism. Many commentators cite Canada as more successfully incorporating immigrant and 'visible' or religious minorities into the national imaginary and being more effective in its multiculturalism policies than any other place (e.g. Kymlicka 2010; Winter 2011: 15–20; Jakubowicz 2013). So even if we say that Canadian multiculturalism is liberal nationalist in the same sense of being driven by a commitment to 'duality' rather than to 'diversity' (in Bouchard's terms), there still may be warrant to distinguish between the Australian and Canadian experiences in the degree to which they have insisted on this duality in practice as well as rhetorically.

References

Bader, V. (2007), *Secularism or Democracy? Associational Governance of Religious Diversity*, Amsterdam: Amsterdam University Press.

Bouchard, G. (2011), 'What Is Interculturalism?', *McGill Law Journal*, 56 (2), 435–68.

Bouchard, G., and C. Taylor (2008), *Building the Future: A Time for Reconciliation*, Report of the Consultation Commission on Accommodation Practices Related to Cultural Difference, Quebec City: Government of Quebec.

Cahill, D., G. Bouma, H. Dellal and M. Leah (2004), *Religion, Cultural Diversity and Safeguarding Australia*, Melbourne: Australian Multicultural Foundation.

Canovan, M. (1996), *Nationhood and Political Theory*, Cheltenham: Edward Elgar.

Cantle, T. (2012), *Interculturalism: The New Era of Cohesion and Diversity*, Basingstoke: Palgrave Macmillan.

Carpay, J. (2009), 'Quebec's Parents Have Lost the Freedom to Choose Religious Education', *The Globe and Mail*, 11 May.

Council of Europe (ed.) (2003), *Declaration on Intercultural Dialogue and Conflict Prevention (The Opatija Declaration)*, Conference of the European Ministers Responsible for Cultural Affairs, Opatija (Croatia), 22 October, <http://www.coe.int/T/E/Com/Files/Ministerial-Conferences/2003-Culture/dec laration.asp> (last accessed 24 June 2015).

Council of Europe, Committee of Ministers (2008), *Living Together as Equals in Dignity: White Paper on Intercultural Dialogue*, Strasbourg: Council of Europe.

Crowder, G. (2002), *Liberalism and Value Pluralism*, London and New York: Continuum.

Department of Immigration and Citizenship (DIAC) (2011), *The People of Australia: Australia's Multicultural Policy*, Canberra: DIAC.

Fraser, N. (2002), 'Recognition without Ethics', in S. Lash and M. Featherstone (eds), *Recognition and Difference: Politics, Identity, Multiculture*, London: Sage, pp. 21–42.

Gaita, R. (2011), 'Multiculturalism, Love of Country and Responses to Terrorism', in R. Gaita (ed.), *Essays on Muslims and Multiculturalism*, Melbourne: Text, pp. 187–220.

Gans, C. (2003), *The Limits of Nationalism*, Cambridge: Cambridge University Press.

Glazer, N. (1998), *We Are All Multiculturalists Now*, Cambridge, MA: Harvard University Press.

Gundara, J. S. (2012), *Interculturalism, Education and Inclusion*, Thousand Oaks, CA: Sage.

Howard, J. (2006), 'Australia Day Address to the National Press Club', Parliament House, Canberra, 25 January, <www.theage.com.au/news/national/pms-speech/2006/01/25/1138066849045.html?page=fullpage> (last accessed 12 June 2015).

Jakubowicz, A. (2013), 'Comparing Australian Multiculturalism: The International Dimension', in A. Jakubowicz and C. Ho (eds), *'For Those Who've Come across the Seas. . .': Australian Multicultural Theory, Policy and Practice*, Melbourne: Australian Scholarly Publishing, pp. 15–30.

Kymlicka, W. (1995), *Multicultural Citizenship: A Liberal Theory of Minority Rights*, Oxford: Clarendon Press.

Kymlicka, W. (2001), *Politics in the Vernacular: Nationalism, Multiculturalism, and Citizenship*, Oxford: Oxford University Press.

Kymlicka, W. (2003), 'Multicultural States and Intercultural Citizens', *Theory and Research in Education*, 1, 147–69.

Kymlicka, W. (2010), *The Current State of Multiculturalism in Canada and Research Themes on Canadian Multiculturalism 2008–2010*, Ottawa: Citizenship and Immigration Canada.

Levey, G. B. (2008), 'Multiculturalism and Australian National Identity', in G. B. Levey (ed.), *Political Theory and Australian Multiculturalism*, New York: Berghahn Books, pp. 254–76.

Levey, G. B. (2012), 'Interculturalism vs. Multiculturalism: A Distinction without a Difference?', *Journal of Intercultural Studies*, 33 (2), 217–24.

Levey, G. B. (2014), 'Liberal Nationalism and the Australian Citizenship Tests', *Citizenship Studies*, 18, 175–89.

Levey, G. B. (2015), 'Authenticity and the Multiculturalism Debates', in G. B. Levey (ed.), *Authenticity, Autonomy and Multiculturalism*, New York: Routledge, pp. 1–23.

Margalit, A., and M. Halbertal (1994), 'Liberalism and the Right to Culture', *Social Research*, 61, 491–510.

Margalit, A., and J. Raz (1990), 'National Self-Determination', *Journal of Philosophy*, 87, 439–61.

Martínez, D. O. (2013), 'Intellectual Biography, Empirical Sociology and Normative Political Theory: An Interview with Tariq Modood', *Journal of Intercultural Studies*, 34, 729–41.

Meer, N., and T. Modood (2012), 'How Does Interculturalism Contrast with Multiculturalism?', *Journal of Intercultural Studies*, 33 (2), 175–96.

Miller, D. (1995), *On Nationality*, Oxford: Clarendon.

Modood, T. (1994), 'Establishment, Multiculturalism and British Citizenship', *Political Quarterly*, 65, 53–73.

Modood, T. (2005), *Multicultural Politics: Racism, Ethnicity, and Muslims in Britain*, Minneapolis: University of Minnesota Press.

Modood, T. (2007), *Multiculturalism: A Civic Idea*, Cambridge: Polity Press.

Modood, T. (2013), *Multiculturalism: A Civic Idea*, 2nd edn, Cambridge: Polity Press.

Modood, T. (2014), 'Multiculturalism, Interculturalisms and the Majority', *Journal of Moral Education*, 43, 302–15.

Mookherjee, M. (2011), *Women's Rights as Multicultural Claims: Reconfiguring Gender and Diversity in Political Philosophy*, Edinburgh: Edinburgh University Press.

Office of Multicultural Affairs (OMA) (1989), *National Agenda for a Multicultural Australia*, Canberra: AGPS.

Pampanini, G., F. Adly and D. Napier (eds) (2010), *Interculturalism, Society and Education*, Rotterdam: Sense.

Parekh, B. (2000), *Rethinking Multiculturalism: Cultural Diversity and Political Theory*, Basingstoke: Macmillan.

Solano-Campos, A. T. (2013), 'Bringing Latin America's "Interculturalidad" into the Conversation', *Journal of Intercultural Studies*, 34, 620–30.

Soutphommasane, T. (2012), *The Virtuous Citizen: Patriotism in a Multicultural Society*, Cambridge: Cambridge University Press.

Sunday Mail (Brisbane) (2005), 'Season for All', 4 December.

Tamir, Y. (1993), *Liberal Nationalism*, Princeton: Princeton University Press.

Taylor, C. (1992), 'The Politics of Recognition', in A. Gutmann (ed.), *Multiculturalism and 'The Politics of Recognition'*, Princeton: Princeton University Press, pp. 25–73.

Taylor, C. (2012), 'Interculturalism or Multiculturalism?', *Philosophy and Social Criticism*, 38 (4–5), 413–23.

Tubino, F. (2013), 'Intercultural Practices in Latin American Nation States', *Journal of Intercultural Studies*, 34, 604–19.

Winter, E. (2011), *Us, Them, and Others*, Toronto: University of Toronto Press.

Wood, P., and C. Landry (2007), *The Intercultural City*, London: Routledge.

Wood, P., C. Landry and J. Bloomfield (2006), *Cultural Diversity in Britain: A Toolkit for Cross-Cultural Co-Operation*, York: Joseph Rowntree Foundation.

Young, I. M. (1990), *Justice and the Politics of Difference*, Princeton: Princeton University Press.

Zapata-Barrero, R. (ed.) (2015), *Interculturalism in Cities: Concept, Policy and Implementation*, Cheltenham: Edward Elgar.

10

Towards an Intercultural Sense
of Belonging Together:
Reflections on the Theoretical and Political Level

Patrick Loobuyck

Introduction

During the last decades, the concept of interculturalism has increasingly been used in the philosophical, political and public debates on diversity issues. Especially as an answer to the so-called failures of multiculturalism, it gets more and more positive attention. In Quebec the concept is mainly used against the Canadian multicultural model wherein there is no place for majority precedence and the idea of a foundational (national) culture is absent (Bouchard 2011: 462ff; see also Weinstock 2013, Bouchard 2012, Taylor 2012, Gagnon and Iacovino 2007, Gagnon 2000). This position is close to what Will Kymlicka (2001) defended as a combination of liberal nationalism and multiculturalism. In Europe the Council of Europe (2008) played a leading role in the advocacy of interculturalism as a full-fleshed critical alternative for multiculturalism. Interculturalism has been presented as a new approach to managing culturally diverse societies by focusing on integration and social inclusion, interconnectedness and intercultural dialogue, interaction and exchange (especially at school), social cohesion and desegregation. However, on the policy level the arguments for the superiority of interculturalism are intellectually weak (Meer and Modood 2012), and often the term has been used as an interesting rhetoric trick to save some multicultural policies (Kymlicka 2012). Where multiculturalism became a poisoned and caricatured concept, it can be strategically better to relabel some multicultural measures as intercultural politics. Interculturalism, then, suggests some change, but in fact it is used to keep political and societal support for multicultural diversity politics. This was for instance the case in Belgium, where several recommendations of the Round Tables on Interculturalism (2011) were recommendations for multicultural measures such as concerted adjustments and reasonable accommodation, allowance for pupils to wear religious symbols in schools, the acceptance of religious symbols in the public service sector, and the rearrangement of the until now Christian-inspired calendar of paid holidays.

In this chapter I do not want to carry out another analysis of how the term 'interculturalism' appears in policy documents and academic texts. Instead I argue for a new interpretation. Interculturalism is presented and defended here as an additional strategy, next to, for example, liberal nationalism and constitutional patriotism, to create a sense of belonging together as a necessary condition for solidarity and deliberative democracy in multicultural societies.

To clarify my understanding of interculturalism, the chapter starts with a brief reconstruction of how the sense of belonging together became an important issue in the post-Rawlsian political philosophy (§1). The most important strategies to foster a sense of belonging together – the cultural and civic nationalist strategy – came to the fore as an answer to the communitarian critique on standard liberalism. However, it seems that there is also a third strategy, which I will call interculturalism (§2). From this perspective interculturalism and multiculturalism can be reconciled: while the latter focuses on equal rights, recognition and justice, interculturalism focuses on interaction, social cohesion and shared participation on the basis of a sense of belonging together (§3). To illustrate my theoretical position, three intercultural policy applications are briefly mentioned: the importance of social mix, language and civic integration programmes, and integrative religious education (§4). Finally, I open the discussion on how multicultural and intercultural policies can be related to each other. Despite the fact that some tensions can arise, it seems that multicultural and intercultural policies can and should be implemented simultaneously, as two complementary partners, each correcting the other in a fruitful way (§5).

1. Two liberal accommodations of the communitarian critique

One of the consequences of the communitarian critique on Rawlsian liberalism is that many liberal authors are now aware of the importance of social cohesion and a sense of belonging together to establish a deliberative, egalitarian democracy with welfare programmes and other policies based on solidarity and reciprocity. According to the so-called communitarians such as Michael Sandel and Charles Taylor, the standard Rawlsian liberals were sociologically naive: the fact that individual citizens share similar beliefs about justice is not a sufficient condition for democratic deliberation and sustainable egalitarian policies. Democracy and especially sustainable schemes of redistribution imply trust and social solidarity, and this must be established by a strong sense of belonging together (Taylor 1995: 184). For communitarians, however, this sense of belonging together can only exist when the members share some community values and a common form of life. Therefore, the idea of a neutral state should be replaced by a non-neutral politics of the common good.

The work of the so-called liberal nationalists (like Yael Tamir, David Miller and Will Kymlicka) reflects a sincere attempt to accommodate this communitarian critique (Kymlicka 2002: 261–8; 2001). They reject both the traditional liberal view that shared beliefs in universal principles of justice are sufficient for a sustainable practice of democracy and social justice, *and* the communitarian view that shared beliefs in a particularistic conception of the good – and thus a non-neutral politics of the common good – are necessary for the practice of democracy and social justice. Liberal nationalism is something in between: distributive justice and deliberative democracy require that citizens share more than simply political principles, but less than a shared conception of the good life. A shared but 'thin' national identity should and can be sufficient.

Next to liberal nationalism, a post-nationalist conception of solidarity has been proposed, partly because globalisation and immigration challenge the relevance of the traditional idea of a national identity based on a shared history, language and culture. According to this post-nationalist thesis the creation of a sense of belonging together should be independent from the cultural

227

integration in a particular national framework, and citizenship should be independent of particular (ethno-)cultural and historical characteristics (Habermas 1996: 264–71; 2001). The problem of community-building should be solved by appeal to the citizens' loyalty to their political institutions, their identification with liberal values locally embedded and codified in the constitution of the state, and a shared 'praxis of citizens who actively exercise their civil rights' (Habermas 1992: 3). Each country has its own constitutional tradition and this can be the basis for a shared political practice that creates a sense of belonging together. Through political participation and engagement in liberal democratic procedures, people come to see themselves as 'co-authors' of their own laws and institutions. This idea of co-authorship creates a sense of collective ownership and collective identity. Habermas insists, therefore, on 'the republican model of citizenship' wherein citizens are 'well-versed in adopting the we-perspective of active self-determination' (Habermas 1996: 263). To avoid any reference toward nationalism, Habermas coined the concept *Verfassungspatriotismus*, or constitutional patriotism. Other authors, who argue that the identification with the nationally coloured implementation of rather abstract principles of justice and politico-legal values must be sufficient as condition for trust, solidarity, democratic deliberation and social justice, keep the term 'nationalism' and use the concept of 'civic nationalism'. They emphasise that a shared nationality may not imply something more than a civic tie. This civic nationality is more than legal citizenship 'embodied in a passport', but less than the ethnic and cultural interpretation of nationality (Barry 2001: 80; Bauböck 1994; Laborde 2002).

While liberal nationalists argue that the standard liberal model of social unity and civic friendship is too abstract and sociologically naive, the civic nationalists argue that the idea of a shared cultural national identity is sociologically naive, especially in our context of globalisation, immigration and diversity. And, indeed, the liberal nation-building policies may be important (and they are), but in the end their scope and effectiveness is sometimes limited and rather modest. Especially in immigration societies – societies where newcomers are a permanent phenomenon – and multinational constellations such as Belgium and the EU, liberal nation-building projects are limited in their scope and effectiveness (Loobuyck 2012; Loobuyck and Sinardet, forthcoming). Therefore we should try to find alternatives and additional strategies to establish a sense of belonging together. Nobody will deny that a shared national culture is particularly well suited to creating a sense of belonging together; however, this does not imply that liberal nationalism is the one and only strategy to create a sense of belonging together. This is what I call 'the weak nationalist thesis': a shared national identity is a facilitating condition for solidarity and social justice sustained over a long period, but it is not a *conditio sine qua non* (see also the position of Mason 1999: 278; Mason 2000: 134; Moore 2001: 2, 17). Therefore, it would be unwise not to stimulate a shared national identity when it is possible to do this within the liberal constraints of state neutrality and respect for citizens as equal and free individuals. However, it would be even more unwise to deny that there are other additional strategies. Civic and cultural nationalism should not exclude each other. In immigration countries it can be a good idea to use the strategy of constitutional patriotism or civic nationalism as a supplement to cultural nation-building policies, and at the level of the EU, where cultural nation-building policies are impossible, a form of constitutional patriotism can still try to establish a (modest) sense of belonging together.

2. Interculturalism as a third strategy

Interculturalism can now be defined as a third and completely different strategy to create a sense of belonging together. It can be used especially in contexts of (deep or super-) diversity as an additive, complementary strategy alongside the civic and/or cultural liberal nationalist strategy. Compared with the other two strategies, interculturalism does not focus on solidarity on the macro level of the nation-state or as a result of a shared political praxis based on common constitutional values. Interculturalism focuses on solidarity that can develop in an entirely different spatio-temporal register, namely that of everyday place-based practices in which people are engaged across ethnic and cultural boundaries (cf. Oosterlynck et al. 2014). The aim is to create a sense of belonging together 'here and now', by (informal) social interactions and encounters, shared participation and interests, and co-operation at the meso and micro level. This strategy is already described in the work of the German sociologist Georg Simmel (1858–1918) and further elaborated by the urban sociologists of the Chicago School. But in political theory this strategy is neglected. Especially in light of the challenges for solidarity brought about by migration, increased ethnic, religious and cultural diversity, globalisation and individualisation, this third strategy seems to be quite promising (see also Loobuyck 2012; Levrau and Loobuyck 2013). Interculturalism facilitates interpersonal contact and intercultural competences to break down prejudices, stereotypes and misconceptions of others, and to generate mutual understanding, reciprocal identification, societal trust and solidarity.

The whole idea is based on the insights of social-psychologists that co-operative and fair interpersonal interaction between members of different groups reduces intergroup conflict and prejudice, and promotes tolerance and positive intergroup attitudes (Allport 1954; Gaertner and Dovidio 2000; Oliver and Wong 2003). It is indeed plausible to think that 'we are less likely to trust people of different backgrounds if we don't have the opportunity to interact with them and to understand their cultures' (Uslaner 2009: 8). Moreover, empirical research has demonstrated that social contact and co-operation between members of different groups ('us' and 'them') is an important element in the process of creating a common identity ('we'). And creating a common group identity also facilitates further co-operation (Gaertner et al. 1990; for reviews of this so-called 'contact hypothesis' see Hewstone and Swart 2011, Dovidio et al. 2003, Pettigrew 1998). However, to reduce prejudice and conflict, and to stimulate trust and solidarity, simple contact between groups is not sufficient. Contact must involve equal status between groups, norms supportive of equality, and co-operative rather than competitive intergroup interaction (Dovidio et al. 2008: 146; Pettigrew 1998: 66).

These social-psychological insights suggest that it must be possible that citizens with different national and cultural identities, with different social backgrounds and native languages, can recognise each other as co-citizens (a political 'we') by *doing things together* because they share the same workplace, they have children at the same school, they live in the same neighbourhood or street, and so on. The precondition for solidarity and a sense of belonging together can be sought in the idea of citizenship by social interaction and shared participation in common practices and institutions, especially when these practices and institutions are not competitive but co-operative. People with children at the same school have the same goals and interests, and this phenomenon can stimulate mutual identification and co-operation – at least when the condition of equality has also been fulfilled.

Maybe the metaphor of the lifeboat, rejected by Miller (1995: 25, 41, 62), can be useful. The occupants of a lifeboat are being thrown together accidentally and in a random way, but they must treat one another decently, they must work together to keep their craft afloat, and they have a sense of shared fate. This form of quasi-accidental connectedness can be the basis for a sense of belonging together and mutual commitment to each other. As such, we can suppose that shared participation and activities, concrete experiences and real-life contact between citizens of different groups can generate a shared consciousness that 'despite our differences we are all in the same boat and have shared interests', which can provide the motivation to work together (also politically) by changing 'the other' from an abstract stranger to a fellow citizen with the same worries and interests.

What we need at the most basic level is not only a broadly shared (civic and/or cultural) national identity, but also the consciousness of shared interests, a shared engagement of all citizens to undertake common projects based on equality and co-operation. It is possible that this project is a national one, but it is also possible on other, more local levels, such as those of the city, neighbourhood, school community or business company. Whether people feel like Belgian-Moroccans, Turks who live in Hamburg, or Americans who live in Europe is of minor importance as long as people have social interaction with each other and are engaged in living together in the same neighbourhood, school, city, country and in Europe.

3. *Multiculturalism* and *interculturalism*

The starting point of interculturalism is the belief that when people act together, meet each other and participate in concrete activities based on equality and fairness, a sense of belonging together and solidarity can evolve even in the absence of a shared national or cultural identity. This argument is already used by scholars who are looking for a post-national idea of community cohesion for the era of globalisation and super-diversity (Cantle 2008, 2012, 2013). However, I do not agree that we should get rid of the other strategies all together. The liberal nationalist, the constitutional and the intercultural strategies to establish a sense of belonging together are complementary, can enforce each other and can be effective in different contexts. If governments can use the liberal nationalist and/or constitutional strategy, they should do so. But where the nationalist strategies fail, or where the nationalist sense of belonging together can be strengthened and reinforced by real-life contact in shared practices and dialogue, the intercultural model should be used and implied as an additional strategy.

My conception of interculturalism is also largely in line with what the Council of Europe (2008) had in mind with interculturalism and with what the European Court of Human Rights has recognised: 'the harmonious interaction of persons and groups with varied identities is essential for achieving social cohesion' (Gorzelik and Others v. Poland, no. 44158/98, 17 February 2004). The difference is that I do not use interculturalism as a critique on or follow-up of multiculturalism. Interculturalism can be defined and presented in a way that is independent of and complementary to multiculturalism.

Analogous to the idea that liberal nationalism is compatible with multiculturalism (the position of Will Kymlicka is well known), so too the intercultural strategy may be compatible with multiculturalism. They are simply two different paradigms, two approaches on different levels with different actors, targets and aims. While multiculturalism is a theory conceived in order to create a more just society by accommodating diversity, the purpose of interculturalism and liberal nationalism is a sense of belonging together and social cohesion as social preconditions for an egalitarian, democratic multicultural policy. The difference with liberal nationalism, then, is that interculturalism does not focus on a shared, thin national identity, but on more locally embedded interaction, dialogue and shared participation.

Multiculturalism and interculturalism have different objects: the latter is focused on social connections between citizens in (civil) society, while the relation of the state to its cultural minorities is the predominant concern of multiculturalism. Multiculturalism can be thought of as a vertical, top-down policy between the state and minority groups, while interculturalism is rather a horizontal issue of everyday engagements between citizens or groups within the society.

The relation between interculturalism and multiculturalism is dialectical. On the one hand interculturalism can increase the societal support for multicultural policies, and as such multiculturalism can be stronger with the side support of interculturalism. If a government were to invest solely in multicultural acknowledgement of differences, it would be impossible to preclude the segregation of groups as an outcome. As observed by Uslaner (2009, 2010), it is segregation that plays an important role in the creation of societal distrust, and not diversity as such. The fact that people live alongside each other in separate groups undermines solidarity and thus the basis for multicultural justice.

On the other hand, the argument that interculturalism is a precondition for multiculturalism does not preclude the reverse logic of multiculturalism as a precondition for interculturalism. As we have seen, the idea of interaction and shared participation can only be effective when the condition of equality is fulfilled. Simply ensuring contact between groups is not sufficient to reduce prejudice and conflict and to stimulate trust and solidarity. From the outset, the founder of this 'contact hypothesis', Allport (1954: 281), argues that 'prejudice . . . may be reduced by equal status contact between majority and minority groups in the pursuit of common goals'. In addition to equal status between groups, contact must involve norms that support equality and co-operative interaction rather than competitive intergroup interaction. The government must therefore fight social exclusion, racism and discrimination in order to guarantee equal opportunities and equal status between groups and to decrease unequal access to public institutions and the public sphere in general. But sometimes this is not enough and multicultural measures (some would say 'minority rights') are also necessary to establish genuine equality. Affirmative action and special multicultural measures resulting in recognition, equality and equal participation are therefore not only in the individual interest of the minorities, but also in the interest of the cohesion of the whole society. As such multiculturalism is also an important precondition for the success of interculturalism. Multiculturalism guarantees that particular groups feel themselves fairly recognised and are not unfairly disadvantaged or excluded from societal participation – which is (the basis for) interculturalism.

4. Intercultural policies

More than multiculturalism, interculturalism focuses on dialogue and interpersonal cultural encounters at the meso and micro level, such as neighbourhoods, youth clubs and schools. However, that does not imply that interculturalism is apolitical (as is suggested by Meer and Modood 2012: 187; Modood 2014: 302). If intercultural dialogue and encounters are valuable not only for the enrichment of the citizens' individual lives, but also for the necessary sense of belonging together to create a sustainable multicultural society, an efficient deliberative democracy and welfare state, then the government/state clearly has a political interest in stimulating and facilitating interculturalism. As a consequence it is worth making the effort to find out how it can be done and to focus on some concrete policy implications.

To make interculturalism work, it is important that there are enough opportunities, encouragements, incentives and support for citizens of different backgrounds to participate in shared practices and to co-operate and meet each other in common projects. Therefore governments can legitimately develop intercultural policies on the fields of social mix, language and education. Without social mix people do not meet each other, without a common language there is no exchange, and without good education people do not know each other and people may not be adequately trained to cope with diversity in an open and democratic way.

Because real-life contact between members of different groups is an important element of the intercultural strategy, the government can legitimately promote policies of social and cultural mix in education, neighbourhoods, employment, trade unions, sports clubs, youth movements, leisure time organisations and other parts of the civil society. The importance of this kind of population mix is in line with recent research findings, pointing out that (against the so-called Putnam hypothesis (2007)) not diversity as such but rather social isolation and (residential) segregation lead to less trust and social cohesion (Oliver and Wong 2003; Uslaner 2002: 229–37; 2009; 2010). Of course, the implementation of a policy of social mix should always take place within the liberal constraints of freedom and equality. This is not always easy, but it is not impossible (Trappenburg 2003). However, it is important to keep in mind that the idea of social and cultural mix should not only or primarily focus on the co-presence of different people in particular 'places' in the public sphere, because this is not enough to guarantee genuine, meaningful interactions (Oosterlynck et al. 2014; Matejskova and Leitner 2011; Valentine 2008; Hewstone et al. 2007; Hewstone and Brown 1986). The ultimate aim is (informal) contact, interaction and exchange as a result of engagement in shared activities based on common interests.

Since dialogue, encounter and doing things together are distinctive features of interculturalism, it is remarkable that language competence does not get more attention than is the case in the discussion about interculturalism (for this critique see Méndez García and Byram 2013). Language should be a central issue. To stimulate shared participation and interaction, the promotion of (the acquisition of) a common language is highly recommendable. For a diversified society in search of social cohesion, solidarity and trust, an attitude of neutrality or laissez-faire concerning language is not an option. This is also the reason why civic nations can support an active language policy to establish a shared language. Language can be seen as 'instrumental to achieving other justified public purposes' and therefore a language policy should not always be interpreted as part of a cultural, nationalistic project (Stilz 2009: 258). Active policies on language acquisition may be important for practical reasons, and can be justified without any reference to the intrinsic worth of the new language or the importance of a shared national identity. I agree here with Anna Stilz (2009: 267) that 'sharing a language may help to develop . . . democratic solidarity and trust'. However, she argues that social solidarity and trust are 'far less compelling state interests than the interests in facilitating economic opportunity and democratic participation' (2009: 267). On this point I disagree, because trust and social solidarity are important social conditions for a sustainable welfare state. The creation of a sense of belonging together is a compelling state interest and as such an additional convincing reason for an active language policy.

As a consequence, language courses as a substantial part of civic integration policies for newcomers can be seen as intercultural measures. Too often, civic integration and language acquisition programmes and tests are labelled as nationalistic assimilationist policies. However, promoting a common language is not necessarily the same as promoting a shared nationhood, and it is definitely not necessarily the same as insisting on full cultural assimilation. They can easily be framed in another way as a substantial part of an intercultural policy, but also, under certain conditions, as multicultural measures to increase equal opportunities for newcomers to contribute actively to society and the labour market – which is a matter of justice (Levrau and Loobuyck 2013: 620–5; Taylor 2012: 414). The reason why liberal governments may ensure that all citizens and permanent immigrants (can) learn the language is that language acquisition is important for the (equality of opportunities of the) citizens themselves and because it is an important condition of increasing the sense of belonging together as a condition for sustainable social and multicultural policies.

Besides a policy of social mix and a language policy, education is a third policy field where the government can facilitate interculturalism. Governments should not only give incentives for schools to create social and cultural mix among their pupils and teachers; they can also require that schools give special attention to intercultural encounters, teaching about other religions and worldviews, living together in diversity, reciprocity and dialogue. The training of people's democratic attitude towards diversity, otherness and living together based on freedom and equality should be part of the regular school curriculum (Loobuyck and Sägesser 2014; Loobuyck 2015; Franken and Loobuyck 2013). It is vital for interculturalism that people acquire the competences to participate in intercultural dialogue and encounters – and education has a key role to play here as the most important means through which pupils' intercultural competences can be enhanced (Barrett 2013; Bekemans 2013). This can be implemented in a separate, compulsory course on citizenship education, or it can be integrated in a religious and moral education course. The former is the case in France, the latter in Quebec, where religious education, *vivre ensemble* and dialogue are integrated in one course. Quebec introduced its ERC (ethics and religious culture) programme in all primary and secondary schools in 2008 (Estivalèzes 2013; Leroux 2007). Besides religious and moral literacy, dialogue is the third aim of this programme. The idea of promoting intercultural dialogue and competences through religious and citizenship education is also present in the White Paper of the Council of Europe (2008). The paper stresses that schools are important for the 'preparation of young people for life as active citizens' in a multicultural democratic society. 'Education for democratic citizenship is fundamental to a free, tolerant, just, open and inclusive society, to social cohesion, mutual understanding, intercultural and interreligious dialogue and solidarity, as well as equality between women and men' (Council of Europe 2008: 29ff).

5. Intercultural versus multicultural policies?

Multiculturalism and interculturalism are compatible and complementary on the theoretical level, and at first sight this seems also to be the case on the policy level. In short, interculturalism is mainly applicable to the level of the civil society, while multiculturalism is more appropriate to the state level. Multiculturalism should be implemented by the government(s), interculturalism by the citizens (Kymlicka 2003). While citizens and minority groups are key actors in the struggle for fair multicultural politics, which can involve protest, challenging racism and discrimination, claims-making, mobilisation, negotiation and dialogue, it is the (local, national and state) governments who have the primary responsibility for implementing multiculturalism (Modood 2007). And as far as multiculturalism is also concerned about dialogue – as Parekh (2000), Taylor (1992) and Meer and Modood (2012) have argued for – intercultural dialogue is still something else (cf. Levrau and Loobuyck 2013: 615–18). Both Taylor and Parekh present the dialogue – or the 'fusion of horizons' – as a concrete alternative to the ideal of procedural liberal politics. Intercultural dialogue, however, is not perceived as primarily an instrument with which to increase fairness and justice in society. Instead, it is an instrument to create mutual identification, trust, social cohesion and self-identification with the host society.

However, the fact that multiculturalism and interculturalism do not contradict each other and are mutually supportive and complementary on both the theoretical and the policy level does not preclude that sometimes the two paradigms may point in different policy directions. In their implementation, some tensions between multicultural and intercultural policy options may arise: in general, we could say that, on the one hand, the recognition of diversity and multicultural (minority) rights can reduce the possibilities for intercultural contact; and, on the other hand, the incentives to establish intercultural interactions can touch the multicultural rights of minorities.

More concretely, multiculturalism is for instance in favour of ethno-cultural civil society organisations and would give supportive arguments for state subsidies for these kinds of organisations, while interculturalism would suggest that governments primarily support and facilitate social and cultural mix in the civil society. In the same vein, Kymlicka (2003: 161–2) mentions the tension between the model of interculturalism that requires a level of intercultural exchange and the multicultural right of isolationist groups to live their own life. These groups will not reject multiculturalism, but they will be very reluctant to accept the ideal of intercultural citizens who participate in (mixed activities of) the majority society. At first sight it seems impossible to combine these two policy directions. However, in the case where ethnic organisations are functioning as a first step toward participation in other organisations, the two policy directions are still complementary. But even without this stepping-stone theory it makes sense to implement multiculturalism and interculturalism simultaneously – indeed, keeping in mind that interculturalism can place a burden on some conservative, isolationist groups and that the recognition of diversity can increase isolation instead of contact and encounters. A government that is in favour of a diversity-sensitive policy should implement and balance both the intercultural and the multicultural policy options. The multicultural perspective can guarantee that the burden of interculturalism on minority groups is not an unfair violation of the rights of these minority groups. The intercultural perspective can intensify the sense of belonging together which is the necessary social basis of a democratic multicultural society. In short, interculturalism should guarantee that multiculturalism does not crumble into merely a compilation of *Parallel-Gemeinschaften*; multiculturalism should guarantee that the idea of interculturalism does not end up with a society where diversity is gone.

Also in the field of language policy the tension between the multicultural and the intercultural perspective may arise. The first tends to recognise the different languages in an attempt to give them a fair place in society, while the second perspective focuses on a shared language that every citizen should speak in the public sphere. However, again the two options can be implemented simultaneously and can balance each other. An active language policy and citizenship trajectories are not necessarily incompatible with respect for – and even the protection of – the languages spoken by ethnic minorities (Miller 1995: 189; Stilz 2009; Patten 2009; vs Barry 2001: 107). The positive attention to minority languages in the school context, for instance, is not an indication that better knowledge of the common language and the acquisition of the official language is less important. Again the combination can be fruitful – even if there is a burden on two sides. The allowance of different languages is a threat for social mix and intercultural encounters; the emphasis on the shared language (of the majority) can push the other languages aside. On the other hand, recognition of one's own (minority) language is an important condition for self-respect, and the common language enhances equal opportunities and social cohesion. Therefore governments, but also local and school policies, should try to find a contextually balanced equilibrium on this issue.

Finally, the application of interculturalism in the field of education can contradict multiculturalism. As Kymlicka (2003: 162) observes, 'The sort of schooling required by norms of intercultural self-development may not be the same sort of schooling required by norms of multicultural fairness.' Interculturalism asks for open, pluralistic schools and integrative religious education – wherein the students are not segregated in separate classes according to their worldview. Multiculturalism, on the other hand, tends to give support for the idea of separate confessional religious education courses in official schools and/or for schools organised and run by religious organisations (such as Jewish, Catholic or Muslim schools). The fact that every minority group has the multicultural right to provide education for its own public might conflict with the intercultural ambition of societal and intercultural mixing and contact.

Here again the government can contextually balance the multicultural and the intercultural perspective. It is possible to allow (optional) confessional religious courses in public schools and at the same time require that all students follow a class of integrative religious education wherein dialogue, reciprocity and intercultural competences are trained. Indeed, this kind of religious education can be a burden for certain (conservative orthodox) religious groups, but as long as these courses are organised in 'an objective, critical and pluralist way', it is not a human rights violation on the freedom of religion (Leigh 2012; Pettigrew 2014; Bosset 2012).

In the three examples, it is the combination of the two perspectives that is the most promising option for those who take living together in diversity seriously. Instead of merely juxtaposing these two policy paradigms, the examples illustrate the extent to which multiculturalism and interculturalism are both different and complementary, as well as why they can and should be implemented simultaneously. Multiculturalism should be adjusted through the adoption of sufficient intercultural policies, which encourage interaction and shared participation. But if the government were to invest solely in interculturalism, this could create a risk that certain legitimate claims or rights of minorities would not be recognised.

In the last two cases, language and education, it seems that interculturalism is more important than multiculturalism. Multicultural policies (special religious education, recognition of the use of minority languages) may be implemented only when there is also enough interculturalism. While the state has a strong duty (toward its own society and toward the individual pupils) to guarantee a shared language, language acquisition for newcomers and intercultural education, the state is more free to decide if it is also desirable to implement multicultural measures concerning language and education. Without a shared language and intercultural skills, there can be no conversation and people cannot work and live together. Without a shared language and intercultural skills, there is almost no society.

In the first example of social mix, however, it seems to be the other way around. The state has a strong multicultural duty to guarantee the freedom of organisation, and the freedom of how and where to live. The intercultural duty to establish social mix and to stimulate intercultural interactions is also important, but weaker and inferior.

Conclusion

In many Western countries our time is characterised by individualism, secularisation, diversity and globalisation. The *Gemeinschaft* became more and more a *Gesellschaft* wherein solidarity, trust and a sense of belonging together are no longer automatically present. On the contrary, they are under pressure, despite the fact that they are important preconditions for fair redistribution programmes, deliberative democracy and stable multicultural policies based on freedom and equality. This means that the search for theoretical and practical input to strengthen the societal sense of belonging together was never so urgent as it is today.

In political philosophy, this issue was a key element in the so-called liberalism-communitarianism debate of the 1980s. Since then, liberalism gives much more attention to the importance of community-building and a sense of belonging together. Liberal nationalism and constitutional patriotism came to the fore as two strategies to foster the necessary sense of belonging together between citizens with a diverse ethnic, cultural, linguistic and religious background. The combination of these strategies with a politics of multiculturalism was quite successful, but did not solve all the problems.

Today the discussion is still going on, not only about the value and consistency of the liberal nationalist and the constitutional strategy, but also about the possibility of other models. Deep diversity within national states (especially in cities) on the one hand and international political constructions such as the European Union on the other is a challenge for the existing strategies and illustrates the need to explore other strategies.

From that perspective, it is surprising that the intercultural way of creating a sense of belonging together, as it is presented here, has for so long been neglected in political theory. Interculturalism, based on well-known insights of social-psychologists about co-operation and the importance of real interaction between people, does not exclude the other strategies, but can be seen as an important supplementary and complementary strategy to strengthen the sense of belonging together. Especially in cases where the other strategies fail or have only a weak effect because there is no thin shared identity or because community-building around constitutional values is too abstract, interculturalism is a valuable additional strategy.

This chapter has also covered some exploratory work on how multicultural and intercultural policies may support each other, and how they may direct in opposite directions. It has been argued that interculturalism and multiculturalism can best be seen as two complementary partners, each correcting the other in a fruitful way. The two policy models can adjust and compensate for possible undesirable outcomes, but in addition they can also be mutually reinforcing. On the one hand, multiculturalism and interculturalism can be reconciled; on the other hand, there is somehow a tension between the multicultural recognition of diversity and the search for a societal belonging together.

And this is, more generally speaking, precisely the challenge for many states: how to recognise diversity without disintegration of the society. How can the state generously protect the rights of newcomers and immigrants without neglecting the fact that a society needs a social cement to keep everybody – minorities and (former) majority – together? Some (mostly progressive political voices) have mainly thought about the recognition of diversity; others (mostly conservative, nationalist, right-wing political forces) have mainly been concerned with the sense of belonging together. The multiculturalism/interculturalism debate can help things to move some steps forward by acknowledging that both elements are equally important. Governments have to balance the two per-spectives and policy goals: diversity and social unity. How this can be done in concrete situations and particular contexts will be an unavoidable part of every future debate about living together in diversity.

References

Allport, G. W. (1954), *The Nature of Prejudice*, New York: Addison-Wesley.

Barrett, M. (2013), 'Intercultural Competence: A Distinctive Hallmark of Interculturalism', in M. Barrett (ed.), *Interculturalism and Multiculturalism: Similarities and Differences*, Strasbourg: Council of Europe, pp. 147–68.

Barry, B. (2001), *Culture and Equality: An Egalitarian Critique of Multiculturalism*, Cambridge: Polity Press.

Bauböck, R. (1994), *Transnational Citizenship: Membership and Rights in International Migration*, Aldershot: Edward Elgar.

Bekemans, L. (2013), 'Educational Challenges and Perspectives in Multiculturalism vs. Interculturalism: Citizenship Education for Intercultural Realities', in M. Barrett (ed.), *Interculturalism and Multiculturalism: Similarities and Differences*, Strasbourg: Council of Europe, pp. 169–87.

Bosset, P. (2012), 'Les droits des parents en matière d'enseignement religieux: pour une mise en perspective du discours juridique', in M. Estivalèzes and S. Lefebvre (eds), *Le programme d'éthique et culture religieuse. De l'exigeante conciliation entre le soi, l'autre et le nous*, Quebec City: Presses de l'Université Laval, pp. 157–74.

Bouchard, G. (2011), 'What Is Interculturalism?', *McGill Law Journal*, 56 (2), 435–68.

Bouchard, G. (2012), *L'interculturalisme: un point de vue québécois*, Montreal: Boréal.

Bouchard, G., and C. Taylor (2008), *Building the Future: A Time for Reconciliation*, Report of the Consultation Commission on Accommodation Practices Related to Cultural Difference, Quebec City: Government of Quebec.

Cantle, T. (2008), *Community Cohesion: A New Framework for Race and Diversity*, Basingstoke: Palgrave Macmillan.

Cantle, T. (2012), *Interculturalism: The New Era of Cohesion and Diversity*, Basingstoke: Palgrave Macmillan.

Cantle, T. (2013), 'Interculturalism as a New Narrative for the Era of Globalisation and Super-Diversity', in M. Barrett (ed.), *Interculturalism and Multiculturalism: Similarities and Differences*, Strasbourg: Council of Europe, pp. 69–91.

Council of Europe, Committee of Ministers (2008), *Living Together as Equals in Dignity: White Paper on Intercultural Dialogue*, Strasbourg: Council of Europe.

Dovidio, J. F., S. L. Gaertner and V. M. Esses (2008), 'Cooperation, Common Identity, and Intergroup Contact', in B. A. Sullivan, M. Snyder and J. L. Sullivan (eds), *Cooperation: The Political Psychology of Effective Human Interaction*, Oxford: Blackwell, pp. 143–59.

Dovidio, J. F., S. L. Gaertner and K. Kawakami (2003), 'Intergroup Contact: The Past, Present, and Future', *Group Processes and Intergroup Relations*, 6 (1), 5–21.

Estivalèzes, M. (2013), 'The Teaching of an Ethics and Religious Culture Programme in Quebec: A Political Project?', in A. Jödicke (ed.), *Religious Education Politics, the State, and Society*, Würzburg: Ergon, pp. 129–47.

Franken, L., and P. Loobuyck (2013), 'The Future of Religious Education on the Flemish School Curriculum: A Plea for Integrative Religious Education for All', *Religious Education*, 108 (5), 482–98.

Gaertner, S. L., and J. F. Dovidio (2000), *Reducing Intergroup Bias: The Common Intergroup Identity Model*, Philadelphia: Taylor and Francis.

Gaertner, S. L., J. A. Mann, J. F. Dovidio, A. Murrell and M. Pomare (1990), 'How Does Cooperation Reduce Intergroup Bias?', *Journal of Personality and Social Psychology*, 59 (4), 692–704.

Gagnon, A.-G. (2000), 'Plaidoyer pour l'interculturalisme', *Possibles*, 24 (4), 11–25.

Gagnon, A.-G., and R. Iacovino (2007), *Federalism, Citizenship and Quebec: Debating Multinationalism*, Toronto: University of Toronto Press.

Habermas, J. (1992), 'Citizenship and National Identity: Some Reflections on the Future of Europe', *Praxis International*, 12 (1), 1–19.

Habermas, J. (1996), *Die Einbeziehung des Anderen*, Frankfurt-am-Main: Suhrkamp.

Habermas, J. (2001), 'Why Europe Needs a Constitution', *New Left Review*, 11 (September–October), 5–26.

Hewstone, M., and R. Brown (1986), 'Contact Is Not Enough: An Intergroup Perspective on the Contact Hypothesis', in M. Hewstone and R. Brown (eds), *Contact and Conflict in Intergroup Encounters*, Oxford: Blackwell, pp. 1–44.

Hewstone, M., and H. Swart (2011), 'Fifty-odd Years of Inter-group Contact: From Hypothesis to Integrated Theory', *British Journal of Social Psychology*, 50 (3), 374–86.

Hewstone, M., N. Tausch, J. Hughes and E. Cairns (2007), 'Prejudice, Intergroup Contact and Identity: Do Neighbourhoods Matter?', in M. Wetherell, M. Lafleche and R. Berkeley (eds), *Identity, Ethnic Diversity and Community Cohesion*, London: Sage, pp. 102–12.

Kymlicka, W. (2001), *Politics in the Vernacular: Nationalism, Multiculturalism, and Citizenship*, Oxford: Oxford University Press.

Kymlicka, W. (2002), *Contemporary Political Philosophy: An Introduction*, Oxford: Oxford University Press.

Kymlicka, W. (2003), 'Multicultural States and Intercultural Citizens', *Theory and Research in Education*, 1 (2), 147–69.

Kymlicka, W. (2012), 'Comment on Meer and Modood', *Journal of Intercultural Studies*, 33 (2), 211–16.

Laborde, C. (2002), 'From Constitutional to Civic Patriotism', *British Journal of Political Science*, 32 (4), 591–612.

Leigh, I. (2012), 'Objective, Critical and Pluralistic? Religious Education and Human Rights in the European Public Sphere', in L. Zucca and C. Ungureanu (eds), *Law, State and Religion in the New Europe: Debates and Dilemmas*, Cambridge: Cambridge University Press, pp. 192–214.

Leroux, G. (2007), *Éthique, culture religieuse, dialogue. Argument pour un programme*, Quebec City: Fides.

Levrau, F., and P. Loobuyck (2013), 'Should Interculturalism Replace Multiculturalism? A Plea for Complementariness', *Ethical Perspectives*, 20 (4), 605–30.

Loobuyck, P. (2012), 'Creating Mutual Identification and Solidarity in Highly Diversified Societies: The Importance of Identification by Shared Participation', *South African Journal of Philosophy*, 31 (3), 560–75.

Loobuyck, P. (2015), 'Religious Education in Habermasian Post-Secular Societies', in M. Rectenwald et al. (eds), *Global Secularisms in a Post-Secular Age*, Berlin and Boston: Walter de Gruyter Publications.

Loobuyck, P., and C. Sägesser (2014), *Le vivre-ensemble à l'école. Plaidoyer pour un cours philosophique commun*, Brussels: Espace de Libertés (Éditions du Centre d'Action Laïque).

Loobuyck, P., and D. Sinardet (forthcoming), 'Belgium: A Hard Case for Liberal Nationalism?', in W. Kymlicka and K. Banting (eds), *The Strains of Commitment*, Oxford: Oxford University Press.

Mason, A. (1999), 'Political Community, Liberal Nationalism, and the Ethics of Assimilation', *Ethics*, 109 (2), 261–86.

Mason, A. (2000), *Community, Solidarity and Belonging*, Cambridge: Cambridge University Press.

Matejskova, T., and H. Leitner (2011), 'Urban Encounters with Difference: The Contact Hypothesis and Immigrant Integration Projects in Eastern Berlin', *Social and Cultural Geography*, 12 (7), 709–33.

Meer, N., and T. Modood (2012), 'How Does Interculturalism Contrast with Multiculturalism?', *Journal of Intercultural Studies*, 33 (2), 175–96.

Méndez García, M. del C., and M. Byram (2013), 'Interculturalism, Multiculturalism and Language Issues and Policies', in M. Barrett (ed.), *Interculturalism and Multiculturalism: Similarities and Differences*, Strasbourg: Council of Europe, pp. 133–46.

Miller, D. (1995), *On Nationality*, Oxford: Clarendon Press.

Modood, T. (2007), *Multiculturalism: A Civic Idea*, Cambridge: Polity Press.

Modood, T. (2014), 'Multiculturalism, Interculturalisms and the Majority', *Journal of Moral Education*, 43 (3), 302–15.

Moore, M. (2001), 'Normative Justifications for Liberal Nationalism: Justice, Democracy and Nationality', *Nations and Nationalism*, 7 (1), 1–20.

Oliver, J. E., and J. Wong (2003), 'Intergroup Prejudice in Multi-Ethnic Settings', *American Journal of Political Science*, 47 (4), 567–82.

Oosterlynck, S., et al. (2014), 'Putting Flesh to the Bone: Looking for Solidarity, Here and Now', DieGem Working Paper, Antwerp University.

Parekh, B. (2000), *Rethinking Multiculturalism: Cultural Diversity and Political Theory*, Basingstoke: Macmillan.

Patten, A. (2009), 'The Justification of Minority Language Rights', *Journal of Political Philosophy*, 17 (1), 102–28.

Pettigrew, J. (2014), 'Le progam Éthique et culture religieuse et le jugement de la Cour suprême du Canada dans l'affaire S.L. c. *la Commission scolaire des Chênes*', in J.-P. Willaime (ed.), *Le défi de l'enseignement des faits religieux à l'école. Réponses européennes et québéqoises*, Paris: Riveneuve éditions, pp. 223–37.

Pettigrew, T. F. (1998), 'Intergroup Contact Theory', *Annual Review of Psychology*, 49 (1), 65–85.

Round Tables on Interculturalism (2011), 'Final Report', in M.-C. Foblets and J.-P. Schreiber (eds), *The Round Tables on Interculturalism*, Brussels: Larcier, pp. 493–581.

Stilz, A. (2009), 'Civic Nationalism and Language Policy', *Philosophy and Public Affairs*, 37 (3), 257–92.

Taylor, C. (1992), 'The Politics of Recognition', in A. Gutmann (ed.), *Multiculturalism and 'The Politics of Recognition'*, Princeton: Princeton University Press, pp. 25–73.

Taylor, C. (1995), 'Cross-Purposes: The Liberal-Communitarian Debate', in *Philosophical Arguments*, Cambridge, MA: Harvard University Press, pp. 181–203.

Taylor, C. (2012), 'Interculturalism or Multiculturalism?', *Philosophy and Social Criticism*, 38 (4–5), 413–23.

Trappenburg, M. (2003), 'Against Segregation: Ethnic Mixing in Liberal States', *The Journal of Political Philosophy*, 1 (3), 295–319.

Uslaner, E. (2002), *The Moral Foundations of Trust*, New York: Cambridge University Press.

Uslaner, E. (2009), 'Trust, Diversity, and Segregation', <http://ssrn.com/abstract=1523721> (last accessed 22 June 2015).

Uslaner, E. (2010), 'Segregation, Mistrust and Minorities', *Ethnicities*, 10 (4), 415–34.

Valentine, G. (2008), 'Living with Difference: Reflections on Geographies of Encounter', *Progress in Human Geography*, 32, 323–37.

Weinstock, D. (2013), 'Interculturalism and Multiculturalism in Canada and Quebec: Situating the Debate', in P. Balint and S. Guérard de Latour (eds), *Liberal Multiculturalism and the Fair Terms of Integration*, Basingstoke: Palgrave Macmillan, pp. 91–108.

11

Multiculturalism, Interculturalisms and the Majority

Tariq Modood

Introduction

In this chapter I try to do two things.[1] Firstly, in response to those Quebecan intellectuals who say that Europeans do not consider their significant contribution to the theory and politics of interculturalism, I do that. Secondly, and more substantively, I acknowledge that Quebecan interculturalists have raised the question of the normative significance of the majority in the way that multiculturalists have not, and that multiculturalists can learn from those interculturalists here. I show, however, that multiculturalists can take on board this concern with the majority without changing or adapting multiculturalism, and I conclude by reaffirming a commitment to accommodate ethno religious minorities that is very different from what is advocated by Quebecers.

In Chapter 2 Nasar Meer and I identified four ways in which (mainly European) interculturalism is alleged to contrast positively with multiculturalism in contexts of cultural diversity:

1. More than co-existence, more geared toward interaction and dialogue than multiculturalism.
2. Less 'groupist' or more yielding of synthesis than multiculturalism.

[1] This is a modified version of T. Modood (2014), 'Multiculturalism, Interculturalisms and the Majority', Kohlberg Memorial Lecture, *Journal of Moral Education*, 43 (3), 302–15. I am grateful for comments on an earlier draft from Joe Carens, Terrell Carver, Nicole Hossan, Geoff Levey, David Miller, Bhikhu Parekh and Varun Uberoi.

3. Committed to a stronger sense of the whole (Quebecan primarily).
4. Critical of illiberal cultural practices (as part of the process of intercultural dialogue).

The conclusion was that these contrasts could not on closer inspection be substantiated, so while interculturalism (IC) (in both its European and Quebecan variants) could be said to offer a difference in emphases or a revision of MC, it was less an alternative, more a modification of multiculturalism (MC).

In this chapter I consider whether that argument needs to be augmented in the light of three important recent statements or restatements of Quebecan and European IC:

- Ted Cantle (2012), *Interculturalism: The New Era of Cohesion and Diversity*; see also Cantle, this volume, Chapter 6.
- Gérard Bouchard (2011), 'What Is Interculturalism?', *McGill Law Journal*, 56 (2); see also Bouchard, this volume, Chapter 4.
- Charles Taylor (2012), 'Interculturalism or Multiculturalism?', *Philosophy and Social Criticism*, 38 (4–5).

Interculturalisms

The central argument of Ted Cantle's book is that mass migrations and urban super-diversity are inevitable in an age of globalisation, and so national, ethnic and communal identities will seem irrelevant as individuals – through diverse neighbourhoods, foreign travel, work abroad, global media and online social networks – will be in constant interaction across cultural and national boundaries, which inevitably will decompose and individuals will come to have and be comfortable with hybridic, fluid and multiple identities of their own and of others (Cantle 2012a; for Cantle's own summary, see Cantle 2012b; see also his chapter in this book).

I do not think Cantle's book occasions any revision of my previous views. I hope it is quite clear from the very brief summary that I have offered that Cantle's IC is a version of cosmopolitanism, that is to say, the view that people are rightly increasingly thinking of themselves as global citizens and identifying with humanity in a post-national way. As such it has certain normative and sociological strengths but does not analytically capture the full range of contemporary ethnic, religious and national identities and their legitimate claims, no less than that of cosmopolitans, to be politically recognised (Modood 2012). It is not an alternative to MC but a valuable complement to a communitarian multiculturalism and, indeed, to other modes of integration.

My main purpose in this chapter is to examine the radically different understanding of interculturalism presented by Gérard Bouchard and Charles Taylor.[2] A preliminary remark is that whilst it is clear that this version of IC owes considerably, perhaps everything, to a Québécois struggle for the rest of Canada to recognise it as a founding nation and refusal to be defined within the terms of Canadian multiculturalism, my interest is not in this provenance (on which see Weinstock 2013). Indeed, one of the striking features of these two texts, especially Bouchard's, is that IC is not defined in terms of its aptness in contexts of minority nationhood, where a nation, like Quebec, is a minority within a larger state (though in his chapter in this book Bouchard emphasises that the primary reason for the Quebecan rejection of federal Canadian MC and development of an alternative, oppositional IC was that the former had no place in it for Quebecan national identity, and so more closely relates Quebecan interculturalism (IC-Q) to minority nationalism). Furthermore, while IC is presented as an alternative to and superior to Canadian multiculturalism, it is not conceptualised in terms of the relation of one nation to another. Bouchard does not mention minority national identity in his account of IC, which he says distinctively 'concerns itself with the interests of the majority culture' (2011: 438), and Taylor explicitly concludes his discussion of the meaning of IC in Quebec by suggesting that it may fit majoritarian anxieties in Europe (2012: 420). My interest in IC is at this level of general applicability, regardless of its origins, though I note that this has a certain real world logic too. If Quebec were an independent state, its government and publics would pre-

---

[2] Bouchard and Taylor (2008: 118) state that the first record of the term 'interculturalism' in Quebec is in 1985, prior to which they could find only two references, a Council of Europe document and a Belgian government document, both dated 1981. The term 'intercultural education' was being used by Germans and others from the late 1970s (Kraus and Schönwälder 2006). So it seems that 'interculturalism' is only about fifteen years behind the emergence of 'multiculturalism' in the late 1960s, originated in Europe, and was soon followed by Quebec. Moreover, 'intercultural education' also seems to have European origins and seems to be of the same vintage as 'multicultural education'.

sumably continue to subscribe to interculturalism. They would not say that interculturalism was no longer more suited to Quebec than multiculturalism just because Quebecers had a state of their own. IC-Q is thus about integration in relation to a national state and not in relation to a minority nation; it is because so many Quebecers understand themselves as a nation and a semi-nation state that IC has developed in Quebec. It is however worth noting that while Taylor now uses 'interculturalism' to capture the desire of the Quebecan *majority* to preserve its culture, in his famous essay on multiculturalism Quebecers are the central illustration of the right of a *minority* to preserve its culture (Taylor 1994).

Explicitly drawing on 'authors from Quebec who have a long history of reflecting on the topic', Bouchard (2011: 439) considers interculturalism to be a model that 'aims at integration within a single nation', which, as a pluralist model, 'concerns itself with the interests of the majority culture, whose desire to perpetuate and maintain itself is perfectly legitimate, *as much as* it does with the interests of minorities and immigrants' (438; my emphasis). As an aside, it is worth reflecting upon the highlighted 'as much as'. It seems reasonable but it is not usually how egalitarian perspectives are stated; such perspectives normally assume a starting point where one party's interests need to be highlighted. Feminism, for example, does not normally consist of the view that men do not have legitimate interests but rather that they are in the main already catered for, or over-catered for, or can best be met by considering the interests of women more than hitherto. Hence, IC is being presented as a rectification of MC's unbalanced concern with the rights of minorities or the disadvantaged.

Of the various characteristics of IC offered by Bouchard, I wish to consider only two, the two that I believe are distinctive to his version of IC: a *diversity/duality distinction* and a *majority cultural precedence*, which presupposes an assumption of duality. My purpose, then, is not to summarise Bouchard's multi-aspected position but to bring out, explore and learn from what I think is distinctive about his interculturalism and challenging for multiculturalism as I understand it. While Bouchard's conception of IC is based on a contrast with MC, and this contrast is rooted in his understanding of the discourses and policies of federal Canada and Quebec, nevertheless he wants to theorise at a more general level and illustrates his argument by reference to a number of countries. For example, in relation to the first point I am interested in, he holds that MC takes different forms in different countries and changes over time (and not just in one direction) but to the extent that it is MC then it exists in a 'diversity' model. The central feature of a diversity paradigm is 'there is no recognition of a majority culture and, in consequence, no minorities per se' (2011: 441). Bouchard sometimes refers to the inherently individualistic character of MC (2011: 464) – which for a European is very confusing, as in Europe IC is the individual-friendly correction of 'groupist' MC, e.g. Council of Europe 2008 – but that is not the issue. The key idea of diversity is that all individuals and groups are on an equal footing. Taylor, without using the same analytical framework or vocabulary, takes the same view: 'the "multi" story decentres the traditional ethno-historical identity and refuses to put any other in its place. All such identities coexist in the society, but none is officialised' (Taylor 2012: 418). They are both clearly thinking of federal Canadian multiculturalism as put by Pierre Trudeau: 'although there are two official languages, there is no official culture, nor does any ethnic group take precedence over any other' (House of Commons 1971).

IC, by contrast, 'as a global model for social integration . . . takes shape within the duality paradigm' (Bouchard 2011: 445): a recognition of 'the majority/minorities duality', 'an us-them divide' (443). 'More precisely,' Bouchard says, 'I am referring to the anxiety that the majority culture can feel in the face of cultural minorities. Indeed, they can create a more or less acute sense of threat within the majority culture not only in terms of its rights, but also in terms of its values, traditions, language, memory and identity (not to mention its security)' (445).

This is an interesting contrast but I do not think it does the work that Bouchard wants it to do. Firstly, it is not clear to me that it adequately distinguishes different states. Bouchard believes that a number of countries have at some time or other during the past fifty years or so, partly or fully, embraced diversity, that is, have denied that there are minorities/majorities and have disavowed an official recognition of a (historical) culture: the USA, federal Canada, Australia and Britain are explicitly mentioned. This characterisation of each of these countries can be disputed, though I will not pursue that here. Note, however, that Bouchard thinks that they have been moving away from diversity to duality in recent years

– exactly the opposite to the sense that Cantle and cosmopolitan interculturalists have of where the world is going.[3]

Related to this, and secondly, the term 'diversity' is often appropriated by certain critics of MC. Bouchard has chosen a term to characterise MC which is the term of choice of those who offer an anti-groupist and individualist alternative to MC (cf. Faist 2009). Similarly, its presence in the approach known as 'diversity management' is to positively express an individualistic understanding of 'difference' as an alternative to MC and related egalitarian approaches (Kandola and Fullerton 1994; Wrench and Modood 2001), and not just in the anglophone sphere, but also in France (La Charte de la diversité en enterprise 2014). So, at a minimum, Bouchard's diversity/duality distinction risks cross-national misunderstandings.

Whilst my first reservation about whether any Western country has in practice ever denied the existence of a foundational or official culture in the name of multiculturalism might be countered by saying that some intellectuals and politicians have flirted with this idea, my second point that Bouchard's vocabulary confuses multiculturalism with those of its critics who self-define around a concept of 'diversity' may be regarded as unfortunate but not a major objection. My third point is the one I want to press here. This is that the diversity/duality contrast does not distinguish IC-Q from MC at a conceptual level.

It is true that an emphasis on majoritarian anxieties is a radically different starting point from MC. The latter originates in a sensitivity to the condition of minorities: with negative perceptions and treatment of minorities in the form of racist stereotypes, group labels, misrecognition, discrimination, exclusion, marginalisation and various other forms of inequality that are centred around the existence of a public space that is reflective of the culture of some citizens and not of other citizens (Modood 2007: 37–41; 2013: 34–7). Nevertheless, it should be apparent from the last sentence that MC is framed within the majority/minority duality; at the very least its starting point is 'an us-them divide'. My own way

---

[3] These issues are matters of debate in Europe too but no European country has come close to the view that there is no such thing as a national historic culture, and few MCs are demanding that they do, a position that comes closer to cosmopolitanism than multiculturalism; the same tensions actually exist within IC-Q too (Maxwell et al. 2012).

of expressing this is that MC begins with 'the fact of negative difference . . . an unequal "us-them" relationship' (2007: 37; 2013: 34). I begin with 'difference' and speak of minorities (as do all the MC positions that I know) so, once again, it is not MC but IC-E (European interculturalism) or cosmopolitanism that seems to fit 'diversity' and seems to be Bouchard's unintended target. Perhaps the difference between IC-Q and MC is that the former is framed in terms of a duality, an 'us-them' that the majority is uncomfortable with, even threatened by; while MC is framed simultaneously in terms of an us-them and a certain conception of equality.

Majority precedence

I turn now to the second of Bouchard's two defining ideas of IC: 'While seeking an equitable interaction between continuity and diversity, interculturalism allows for the recognition of certain elements of ad hoc (or contextual) precedence for majority culture' (2011: 451). Lest there is a misunderstanding, he immediately adds: 'I say ad hoc because it is out of the question to formalise or establish this idea as a general legal principle, which would lead to the creation of two classes of citizens.' Taylor seems to be making the same qualified claim when he writes: 'The "inter" story starts from the reigning historical identity but sees it evolving in a process in which all citizens, of whatever identity, have a voice, and no-one's input has a privileged status' (2012: 418). It is being suggested that central to IC is a certain legitimate majority precedence but not a legal privileging of majority citizens.

So, while for some European authors intercultural dialogue and exchange are the key characteristics of interculturalism and the best characteristics of multiculturalism (Rattansi 2011: 152, 160), these are not the key features of the interculturalism of Bouchard and Taylor. The idea of majority precedence I believe is a significant difference from most accounts of MC.[4] Moreover, it is differ-

---

[4] In a private communication Bouchard has said that he thinks I am 'making way too much of the idea of precedence'. He says that he sees it as 'stemming from a sociological necessity . . . every society, in order to function and to survive, needs a strong symbolic foundation' and his 'point is that it should be preserved not as the culture or identity of the majority . . . but as a necessary social feature'. I have reread his article in the light of this communication and do not feel the need to make any changes to my text; see also his chapter in this book.

ent from classical assimilation and liberal individualism which do not so much seek a lower status for minorities but their gradual dissolution and the confinement of 'difference' to private spaces and weekends. Moreover, while Bouchard in several places contrasts his perspective with liberalism, it could be said that his ideas here are within touching distance of at least one version of liberal nationalism, namely that expressed very recently by Tim Soutphommasane, which includes the claim that 'the liberal nationalist suggests that any minority cultural identity should be subordinated to the national identity' (Soutphommasane 2012: 76), and Geoff Levey has expressly argued that Australian multiculturalism as state policy has always recognised the foundational character of Anglo-Australian majority culture (Levey 2008).

Bouchard argues that it is difficult, given that it is emphatically not to be given a legal or official status, to express what this precedence means in the abstract, hence he gives some examples of legitimate and illegitimate precedence from the Canadian and Quebec context. I do not have the space here to consider such nationally specific examples, and to do so would distract from the idea of majority precedence as such and the way in which it is different from and a challenge to MC. Bouchard's emphasis on majority precedence, while by no means the only point of interest in his complex position, is most challenging for multiculturalists, as it is fair to say they have not addressed the issue about the majority and do need to do so. Of course, multiculturalists have written a lot on the remaking of a national citizenship in order to make it more inclusive (Modood 2007/2013), as that is central to multiculturalism as I understand it, so perhaps it is not entirely accurate to say that multiculturalists have neglected to note the normative significance of the majority *tout court*. In so far as multiculturalists distinguish between the majority culture and the public or civic culture, it is about its tendency to dominate and pass itself off as the whole of the national culture. It is assumed that a minority culture can be identified as distinct from what it needs to be included in, but much less is said about the majority culture in this respect. I confess to being guilty here. Stimulated by this sense of neglect, I would like to reflect on the place of the majority in MC.[5]

---

[5] I appreciate that examples are necessary to understand general propositions and offer two detailed examples below.

Having admitted that multiculturalists like myself have not engaged much with the concept of 'the majority', I think a good way to approach Bouchard's view on this topic and to consider what multiculturalists may learn from it is to ask what might be the current view of the concept of the majority implicit in MC. I think what I have said to date about minorities in relation to the majority can be summarised in terms of two 'protectionist' statements and two positive statements:

1. There should be protection from racism, cultural racism and Islamophobia (not from majority culture per se).
2. There should be no insistence on assimilation, nor should there be any hindrance to uncoercive social processes of assimilation or self-chosen assimilation; different modes of integration should be equally welcomed.
3. There should be multicultural accommodation of minorities within shared public institutions.
4. Minorities should be able to make claims on national culture and identity in their own ways. This remaking of national identity is part of multicultural citizenship and should be welcomed and encouraged by the majority.

So, while multiculturalists may need to think more about 'the majority', it is not the case that existing theories are negative about majority culture per se, or even that multiculturalism is about protecting minorities from majority culture.

Let me consider what I think are the three main arguments for 'majority precedence'. Bouchard's distinctiveness is not in the arguments as such but in their deployment to support the idea of majority precedence. I accept the starting points of the arguments but not the conclusions. The arguments show that the majority culture has a normative significance, but not normative precedence if that means the majority is able to make normative claims that minorities are not, or that there is always some prima facie presumption in favour of the majority culture.

No neutral space

Here the idea seems to be that liberal or democratic or secular states, 'beyond their founding principles, values, norms and laws', 'typically incorporate a number of contextual and historical elements' (Bouchard 2011: 453). Such states have a national identity that is not reducible to universal laws and norms, or even to a legal-political framework, but also have a cultural aspect – such as language(s), a specific history, a religion or set of religions, national memories and an official calendar, ceremonies, memorials and other symbols marked by these religions and histories – and this culture is central to what state-funded schools are required to teach. Whilst these national identities should be common to all citizens, they are inevitably deeply shaped by 'the majority culture', parts of which sometimes may even be indistinguishable from the 'national culture'. Liberal states may aspire to be culturally neutral but all societies must have a symbolic-normative core which acts as an integrative mechanism, and liberal states are no exception. In short, liberal democratic states are not a neutral public space but have a cultural character in which the majority culture has a legitimate precedence.

I fully endorse the impossibility of a neutral public space but query the implication of precedence. I can see that by the mere fact of what I might call 'sociological privilege', members of the majority culture will enjoy advantages of identification, access, discursive and other capabilities – in short, a certain kind of cultural capital or cultural power – over those less steeped in the majority and therefore the national culture. Yet while it does not follow that those advantages are unfair, given that there is not a neutral public space some will always have some advantages of that kind relative to others. Neither, however, does it follow that some particular normative precedence should be acknowledged by all in addition to these socio-cultural advantages. If Bouchard means that the sociological precedence, the fact of the power imbalance, the mechanisms by which the majority culture reproduces itself and incorporates minorities and manages change, is not illegitimate per se, is not necessarily illegitimate, that would be right – and is a useful point to make if some multiculturalists and theorists imply that it is necessarily illegitimate. But it is not legitimate in all instances either. In talking of national culture and citizenship we necessarily invoke a concept of equality and therefore have to formulate concepts of intercultural dialogue, as Bhikhu Parekh does (2000/2006), or of oppression in relation to public culture, as Iris Young does (Young 1990), or concepts such as misrecognition, as

255

Taylor does (1994), in order to identify the ways in which minorities can have their claim to equal dignity and equal respect ignored or compromised. Positive aspects of this equality can include the expunging of racist language and imagery from the public space or widening the register of symbolic prestige to include demeaned and marginal groups. The fact that a polity cannot be culturally contentless or neutral between all cultures does not mean that the concept of equality becomes secondary to majority precedence.

IDENTITY PRESERVATION

This argument is that '[i]n order for the majority group to preserve the cultural and symbolic heritage that serves as the foundation of its identity and helps to ensure its continuity, it can legitimately claim some element of contextual precedence based on its seniority or history' (Bouchard 2011: 451).

Here I query if the right to identity preservation – with which I have no quarrel – depends on 'seniority or history'? If yes, then by definition no new minority has a right to identity preservation, which is a very extreme view, and I do not think there is anything to indicate that it is Bouchard's view. If, however, minorities do have a right to identity preservation, then such a right does not depend on 'seniority or history' but upon being a group that is not harming anyone – in which case, the majority does have this (qualified) right, but so do the minorities. Sometimes there will be clashes and we will have to work out ways to handle them, but automatic precedence of one party over the other does not emerge simply because of seniority or history, as there will be other considerations to take into account, such as individual rights, marginal utility, the vulnerability of a culture, and some sense of fairness and even-handedness such that one argument like historical precedence does not unduly trump all others.

Indeed, the relatively secure place of the majority, their enjoyment of 'sociological privilege' and cultural power to reproduce themselves and wanting to extend to minorities what majorities claim for themselves, is one of the origins of multiculturalism. Every group and not just a majority should have a prima facie right to identity preservation (as long as the rights and interest of others – groups and individuals – are taken into account, the cost is not too high, and so on). Multiculturalists are mindful of how minorities can be under various pressures to assimilate and can become anxious about their identities and so argue that minorities should be allowed to preserve, change and adapt in their own way and at their own pace. Bouchard usefully alerts us to the fact that under some conditions, which seem to be growing today, the majority may feel anxious about a sense of cultural loss, of losing control, about the pace of identity change. Multiculturalists normally assume that the majority already has what the minority is seeking, but suppose it has not? Or parts of it – such as, say, parts of the white working class – has not? As a matter of fact, the growing presence and empowerment of minorities, the multiculturalist project, itself may be a cause for identity anxiety amongst the majority (Jones 2011). Where this is the case, multiculturalists need to show the same sensitivity to change and identity anxiety in relation to the majority as to the minority. This may lead to some political difficulties at times, but I do not think there is a theoretical problem as such. After all, one of the fundamental philosophical arguments for minority recognition is based on a dialogical or relational sense of identity that posits that it is not only members of minorities whose sense of self and self-worth is dependent on the perceptions and treatment by the majority, but also vice versa (Taylor 1994: 60–3). So, where appropriate, emphasising mutual recognition – or, as Bouchard puts it, reciprocity – and not merely minority accommodation may be a political adjustment but is not a philosophical difficulty for multiculturalists. Multiculturalists can, therefore, acknowledge that the majority and minorities have a right to be supported through state structures and policies without conceding that the majority has an exclusive right to identity preservation or the precedence of seniority, let alone the right to suppress a minority's right to publicly express and preserve its identity simply because that would mean the public space is less reflective of majority culture.

National culture as 'useful and necessary'

The last argument I will examine is the suggestion that the fact of non-neutrality, which means that every liberal democratic state has a distinctive national-cultural identity, can be 'useful and necessary even in a liberal democratic state. For example, it allows for the consolidation of national identity, which is at once a source of solidarity and a foundation for responsible citizen participation and social justice' (Bouchard 2011: 452). Bouchard cites a number of authors who hold this view, including several multiculturalists (myself included) and also liberal nationalists such as David Miller, who is amongst those who have argued this most fully (Miller 1995). Some of us have utilised this argument without the implication of majority precedence. The argument establishes that a national-cultural identity, because of its linkage with a national citizenship, has some political and normative significance but is only acceptable as such if interpreted in a very liberal way, for example if racist or intolerant aspects of the national culture get dropped. Individuals and groups have some freedom in emphasising different aspects of the national identity, which is differently and freely interpreted and allowed to change over time and through the inclusion of new groups. State-manufactured identities are not imposed on people and there is not an expectation that a national identity – shared with minorities but largely reflective of the majority – has to be everyone's most important and cherished identity and must always trump all other identities.

In this way the national identity and its component parts, including key aspects of the majority culture, has to be made consistent with democratic values such as liberty, equality and fraternity and can therefore in principle also be consistent with multicultural citizenship. In this formation the majority culture again does not enjoy a unique position. Minority identities, such as that of Catholics or of black people, or, specifically in relation to my own work, Muslim civic identities also participate in and thereby both potentially adapt and support the shared citizenship (Modood 2007/2013). Of course they may do so in different ways and in the process extend and complexify the relevant conception of national citizenship, giving it a multicultural character. I think that in principle all group identities can and should be encouraged (but not pressured) to support and adapt citizenship in this way. This is best done through dialogues or multilogues in which conceptions of citizenship and corresponding national identities are contested and reworked. Dialogue is indeed an idea central to multicultural citizenship and, *pace* certain versions of IC, it is not thought of only in relation to micro, everyday interactions but also in relation to controversies, as, for example, Bhikhu Parekh demonstrates in relation to the *Satanic Verses* affair, where the majority has a chance to make its point but often does so in a tone that is not conducive to dialogue or mutual learning (Parekh 2000/2006).[6] Parekh shows that such dialogues inevitably have a majoritarian or status quo starting point because, even while wanting to express unfamiliar sensibilities and bring in new arguments, minorities are primarily trying to persuade the majority that what they are seeking is not so different from what the majority at one time or another has sought for itself, and in so arguing the minority must justify itself by appealing to – even while seeking to modify – the existing 'operative public values' which structure public debate and what is thought to be legitimate or reasonable in that polity at the time (Parekh 2000/2006).

These three arguments (no neutral space; identity preservation; national culture as useful and necessary), then, press multicultural- ists to acknowledge not just recognition of minorities but mutual or multilogical recognition and thereby to be sensitive to anxie- ties about threats to identity on the part of the majority as well as minorities. They also remind us that the power of the majority to preserve its culture and to enshrine it within a national identity supported by the state is not necessarily illegitimate, though it does not invalidate multicultural concerns about the ways majorities can oppress, misrecognise and marginalise, formally and infor- mally. These arguments that I have been discussing do not establish a majority precedence and are not a basis from which to repudi- ate the multiculturalist project of remaking national citizenships so that all citizens can see themselves in the national identity and achieve a sense of belonging together. A living national identity is a work in progress, a conversation between where we are coming from and where we are going. The past is central to the sense of nationhood today – we have to be able to see it as our past, as how it has formed us – but equally we must appreciate the country we are becoming. It is a story in which the white or ethnic major- ity is central but it is a developing story, and one in which new

---

[6] Dialogue is one of the foundational ideas of MC (Parekh 2000/2006; Taylor 1994) in contrast to political and social theories which centre on logics of conflict, abstract rationality, market choices, legal mechanisms and so on. Multiculturalists have mainly thought of dialogue at the level of public discourses and political controver- sies; interculturalists have added the micro in terms of interpersonal cultural encoun- ters and group dynamics at the level of youth clubs, neighbourhoods, and towns and cities (Meer and Modood 2012).

minorities too are characters and not just replicas of the majority or mere 'add-ons'.

Given that I do not think that the priority of the majority culture in the national identity and public culture is necessarily illegitimate and Bouchard is explicit that the principle of precedence can be abused, it may well be asked how substantive are our differences? I mentioned that Bouchard draws on some of the controversies today in Quebec and Canada to illustrate what he thinks is legitimate and illegitimate majority precedence. While I do not want to get drawn on the specifics of those cases, I nevertheless do owe some examples in order to give content to my own position, and that is what I would like to do by way of concluding, taking the examples from education.

Two examples

Many liberal democratic countries have a statutory national curriculum for all state schools.[7] That is a legitimate thing for a state to do. It is also legitimate for the nation to be the reference point for most of the curriculum rather than a region or a locality or the composition of a specific school, though they too may be relevant. Yet that still leaves open the question of the content of the national curriculum. For a start, the national curriculum must not be reducible to the majority culture or be a synonym for it: the national curriculum must seek to include aspects of the presence of minorities and their contribution to the ongoing development of the country. So, in relation to history, it would be illegitimate for the curriculum to cover just what some people in the UK (perhaps mainly in England) call 'our island story'. There must be a narrative of the various peoples, ancient and modern, who have come to and settled in Britain – mainly violently up to 1066, and peacefully since then – thus continually changing and shaping and being absorbed by what today we may call 'majority culture'. It should in the British case include histories of how the British encountered and conquered various peoples, along with something about the histories of those people before and after these encounters and

---

[7] I accept that my two examples run against US practice and sensibilities but they are nevertheless consistent with educational policy and practice in most liberal democratic states.

conquests. It should show how the history of the country was changed by the encounter and so how today we have come to have the ethnic composition that we do ('we are over here because you were over there'), how the national identity has become multi-stranded and has expanded and contracted over time, as one-time minorities, like various waves of refugees, have become part of the nation, or as some have sought to leave the Union, such as most of the island of Ireland, and others have sought to change the terms of membership and to adjust majority/minority relations, usually in the direction of greater equality.

The national history will therefore not be simply a history of the majority; indeed, it will show how compositions of the majority are themselves a feature of historical evolution and so cannot be 'reduced to a simple tale of essential and enduring national unity' (CMEB 2000: 2.9, 16). Jews, for example, were and are a minority when we conceive the majority to be Christians, but they are part of the majority if we think in terms of white, black, brown, red and yellow. Moreover, each new generation does not simply add a new chapter to an ever-expanding book, but rethinks the whole story; new emphases, under-appreciated themes and storylines, and the significance of certain actions, such as the British Empire, emerge and grow. In the absence of the mass migrations from countries like India and Jamaica, certain events of the past – such as the large contribution of Indian soldiers in the two world wars – may seem marginal but should come to be significant in the national narrative today. While a national history will be for the most part what today's majority thinks of as its history, it is legitimate to prescribe it alongside – indeed, as part of – the national goal of producing citizens for a multicultural nation of tomorrow. It would be illegitimate if the national history was simply identified as the history of the majority and the national identity was presented as less than open to and inclusive of minority citizens, and no effort was made to revise the history syllabus so that all the citizens-to-be can see how the minorities are part of the national story.

Let me take one other school subject: religion. It is clear that in the present phase of multiculturalism debates, religion has come to have a centrality and is the subject of most of the controversy associated with multiculturalism. Most people accept a distinction between religious instruction (RI), the teaching of how to become a member of a certain faith, and religious education (RE), the learning of a variety of faith traditions and their past and current effects upon individuals and societies, upon the shaping of humanity, taught to classes comprising those of all religions and those of none. It is fairly uncontroversial in many countries that religious education should be part of a national curriculum,[8] so the main issue in relation to majority precedence is with regard to religious instruction. Broadly speaking, there are two majoritarian possibilities. First, we have a society where there is a majority religion and that alone is allowed as RI; minorities might be exempted from those classes but no alternative religious instruction is provided. Second, the majority view is that there should be no RI in state schools, as in the USA. Is it fair to impose either of these policies on minorities that do want RI?

That is certainly an appropriate subject for a national dialogue, but if, after that, certain minorities want RI as well as RE, then a truly national system – certainly a multicultural system – must make an effort to accommodate minority RI. In my understanding, then, under both the majoritarian possibilities the minorities should have their religions instructed or worshipped within the national system. On the other hand, minorities do not have the right to stop the majority from including the instruction of their religion. We should not, for example, ask schools to cease Christian RI or worship or celebrating Christmas because of the presence of Muslims or Hindus; rather, we should extend the celebrations to include, for example, Eid and Diwali. Muslims and other religious minorities in Europe are seeking accommodation within something resembling the status quo, not a dispossession of Christian churches, and so what we are really seeing is an *additive* not a *subtractive* view of inclusivity (Modood 2007/2013, 2016). The challenge is not how to de-Christianise Western states, but how to appropriately add the new faiths alongside the older ones in ways that are faithful to national cultures but also adapting them so they are inclusive in this additive sense. All the evidence suggests that this is what most minorities, especially Muslims, want, certainly in Britain (Modood 1997). It is not the case, as a

---

[8] Again, I appreciate that this will read oddly to US readers. They should bear in mind that the US is not typical of how religion is treated in schools in the Western democracies. For example, all states of the European Union give funding either to religious schools or for religious education in state schools.

political scientist recently put it, that 'accommodating Muslims in the political sphere certainly requires abandoning a commitment to the Christian norms that have, historically, defined European states' (Lennard 2010: 317). As I have said, the challenge is not to de-Christianise states but to add the new faiths alongside the older ones. This is what is gradually happening across much of Western Europe, albeit in an ad hoc and uneven way. What is interesting is that those most uncomfortable with this are not Christians or Churches but ideological secularists.

These two examples, then, illustrate what I take to be a multiculturalist recognition of the legitimate claims and limits of majority culture. The majority may insist that the history curriculum centre on how the majority came to be formed as a nation and a polity, but it may not exclude the minorities from that story. The majority may – in addition to, not as a substitution for, an RE which includes all religions – include the instruction of the majority religion(s) or the majority may choose to not have its religion(s) instructed in state schools, but it cannot impose its preference in this regard upon minorities, who must be given the option to have their religion instructed in state schools, independently of what the majority may decide for itself. The national identity, then, must aspire to be more than merely the majority or merely 'difference blind'; it must be genuinely inclusive. If IC-E is for dethroning the inherited national identity and leaving that space blank, and IC-Q is for embracing while opening up the national identity, MC is about opening up and replacing the national identity if closed and for embracing it if plural. In the national identity the majority clearly has a centrality, but it is only legitimate if we work to make the national identity a true reflection of the citizenship and so to extend 'precedence', not hoard it.

Conclusion

The idea of majority precedence as found in the work of Bouchard and Taylor and within Quebecan IC more generally is a significant difference from most accounts of MC. Multiculturalists can and should learn from it. I have suggested that I accept the starting points of the argument in question but not the conclusions. The arguments show that the majority culture has a normative significance, but not normative precedence if that means the majority is able to make normative claims that minorities are not or that there is always some prima facie presumption in favour of the majority culture. I have concluded with educational examples in relation to religious minorities in which I make what I believe is a multiculturalist claim that minority religions are entitled in some circumstances to have religious instruction classes in state schools even if the majority does not want this for itself. I suggest that this is consistent with everything I have argued in relation to majority/minority relations but am aware that this is something that is inconsistent with Bouchard and Taylor's understanding of Quebec's interculturalism and 'open secularism' (Bouchard and Taylor 2008) and with the practice and public opinion in Quebec. Hence, I hope I have made evident that while there are overlaps and dialogical connections between Quebecan interculturalism and my understanding of multiculturalism, they clearly differ on majority and minority entitlements too.

References

Bouchard, G. (2011), 'What Is Interculturalism?', *McGill Law Journal*, 56 (2), 435–68.

Bouchard, G., and C. Taylor (2008), *Building the Future: A Time for Reconciliation*, Report of the Consultation Commission on Accommodation Practices Related to Cultural Difference, Quebec City: Government of Quebec.

Cantle, T. (2012a), *Interculturalism: The New Era of Cohesion and Diversity*, Basingstoke: Palgrave Macmillan.

Cantle, T. (2012b), 'Interculturalism: For the Era of Globalisation, Cohesion and Diversity – a rejoinder to Modood and Meer', *Political Insight*, December, <http://tedcantle.co.uk/wp-content/uploads/2013/03/071-Political-Insight_Interculturalism-Dec-2012-Cantle-2012a.pdf> (last accessed 25 June 2015).

Charte de la diversité en enterprise (2014), The French Diversity Charter, available at <http://www.diversity-charter.com/> (last accessed 16 June 2015).

Commission on Multi-Ethnic Britain (CMEB) (2000), *The Future of Multi-Ethnic Britain*, London: Profile Books.

Council of Europe, Committee of Ministers (2008), *Living Together as Equals in Dignity: White Paper on Intercultural Dialogue*, Strasbourg: Council of Europe.

Faist, T. (2009), 'Diversity – A New Mode of Incorporation?', *Ethnic and Racial Studies*, 32 (1), 171–90.

House of Commons (1971), *Debates*, Ottawa: Queen's Printer.

Jones, O. (2011), *Chavs: The Demonization of the Working Class*, London: Verso Books.

Kandola, R., and J. Fullerton (1994), *Managing the Mosaic: Diversity in Action*, London: Chartered Institute of Personnel and Development.

Kraus, P. A., and K. Schönwälder (2006), 'Multiculturalism in Germany: Rhetoric, Scattered Experiments, and Future Chances', in K. Banting and W. Kymlicka (eds), *Multiculturalism and the Welfare State: Recognition and Redistribution in Contemporary Democracies*, Oxford: Oxford University Press, pp. 202–21.

Lennard, P. T. (2010), 'What Can Multicultural Theory Tell Us about Integrating Muslims in Europe?', *Political Studies Review*, 8, 308–21.

Levey, G. B. (2008), 'Multiculturalism and Australian National Identity', in G. B. Levey (ed.), *Political Theory and Australian Multiculturalism*, New York: Berghahn Books, pp. 254–76.

Maxwell, B., D. I. Waddington, K. McDonough, A.-A. Cormier and M. Schwimmer (2012), 'Interculturalism, Multiculturalism, and the State Funding and Regulation of Conservative Religious Schools', *Educational Theory*, 62 (4), 427–47.

Meer, N., and T. Modood (2012), 'How Does Interculturalism Contrast with Multiculturalism?', *Journal of Intercultural Studies*, 33 (2), 175–96.

Miller, D. (1995), *On Nationality*, Oxford: Oxford University Press.

Modood, T. (ed.) (1997), *Church, State and Religious Minorities*, London: Policy Studies Institute.

Modood, T. (2007/2013), *Multiculturalism: A Civic Idea*, Cambridge: Polity Press.

Modood, T. (2012), *Post-Immigration 'Difference' and Integration: The Case of Muslims in Western Europe*, London: The British Academy.

Modood, T. (2016), 'State-Religion Connexions and Multicultural Citizenship', in J. Cohen and C. Laborde (eds), *Post-Postsecularism?*, New York: Columbia University Press.

Parekh, B. (2000/2006), *Rethinking Multiculturalism: Cultural Diversity and Political Theory*, Basingstoke: Macmillan.

Rattansi, A. (2011), *Multiculturalism: A Very Short Introduction*, Oxford: Oxford University Press.

Soutphommasane, T. (2012), *The Virtuous Citizen: Patriotism in a Multicultural Society*, Cambridge: Cambridge University Press.

Taylor, C. (1994), 'The Politics of Recognition', in A. Gutmann (ed.), *Multiculturalism and 'The Politics of Recognition'*, Princeton: Princeton University Press, pp. 25–73.

Taylor, C. (2012), 'Interculturalism or Multiculturalism?', *Philosophy and Social Criticism*, 38 (4–5), 413–23.

Weinstock, D. (2013), 'Interculturalism and Multiculturalism in Canada and Quebec: Situating the Debate', in P. Balint and S. Guérard de Latour (eds), *Liberal Multiculturalism and the Fair Terms of Integration*, Basingstoke: Palgrave Macmillan, pp. 91–108.

Wrench, J., and T. Modood (2001), *The Effectiveness of Racial Equality Employment Policies in the UK*, Geneva: International Labour Office.

Young, I. M. (1990), *Justice and the Politics of Difference*, Princeton: Princeton University Press.

Afterword: Multiculturalism and Interculturalism – A Critical Dialogue

Bhikhu Parekh

This fine collection has the unique merit of bringing together and setting up a stimulating dialogue between multiculturalism and interculturalism represented by uniformly impressive essays. The editors' excellent introduction skilfully signposts the direction of the dialogue and highlights the issues lying at its heart. In recent years multiculturalism has been subjected to considerable criticism and held responsible for all sorts of ills such as social fragmentation, ghettoisation, lack of patriotism and absurdly even terrorism. The criticism is deeply misguided. It homogenises its target and ignores its internal diversity. Secondly, it gives a misleading account of multiculturalism and virtually borders on a caricature. I shall take each in turn.

Multiculturalism appeared on the political and philosophical agenda of the West in the 1960s in response to the cultural diversity introduced mainly but not exclusively by the badly needed immigrants from the developing countries. Various views were canvassed, multiculturalism being one of them. It held that the receiving society's response to cultural diversity should be guided by three principles that were at the heart of liberal democracy, namely liberty, equality and unity. The minorities should not be subjected to coercive assimilation and should be left free within the limits of the law to lead their freely chosen ways of life including maintaining their identity. Secondly, minorities were entitled to equal treatment, their right to their cultures deserved equal respect, and they should not be subjected to discrimination and disadvantages on cultural grounds. Thirdly, cohesion and stability of the receiving society required that the minorities should be integrated

266

into it, become its valuable members like the rest, and play their full part in it. The central concern or problematic of multicultural-ism then was how to combine diversity and unity without violating the liberty and equality of minorities. It was not about creating unity out of diversity because the wider society was already united, but rather about how to accommodate diversity within that unity by expanding and redefining its basis.

The multicultural problematic raised three important sets of questions. At the philosophical level they were about the nature and importance of culture, why it deserved respect and what that meant, why newcomers' cultures should be accorded equal treat-ment, what it entailed, and whether and how it differed from the more familiar idea of equality of individuals. The second set of questions related to the nature and basis of social unity and the vision of society that best reconciled the demands of unity and diversity. The third set of questions had to do with the policies most likely to achieve such a society.

Different writers answer these questions differently. Furthermore those agreed on their answers to one set of questions do not always agree on their answers to either or both of the other two. Like lib-eralism, socialism and any other body of thought, multiculturalism thus contains much internal diversity of views. It is therefore wrong of its critics to essentialise it, especially when they themselves accuse it of essentialising cultures and groups. They also make two other related mistakes. They think that if one version or view of multiculturalism is shown to be misguided, the case for multicul-turalism itself collapses. Furthermore they do not appreciate that although the answers to the three sets of questions are related, they are distinct and the inadequacy of one does not necessarily entail that of the other two. It is therefore wrong to argue, as some of them do, that if, say, the policies recommended by a theorist or followed by a society are shown to be mistaken, multiculturalism itself stands discredited. Just as a policy is not discredited because it is wrongly implemented by an overenthusiastic official, a case for multiculturalism is not damaged because the writer or the society concerned has not carefully thought out the policies or vision of social unity.

Despite the differences in their philosophical accounts of culture, visions of multicultural society and policies, multiculturalists are broadly agreed on the following (Modood 2007). First, human beings understand and organise themselves and their world in terms of a particular system of meaning and significance, a lived framework of beliefs and practices, a culture. They can and do revise and change it but they cannot dispense with it altogether and lead a culture-free life of pure reason.

Second, every society has a broadly shared culture. Although the latter generally contains different strands and elements derived from different sources and historical periods and is never free of internal tension, it has at least some degree of coherence. It shapes society's institutions and practices and gives them a certain character. It also informs its political life including the design of the state, its vocabulary, laws, mode of reasoning, what activities are considered a matter of public concern and fall within the purview of the state, its ideas of fairness, and so on. Every state is culturally embedded and reflects and reinforces that culture.

This is as true of immigrant societies as of those with a strong historical identity. The former cannot sustain themselves for generations without developing some conception of who they are and what they stand for, how to understand and organise their collective lives, how to nurture public institutions and the qualities of character they presuppose, some unifying symbols, rituals and ceremonies, and a national story. To be sure, their culture is generally less 'thick' or substantive, more self-conscious, more oriented towards the public sphere of life, than that of those with a strong historical identity, but that neither denies its existence and importance nor permits a sharp qualitative distinction between the two. It is therefore wrong to draw too neat a contrast, as some earlier chapters do, between, say, Canada and Quebec in this respect.

Third, cultural minorities should be treated equally with the rest. They should obviously enjoy equal rights as citizens and these include not only the usual civil and political ones but also cultural rights. Since the major institutions of society embody and throw their considerable weight behind its culture, they run the risk of discriminating against and disadvantaging the minorities. If the latter are to enjoy equality, their cultural differences should be suitably accommodated and their cultural disadvantages overcome by judicious application of such means as exemptions, additional assistance, affirmative action and special provisions. No multiculturalist argues that culture is the sole source of minorities' disadvantages but it is one of them and is often ignored by liberals.

268

Fourth, while minority identities deserve respect, it cannot be uncritical and indiscriminate. If some minority beliefs and practices are outrageous and morally unacceptable, they may not be respected or even tolerated. The majority makes such a judgement on the basis of its own cultural norms and values. Since the minorities might not share the latter, they disagree and the matter should be resolved by a dialogue resulting in either the majority insisting on its values or some kind of compromise and accommodation.

Fifth, while giving the minorities equal opportunity to express and maintain their identity, the wider society should also integrate them, that is, help them acquire the linguistic and cultural competence to find their way around in it and develop some degree of identification with it. For the multiculturalist, integration and respect for minority identity are closely related. The latter without the former leads to social fragmentation; the former without the latter is oppressive and fragile. There is thus an implicit understanding or covenant between the receiving society and its minorities entailing mutual claims and obligations.

Multiculturalists argue that integration is a matter of degree. It is possible that some minorities or some of their members wish to limit most of their significant relations such as marriage, friendship and neighbourhood to their fellow members and lead a relatively self-contained life. If that is their choice and not forced on them by their circumstances or the attitudes and actions of the majority, multiculturalists think that it should be respected. Barring such cases and allowing different forms and levels of integration, multiculturalists aim at a society in which its majority and minorities interact as equals in all spheres of life and develop a common sense of belonging.

Finally, multiculturalists see integration as a two-way process involving changes in both the majority and the minorities. The majority should make space for them by suitably restructuring itself, and they in turn should adjust themselves to its basic institutions and practices. As the minorities integrate and interact with the majority, they influence each other and facilitate the emergence of a shared culture and identity carrying the imprints of both. Such a common culture and identity reinforces the shared political and legal institutions and principles, and the two together form the basis of social unity.

These and related beliefs lie at the basis of multiculturalism and define its identity. In their own different ways and in different degrees, all multiculturalist thinkers and societies stress the cultural basis of human life, respect and accommodate minority cultural identities, judge them, disallow morally unacceptable practices, advocate interaction between them and the majority, value the cultural identity of the receiving society, stress dialogue to resolve inevitable differences, see integration as a two-way progress, and aim for a shared public culture and national identity.

Canada, the first country officially to call itself multicultural, emphasises the maintenance and promotion of minority cultural identities, 'creative encounters and interchange' between them and the majority community, and their integration in the wider society through its language policy, equality of opportunity and subscription to common values as embodied in its Charter of Rights and Freedoms. Australia, another multicultural society, values and nurtures minority identities, disallows their morally unacceptable features, stresses intercultural dialogue, and seeks national unity by integrating them in a suitably redefined and broadened 'Australian British heritage' or 'Australian values, customs and beliefs'. In Britain the influential Swann Report, widely regarded as articulating the country's multiculturalism, wants the country to be 'both socially cohesive and culturally diverse', strike a 'balance' between the 'essential elements' of minority identities and the 'shared values distinctive of the society as a whole', and 'recast the [traditional] mould' in a manner that both preserves its integrity and pluralises it (Swann Report 1985: 6–7). The Runnymede Trust report on *The Future of Multi-Ethnic Britain*, yet another statement of British multiculturalism, aims to create a 'country in which the spirit of civic friendship, shared identity and common sense of belonging goes hand in hand with respect for diversity' (2000: x).

In the light of what I have said, the usual criticisms of multiculturalism, some found even in the earlier chapters, rest on a highly misleading account, almost a caricature, of it. Multiculturalism is supposed to involve cultural relativism or the view that each culture is a self-contained whole, a world unto itself, and cannot be judged from outside it. No multiculturalist has advanced such a view (cf. Bromwell 2008; Murphy 2012). Indeed, they cannot. They respect minority cultures for non-relativist reasons such as the importance of culture to individual identity, human rights, human need for public recognition and the benefits of cultural diversity. Their respect further is not indiscriminate and is based on their judgement of what is or is not morally acceptable. Their plea for the equal treatment of minority cultures and emphasis on common values rests on similar non-relativist grounds.

The critic argues that multiculturalism attributes to culture an unchanging essence. Few if any multiculturalists take this view. They do say that a culture has a measure of inner coherence and a recognisable identity but not that it is unchanging because, if it were, they would not expect the majority culture to change and make room for minority identities or require the minorities to make such cultural changes as are required by the process of integration. The charge that multiculturalism sees culture as a determinant of human behaviour is misguided for the same reason. Indeed, if it were true, it would be difficult to explain how a multicultural society with its shared norms and practices is possible at all.

At a different level multiculturalism is said to encourage segregation and social fragmentation. This is strange because, while respecting minority identity, multiculturalism places equal emphasis on integration and social unity and its policies are designed to achieve that end. The policies might be badly designed or implemented but that does not discredit multiculturalism itself. If some groups desire to have only minimum contact with the wider society and segregate themselves, multiculturalism respects them but does not itself seek such an outcome. Multiculturalism is said to be obsessed with cultural differences when in fact it is equally, or even more, concerned with intercultural dialogue, common values and a shared culture. Dialogue, the only way different groups can hope to understand each other, build common bonds and resolve their differences, is at the heart of a multicultural society. Again, multiculturalism is said to be uninterested in fostering common loyalty among the minorities when in fact its policies explicitly aim at it, and it respects minority identities in the hope that, among other things, that would earn their gratitude and loyalty.

Multiculturalism is absurdly accused of leading to terrorism, a charge one would laugh at if it had not been made by the British Prime Minister David Cameron. In his view this is so because multiculturalism encourages different communities to lead separate lives, tolerates behaviour that violates the receiving society's values, fails to provide a vision of society to which the minorities might want to belong, and creates an alienated group readily available for terrorist mobilisation. Cameron's argument is deeply flawed. Multiculturalism allows separate lives but does not encourage them, and aims in various ways to integrate minorities. It disallows unacceptable behaviour and has not hesitated to legislate against it. And it is difficult to see why a multicultural vision that respects both minority and majority identities should not be sufficiently inspiring to minorities and why Cameron's assimilationist 'muscular liberalism' that has no regard for them should have greater success. A multicultural society includes several minority communities, and Cameron does not explain why only the Muslims are involved in terrorist activities, why only a tiny number of their youth, why only in recent years, and why this is also to be found in France, which has, unlike the UK, long followed the policy of strong integration. Lack of integration produces indifference to society, not rage against or hatred of it, and it is the latter that spawns terrorism. On available evidence terrorism is better accounted for in terms of such factors as misguided foreign policies, brutal conduct of wars, callous disregard for civilian lives, and domestic marginalisation and demonisation of Muslims. For obvious reasons these and other factors are not acknowledged, and responsibility is placed on the Muslims themselves and on multiculturalism for 'pampering' them.

Even though multiculturalism has been implemented grudgingly, in a half-hearted manner, and without creating the conditions necessary for its success in most countries, it has been a force for good. Since their identities are respected, minorities are not under a cultural siege, fearful of losing their identity, and seized by a moral panic. They feel relaxed and confident enough to interact with the wider society and take change in their stride. It is not at all implausible that in the absence of multicultural tolerance, the Muslim minorities in the West would have feared for their cultural survival, panicked, built up a powerful current of rage against the wider society, and created a climate in which some of them might have resorted to far more extensive terrorism than we have seen.

Respect for minority identities has also led to the flourishing of their arts, cuisine, literature, music and so on, which are not only valuable additions to the society's cultural resources but have also impacted on and led to new experiments in the majority community. Even in the moral and spiritual sphere, minorities have introduced new or forgotten values such as family loyalty, self-restraint, filial duty and human warmth as well as new forms of piety and spirituality. They have also brought the wider world to the receiving society, expanded the latter's moral and political consciousness, deepened its understanding of global issues, and acted as a valuable political, commercial and cultural bridge between the two. From their different perspectives they have studied the history of the receiving society, brought out its bright as well as dark sides, offered a fresh and sometimes highly critical perspective on it, and contributed to its self-knowledge. One of the reasons why multiculturalism is feared in certain circles has to do with the fact that it destabilises old certainties, deflates nationalist myths, and gives voice to those long silenced or marginalised. Even its bitterest critics acknowledge many of these benefits and, despite their rhetoric, continue with most of its policies.

Since multiculturalism is not vulnerable to the charges levelled against it and is basically a persuasive response to cultural diversity, the question arises why it has provoked acute anxiety and hostility and lost much of its support, particularly in Western Europe where the term itself is seen as a liability.[1] Several factors are responsible for this. Thanks to the hold of the ideology of the nation-state for which a state is unstable unless it is based on a single and collectively shared substantive or 'thick' culture, most people have never been reconciled to multiculturalism and use its occasional aberrations to attack it. Again in a globalising world where the traditional cultural anchors are constantly challenged and immigration changes the social landscape, even those not wedded to the nation-state fear losing their sense of identity and continuity and see multiculturalism as a threatening doctrine.

The minorities' own role in this process should not be ignored. Frightened to make the changes that their new circumstances require and even to interact with the wider society lest that should influence them, some groups of them lead self-contained lives and justify it in terms of their one-sided interpretation of multiculturalism. Anxious to retain their hold over their community and having a vested interest in taking an essentialist view of its culture, their conservative leaders conveniently redefine multiculturalism to mean cultural protectionism. Political establishments in the wider

---

[1] The Council of Europe and UNESCO, which were standard bearers of multiculturalism, have now switched their allegiance to interculturalism.

society and/or the countries of minority origin sometimes find this to their advantage and give it their moral and even financial support.

Although these and other factors have played a part, they would not have been effective if multiculturalism had been properly understood and had not itself contained internal ambiguity and tension. It represents a historically unique way of responding to cultural diversity. It invests minorities with rights, grants them equality with the majority, loosens up the nation-state, and encourages minority participation in reshaping the national culture and identity. The West has never before been confronted with such a radical doctrine, and naturally its understanding and implementation of it was sometimes flawed. The fact that the doctrine involves a delicate and difficult balancing of different, even conflicting, ideas added to the difficulty. I mention three of these to illustrate the point.

First, since multiculturalism arose largely as a reaction against the aggressive assimilationism of the majority, it has a pro-minority orientation. Although it is equally concerned with integrating the minorities, its solicitude for minorities has sometimes received greater emphasis, particularly when the majority seemed intolerant or the nervous minorities sought protection against it. The pro-minority bias has led the majority to believe that it is unequally treated, that it is in danger of losing 'its' country, that its fears and anxieties are ignored, that multiculturalism is only for the minorities, and that it receives nothing in return for the moral and cultural burden it is made to carry. As a result the majority sometimes feels alienated from multiculturalism and hostile to the liberals held responsible for its introduction. Multiculturalism needs to be bifocal, delicately balancing the identity demands of the majority and the minority, and must avoid becoming or giving the impression of being one-sided (see Chapter 11).

The idea of equality that is at the heart of multiculturalism has also raised important issues. As I argued earlier, every state is embedded in the culture of the wider society, which it has itself played an important part in creating, and is not and cannot be culturally neutral. Since it is structured in terms of and is orientated towards a particular culture, its capacity to treat others equally is inherently limited. It can treat them equally only if it is denuded of its identity and rendered bland, which is not only an impossible enterprise but also a recipe for massive resistance. For example, Britain might go some way in this direction by calling Christmas 'winter festival', but that does not alter its Christian majority's attitude to it, let alone take away the deeply inscribed Christian sensibility of its various instructions and practices. This does not mean that the cultural demands of minorities cannot be met but rather that there are structural limits to how far and in what ways they can be treated equally. This has not been appreciated by some advocates of multiculturalism with the result that it has wrongly come to be seen or at least presented as a subtle or crude, well-intentioned or mischievous attempt by a hostile minority to deprive the liberal society of its identity, even as a part of the Muslim imperialist design.

The third area where both the theory and the practice of multiculturalism have thrown up difficult questions has to do with the tension between universal principles and national identity that lies at the heart of every liberal society. Qua liberal it is committed to certain universal principles such as human rights that it shares with other liberal societies. It is also, however, a distinct or particular society with its own unique history and traditions. It reconciles the two by defining, interpreting and prioritising the universal values in a particular way that constitutes the basis of its identity. France, for example, is committed to the right to religion, but in the light of its historical struggle with the Catholic Church and its reliance on the school to produce republican citizens, it interprets and limits that right in terms of the principle of *laicite*. Some French Muslim girls decided to wear the hijab in the classroom and defended it on the grounds of their right to religion. Their defence was correct but it fell foul of *laicite*, a condensed expression of French history and identity, and was overruled. Anticipating such conflicts at various levels, the French government had withdrawn from the relevant provisions of the European Convention on Human Rights, which denied Muslims not only the right to wear the hijab but also the protection of other rights.

A similar situation occurred in Germany, where a Muslim teacher wore a scarf in her class in defiance of school rules. The matter went all the way to the Constitution Court. Although the latter was not happy with her action, it determined that on human rights grounds she was entitled to do so. The bulk of the German public opinion – which, like the Constitution Court, was unhappy with her action – thought that she was using human rights to subvert their deeply cherished and historically justified national tradition. It did not wish to follow France but urged its minorities to respect valued national traditions, accept compromises, and not push universal principles beyond a certain point.

Although such an argument can easily become a way of defending the status quo and denying minorities even the most basic forms of accommodation, it raises an important question. There can be a tension between universal principles and the practices a country greatly values on the basis of its historical experience. Multiculturalism needs to appreciate this more fully than it has done so far and acknowledge that, while national practices should not be allowed to undermine universal principles, they may rightly mediate and modify them. It also needs to recognise that cultural conflicts can become intractable and undermine the society's support for it if they are formulated in the language of rights and judicialised, as the liberal version of multiculturalism tends to do, rather than settled whenever possible through democratic deliberation and accommodation.

Since multiculturalism has not satisfactorily resolved these and related issues, it is vulnerable to misunderstanding and misinterpretation. Indeed, its very name is sometimes taken to gesture in the direction of minority cultural protection and even plural monoculturalism.[2] Its conceptual framework and some of its basic ideas need to be sharpened, and the importance of the balance between unity and diversity firmly stated. Since interculturalism, which mimics and is defined by multiculturalism and paradoxically wants to challenge and replace it, claims to offer a better way of dealing with cultural diversity, we may ask if it redeems the claim (cf. Uberoi and Modood 2015).

In the earlier chapters in this book, two different forms of interculturalism are advocated, the cosmopolitan and the nationalist. Ted Cantle's version of it is individualist in its orientation and cosmopolitan in its scope, suspicious of all collective identities, has only a limited interest in respecting those of the minorities and so on, and virtually amounts to a rejection of multiculturalism. Quebec's version is quite different. It addresses what I have called

[2] I have attempted this in my *Rethinking Multiculturalism: Cultural Diversity and Political Theory*. The first word in the book's title is intended to convey this.

the multicultural problematic, shares some of the basic ideas of multiculturalism, deals with some of the difficulties raised by it, and represents an alternative liberal nationalist form of multiculturalism. The two versions raise very different questions. Since it is difficult to discuss both in a short afterword, and Cantle's version, being hostile to multiculturalism, requires an extended critical response, I shall briefly comment on nationalist interculturalism. For convenience I shall simply call it interculturalism.

The strengths of interculturalism are obvious. It recognises and appreciates the central importance of a society's historically inherited culture, and argues that the question before any culturally diverse society is not to create a common culture *ex nihilo* but rather to open up and suitably broaden that of the majority. It argues rightly that while a society should ensure equal treatment to its minority cultures, it cannot avoid giving some primacy to its 'foundational' culture, and that to ask it not to do so is to denude it of its identity with all its predictable consequences. Nationalist interculturalism insists that social unity or cohesion is one of the most important objectives of any society, and that it can only be achieved by encouraging interaction and co-operation between the various communities at all levels, pursuing common purposes, stressing and developing commonalities rather than just the differences, and evolving a shared identity based on shared experiences, struggles, memories and loyalty to common institutions and values. Most of this is also stressed by multiculturalism, though not always as strongly and unequivocally.

Interculturalism, however, has its limitations. Even as multiculturalism has a pro-minority provenance and orientation, interculturalism is biased towards the majority. While it respects minority cultures it does so within strict limits. It emphasises robust intercommunal exchanges and has little sympathy for the minorities that want to lead relatively self-contained lives. Even when the minorities are keen to participate in the collective life, it is not uncommon for them to feel nervous, diffident, overwhelmed by the all-pervasive majority culture. They then need the space and the resources to build up their self-confidence and strength, to explore and draw inspiration from their heritage, to debate among themselves and form a view of their own on public issues. Multiculturalism is acutely aware of this; interculturalism is not. Multiculturalism appreciates the symbolic significance and cultural value of sponsoring and publicly funding minority or single-identity artistic, religious, linguistic and other organisations and projects; interculturalism is in varying degrees antipathetic to them. While multiculturalism holds that strong minority identities not only do not necessarily subvert or weaken but might positively facilitate their integration and social unity, interculturalism tends to consider the two largely incompatible and limits state support to intercommunal or cross-identity organisations and projects. Multiculturalism is acutely aware of the ease and arrogance with which Western societies have historically judged and condemned non-Western cultures, and urges caution and humility. Interculturalism for the most part shares no such inhibition.

Although interculturalism gives the minorities equal opportunity to express themselves and shape national culture and identity, the scope for doing so is considerably limited. Since the inherited national culture is highly prized and guarded against likely threats, minority choices are limited, as is evident in Quebec's language policy with respect to its English-speaking immigrants. There is also an external pressure on the minorities, at least an internal inhibition, not to press their criticisms and demands beyond a certain point. It is worth observing that even the balanced Bouchard-Taylor report was criticised for being too accommodative of minorities by many in Quebec, including the champions of interculturalism. It is striking that while multiculturalism has wrestled with the big moral and philosophical questions about the nature of culture, its relation to individual identity, limits of its claims and so on, and thrown up a rich body of philosophical literature, the record of interculturalism in this regard is much less impressive. It is equally worth noting that while multiculturalism has analysed the nature of the nation-state, its role in shaping national culture, and other crucial political questions, interculturalism largely ignores them and focuses on intergroup relations at local levels where the full impact of cultural diversity is rarely felt (see Chapter 7).

Multiculturalism and interculturalism, then, have much to learn from each other (see the chapters by Loobuyck and Modood). Each alerts the other to the issues it overlooks or marginalises and corrects its exaggerations. They do so because their starting points and orientations are different. One is primarily concerned with social unity and stresses the centrality of the majority culture. The other is primarily concerned with justice to minorities, stresses their freedom to explore and express their identities, and is more hospitable to diversity. One is orientated towards the nation-state, a state based on a relatively thick though constantly redefined national culture; the other towards a state based on a relatively thin and internally variegated culture born out of intercultural interaction.

The two cannot be mechanically combined into a single allegedly superior form of multiculturalism. Rather each needs to incorporate and use the valid insights of the other to interrogate and organically reconfigure itself, giving rise in one case to a multiculturally sensitive interculturalism and in the other to an interculturally attuned multiculturalism, the latter being the view to which I feel more sympathetic and which I sought to develop in my *Rethinking Multiculturalism*. Although the two share a common theoretical framework, their differences of emphasis and orientation will lead to convergence in some areas and manageable divergence in others. Since they cut across the dualism between multiculturalism and interculturalism, it does not matter whether we call them forms of one or the other or invent a new term altogether. Every culturally diverse society needs to make its own choice between these two and possibly other forms in the light of its history and circumstances.

References

Bromwell, D. (2008), *Ethnicity, Identity and Public Policy: Critical Perspectives on Multiculturalism*, Wellington: Institute of Policy Studies.

Modood, T. (2007), *Multiculturalism: A Civic Idea*, Cambridge: Polity Press.

Murphy, M. (2012), *Multiculturalism: A Critical Introduction*, Abingdon: Routledge.

Parekh, B. (2006), *Rethinking Multiculturalism: Cultural Diversity and Political Theory*, Basingstoke: Macmillan.

Runnymede Trust (2000), *Commission on the Future of Multi-Ethnic Britain*, London: Runnymede Trust.

Swann Report (1985), *Education For All*, London: HMSO.

Uberoi, V., and T. Modood (2015), *Multiculturalism Rethought: Interpretations, Dilemmas and New Directions*, Edinburgh: Edinburgh University Press.

Index

allophones, 110–11
anti-immigrant, 163–4, 167
assimilation, cultural, 108–9
Australia *see* multiculturalism
autonomy, 2, 16–17, 59, 116, 195,
    223; *see also* groups

Berlin, Isaiah, 11, 13
Bouchard, Gérard, 10, 65, 68, 113,
    201–6, 209, 211–17, 219–20,
    248–53, 255–8, 260
Bouchard and Taylor, 3, 15, 205, 221,
    248, 252, 263
    Commission, 70, 85
    report, 7, 163, 215–19, 248
Britain, 2, 31, 34, 70, 135, 171, 203,
    215, 250, 260, 263, 270, 275; *see
    also* United Kingdom

Canovan, Margaret, 168, 208–9
Carens, Joseph, 69, 73, 111, 128, 130,
    246
Charter of Rights and Freedoms,
    Canadian, 86, 121, 202, 214,
    216
citizenship, 3, 19, 29–51, 55, 71,
    105–10, 116, 129, 145, 151, 170,
    181, 185, 228, 258
    education, 42, 236
    intercultural, 11, 53, 55, 58, 63–9,
    71
    multicultural, 5, 45, 55, 58, 71, 171,
    254, 258
    national, 28, 34, 173, 253, 258–9

regimes, 33, 126
status, 105, 109, 115, 117, 127
see also interculturalism; Quebec
cohesion
    community, 5, 19, 42, 65, 133,
    138–40, 231
    social, 42, 64, 67, 98, 109–10, 117,
    158, 181–2, 225–7, 232, 234–5,
    237, 239
communities
    cultural, 44, 111, 115, 119, 128,
    181
    ethno-cultural, 118, 125
    political, 107–8, 110–11, 118, 124,
    126, 169, 207
community-building, 63, 65, 67, 228,
    241
conflict, 29, 63, 65, 79, 82, 108, 113,
    116–17, 128, 134–5, 230, 233,
    239
    cultural, 6
cultural *see* differences; diversity;
    exchange; groups; identities;
    illiberal; pluralism; policies;
    recognition
    mix, 234, 236, 238
    neutrality, 80, 85, 87, 96
culture
    common public, 40–41, 54,
    114–18, 122, 126, 127, 181, 255,
    260
    foundational, 112, 204, 206–7, 211,
    217–18, 221, 277
    religious, 85, 214–15

281

INDEX

283

United Kingdom, 34, 54, 175; *see* also
    Britain
United States, 31, 81, 124, 128,
    180, 184, 190–1, 193, 202,
    215–16

values
    British, 139, 148, 151
    common, 67, 145, 270–1

Weinstock, Daniel, 83, 98